D0948545

DIRTY LITTLE SECRETS of the RECORD BUSINESS

HANK BORDOWITZ

CHICAGO
REVIEW
PRESS

An A Cappella Book

Library of Congress Cataloging-in-Publication Data

Bordowitz, Hank.
    Dirty little secrets of the record business : why so much music you hear
sucks / Hank Bordowitz.
        p. cm.
    Includes bibliographical references (p.   ) and index.
    ISBN-13: 978-1-55652-643-5
    ISBN-10: 1-55652-643-1
    1. Sound recording industry—History. 2. Music trade—History. 3. Music
and technology. I. Title.

    ML3790.B678 2006
    338.4'7781640973—dc22

                                                                    2006023253

Cover and interior design: Rattray Design
Front cover image: Getty Images

Published by Chicago Review Press, Incorporated
814 North Franklin Street
Chicago, Illinois 60610
ISBN-13: 978-1-55652-643-5
ISBN-10: 1-55652-643-1
Printed in the United States of America
5 4 3 2 1

This book is dedicated to:

Dick Thompson, who opened my impressionable eyes to the wider world of music out there

Steve Julty and my cousin Harold, for exposing me to cool stuff early on

all the people who attempted to teach me the guitar, Ron Andriuli and Tom Conners in particular

Kenny Barron, Dan Goode, Joe Zitt, and the Opium Den Mothers, who refined and redefined music for me

John Swenson, Dave Marsh, Dave Sprague, and all my other colleagues who turned me on to so much good music

Marc Jaffee, a music teacher in the mold of Dick Thompson

my wife, Caren, who once accused Ornette Coleman of playing "that cat-swinging music" to his face, in public (I guess you had to be there)

my son Mike, who keeps bringing home these arcane Japanese bands

my son Larry, who has the potential to be a real keyboard prodigy

my son Bill, who, at seven years old, wants to write songs

my late Grandma Goldie, who always wanted to hear me practice

my folks, who always encouraged my music, even though they couldn't stand it

anyone who has ever told me, "Man, you've got to hear this."

As long as there are people like this in the world, music will not suck.

"The music business has always had the nurturing instinct of a great white shark."
—Paul Taylor, *Manchester Evening News*

"The music business is a cruel and shallow money trench, a long plastic hallway where thieves and pimps run free, and good men die like dogs. There's also a negative side."
—Dr. Hunter S. Thompson

"That's not a dirty little secret. It's a fact. Take away the incentive for major or minor financial reward and you dilute the pool of musicians."
—Courtney Love

"When a forest catches fire, you have death, but there's also birth that comes from it. I think that's what we're seeing."
—Sharon Corbitt, Ocean Way Recording Studio, Nashville

Contents

Acknowledgments

I'd like to thank:

Jim Fitzgerald, my extraordinary agent, who went to bat for this book in a big way.

Yuval Taylor, my editor, who had a lot of ideas that I didn't think of, and a lot of ideas I *wouldn't* think of, but who made sure that this book didn't suck; and Devon Freeny, who nitpicked the copy until it made sense, dammit!

The late, great Juggy Gayles, a central character in this book, as he started telling me dirty little secrets and home truths about the music business when I was quite naive. I miss him.

Doug Howard, for vetting some of the stuff that I really needed to know I got right. Doug was always there with a prompt response and a kind word, and he'll never know how much I needed them at the time. He also titled chapter 13 on payola.

Beth Krakower, who unwittingly helped write chapter 12, based on a dog and pony show we've been perfecting for our classes over the course of several years.

Jerry Lembo, Barry Bergman, Dave Seitz, Jack Ponti, and Ed Majewski, for information and issues I hadn't thought of.

Dennis D'Amico, of Lost Audience Records, for the framing concept of chapter 24.

A very special thank you to Vic Steffens, who over a holiday weekend answered a question so thoroughly and thoughtfully, I was in tears.

Ian Coyne, who rescued some critical information at the 11th hour.

Jeff Jacobson, of Jacobson and Colfin, PC, LLC, my legal guardians, for his help on the contracts chapter.

My class on Marketing and Management in the Music Business and Music in Our Time at Ramapo College of New Jersey, for bringing all sorts of information to my attention.

Burt Goldstein at Big Daddy Distribution, my first long-term boss in the biz when he ran Ben-El, who helped with SoundScan numbers, too.

The cast and crew at the New York Public Library for the Performing Arts Dorothy and Lewis B. Cullman Center, Hammerstein Archives of Recorded Sound and Music Division, the *sine qua non* research facility for all matters musical, and the George T. Potter Library, electric and acoustic.

Dasher, May, J-mo and J-9, Laurie, Bego, Top Cat, Meliss, and on for all the encouragement.

The good netizens of the Velvet Rope, whose informed opinions over the course of the years shaped parts of this book.

Introduction

My friends and acquaintances know that for the past 30 years or so, I have worked in one aspect or another of the music business—as a performer, recording artist, journalist, promotion person, marketer, engineer, producer, A&R scout, retailer, critic, crony, gadfly, and guide. Over the last decade, the question most people ask me is "Whatever became of good music?"

Now, I realize "good music" is a pretty subjective phrase, but I also understand the sentiment. Once upon a time, as so many stories begin, you could tune into the radio and hear great things, musical revelations. As "Little Steven" Van Zandt said in the foreword to Richard Neer's excellent (and much cited here) *FM*:

> Rock music had become my religion. Radio my church. And these DJs my priests, rabbis, and gurus. They would preach from the gospel of Dylan, Lennon and McCartney, Jagger and Richards, the Book of Townshend, the Song of the Byrds, and the Acts of Davies. . . . Righteous Rock Radio would continue on a bit longer, struggling valiantly into the eighties, and die quietly in the nineties like a spent stick of incense. In its place, anybody twenty-one years old or younger inherited a wasteland of corporate conservatism tightly controlling lifeless depersonalized deregionalized homogenized DJs spewing out depersonalized deregionalized homogenized playlists.

Now, the real answer to these people is that there is probably more good music available now for the average person's consumption than at any time in history. The problem is *hearing* it, finding it, getting access to it, because no one is going to lay it in your ear any more, though they might try. On the surface, Little

Steven's "wasteland of corporate conservatism" would seem to be in control. But for anyone willing to scratch a little beyond the surface, there's a wealth of great sounds.

In this book I explain just what happened to *easily accessible* good music, music that fans of WNEW in New York and KSAN in the Bay Area remember. It sometimes still exists in odd enclaves like public radio in L.A. and Newark, but you gotta get hipped to know that programs like *Morning Becomes Eclectic* or *Rhythm Review* are out there. Music isn't going anywhere, but music fans who know what they like will have to go into hunter-gatherer mode to get it.

Not long ago, I had the opportunity to poll several classes full of undergraduate college students from a good-sized state college in suburban New Jersey as to their favorite radio stations. The answer genuinely surprised me. Over half of them said that when they listened to the radio at all, they usually listened to the classic rock station out of New York City, which plays much of the music Steve Van Zandt was talking about.

This means that many of these people, just entering their third decade of life, listen to music recorded largely before they were born. It breaks a paradigm that goes back to Socrates and before—that every generation listens to music their parents hate. This generation is listening to the same music their parents listened to and finds it superior to the music of their contemporaries. "Classic rock" is one of the most successful formats on radio today for more reasons than just parental nostalgia. When we examined why, the answer came down to quality, musicianship, and a message. They said that, by and large, the music of their generation lacks these qualities. This boils down to a large number of disenfranchised, shell-shocked music fans who want to know what happened. The book you hold in your hands will explain that, offering dissatisfied music lovers a reason for the fall of popular music.

This book lays out, in very specific terms, how the system that turned music into a commodity ultimately failed, trivializing its product and the user of that product (that would be us, the music fans). Once you finish reading, you will have a better idea of why today's popular music sucks, and maybe even a reason or two to hope that things will improve.

The music business has come up with some fascinating rationales for their slumping sales. Imagine if General Motors started to assess some of the reasons for declining sales and it came up with:

➤ people selling used cars
➤ people buying third-party parts
➤ people buying parts at junk yards

So it started to lobby for laws against the secondhand sale of its products.

Or envision the post office declaring that mail was its intellectual property and starting to sue the providers and users of e-mail.

Sounds ridiculous? It's what the record business has been up to for years. It has spent the last decade trying to find a fall guy to account for declining sales. The upstart technology of the Internet did throw the music business for a loop, but the music business's reaction to this disruptive technology bears scrutiny, if only for how it mirrors the fortunes of other businesses. Is it possible that in reacting like a business—and like many businesses before it had acted—the music industry really couldn't help trying to maintain the status quo?

With several down years behind it, the industry is in big trouble. The powers-that-be blame digital file sharing and CD burning for the business's woes. Yet evidence shows that file sharing might actually help sell physical copies.

The record industry's finger-pointing hides the multifaceted reason for the industry's decline, the dirty little secrets of the record business. The amount of money and energy used to create this smokescreen is just one of the reasons why so much music you hear sucks.

Cognoscenti in the music business point to a host of problems of much longer standing than the World Wide Web to account for their waning fortunes:

➤ There has been consolidation in all aspects of the music business, including
  ➤ the PolyGram-Universal merger
  ➤ the rumored future sale or merger of EMI
  ➤ the buying spree that led to Clear Channel owning nearly half of the U.S. radio business and its offshoot, Live Nation, close to 80 percent of the live music industry
  ➤ would-be songwriter and booze heir Edgar Bronfman getting squeezed out of Universal, "buying" the venerable Warner Music Group, and taking it public
  ➤ the merger of Sony Music and the Bertelsmann Music Group, a record company initially run by a former television executive
➤ The rise of these publicly held companies requires that record labels, as competing parts of these entertainment conglomerates, seek short-term profits to answer quarterly to stockholders. They do this in lieu of developing the career artists that traditionally fueled the business.
➤ Independent promoters maintain a stranglehold on both the radio and record business.
➤ The business continues to concentrate on what they have always regarded as their demographic—12- to 25-year-olds—and ignoring
  ➤ the plethora of entertainment and leisure choices this age group now enjoys

➤ the people who grew up in an era without so many options, who consider music part of their being.

There are many more reasons, though, including systemic problems with the way the record industry does business. This book reveals and analyzes these factors, many of which even industry professionals don't know about, since one facet of the business often doesn't know how the other facets operate.

For example, I once had a student in my Introduction to the Music Business class in New York who worked as the director of A&R for a large, popular, successful record company, run by one of the top young music business entrepreneurs of the 1990s. After the first class I asked him if this might be too basic for him, as he likely made more money from the music business than all the other people in the room—including me—combined. He said that might be true, but he still had no idea what the people in the office next to him were doing.

With one hand not knowing what the other is doing, is it any wonder that the popular music business faces big trouble?

Of course, many take the position that actually making money from music somehow dilutes the music's "purity," that the best music gets made under the rubric of "art for art's sake." And while plenty of the prefabricated music, made only to keep the sluices of the machine lubricated, contributes to why so much music we hear sucks, making music for money is not inherently evil or even a bad thing. The reason the subtitle of this tome reads "Why *So Much* Music You Hear Sucks" and not "Why *All* the Music You Hear Sucks" is that some commercial music actually speaks to people artistically, and some independent music is utter crap. One of the great things about art is that there are no absolutes. Music that ignores the audience *defines* self-indulgence and often borders on (or goes right off into) pretentiousness, while popular—that is, what the people like—defines popular music, and sometimes the reason might even be the music rather than the marketing.

People have made money from music for millennia. Music itself has been around nearly as long as humans have been thinking animals. There are paintings of flute players in Neolithic caves in Tanzania, and it stands to reason that before developing a specialized tool like the flute, people would use their voices, and hit things to keep time for dancing and ceremonies. Playing music would have been mostly an "amateur" activity, dating from the days when humanity began to have time for recreation. Even these early instruments were generally created by the musicians, again as recreation. So when did music "go pro"?

When I pose this question in class, students will often cite Edison, or even point to the advent of rock and roll in the 1950s. But actually, the Bible refers to musicians playing in the courts of King David and Solomon, and one would imagine that such performers would get paid. A millennium after that, the Greek theater used music and paid the musicians who played there. So music became a profession sometime before the Common Era. That's at least 2,500 and probably more like 4,000 years of professional music.

The theater tradition spread to Rome and the entirety of the Roman Empire. The theaters were often used for animal fights and large meetings too, and beyond the tragedy and comedy of the day, ballets and musical performances were held, once again using people who were paid to play. In all of these settings, musicians were divided into two classes—people who played it for money and people who played it for recreation. Very few of the people who played for money could do it as their sole means of support. (Sound familiar?)

In the Middle Ages, there were two chief means of making money, even a living, as a musician. Jongleurs and minstrels tended to be vagabonds, going from town to town, entertaining at weddings and the like. If they were lucky, they could find a wealthy patron. Some of these relationships became longstanding—the former minstrel could become a manor's music master, if the manor could afford such a luxury. Sometimes the relationship would last through the winter, the minstrel entertaining after meals and for company, perhaps giving lessons to other (usually younger) members of the household for room, board, and perhaps a small stipend.

Another major employer of musicians during the Middle Ages was the Church. Their musicians could be from the various orders or from the laity. Johann Sebastian Bach, for example, played and composed church music. Indeed, musical notation as we know it emerged so that music could be sent from church to church, country to country, a sort of *lingua franca* among musicians. This started happening across Europe around the 13th century.

So through the Middle Ages, several classes of musicians emerged, each beholden to one master or another—the court musicians, the direct descendent of the manor musicians, who were treated like servants by the nobility; church musicians, who often pursued other lines of work as well (Bach, for example, sold spirits); and itinerant musicians, the minstrels and *klezmorim*, who went about playing weddings and other events wherever they could.

With the emergence of the Renaissance and a European middle class, and as the craft of playing music well became more rarified and musicians emancipated themselves from the courts, musicians' guilds sprang up across Europe. These guilds weeded out poor musicians (an audition was required to join), offered their members some legal protection and clout, helped them get work, and furthered their training. But mostly they offered a certain level of prestige that allowed musicians to emerge as part of the rising middle class. The guilds set payment standards, stabilizing the market.

About the same time, a goldsmith by the name of Johan Gutenberg created a method for setting type. It was soon discovered that movable type could be set for other symbols, including musical notation. At that point the question became who owns the music, the person who wrote it or the person who printed it? Publishers started to buy compositions from composers, but ultimately the publishers and composers agreed on a royalty situation, splitting the proceeds 50/50, a foreshadowing of the current relationship.

This led to the question of how to protect the creator's interests and how to keep creators creating. In France, the concept of protecting ideas become codified about midway through the 18th century. Nascent America followed suit with its first nationwide set of laws, the Constitution. In article 1, it states that Congress shall have the ability "to promote the Progress of Science and useful Arts, by securing for limited Times to Authors and Inventors the exclusive Right to their respective Writings and Discoveries." With this one line, the concept of copyright and intellectual property came to the New World.

Musically, this was not of much consequence. No major intellectual property issues arose in the music business until 1850, when a piano mechanic named John McTammany invented the "pianola," or player piano. He discovered, however, that making the instrument and marketing it were two different matters, and the pianola didn't really catch on until he sold his patents to the Aeolian Organ Company in 1888. It took 11 years, but at the turn of the century, the pedal-operated player piano, using music "recorded" onto a perforated roll of thick paper, hit the market. Within a few years, you could find them in 75,000 homes and businesses. Over one million piano rolls were sold. By 1920, the pianola had turned into a $20 million annual business. In 1921, of the 341,652 pianos sold, nearly 60 percent were mechanical.

This created a question within the music business: how to pay the composers for these perforated rolls of paper that were playing their music? It wasn't the same thing as sheet music or folios of songs. This was a mechanical reproduction. Eventually, each roll sold entitled the composer and publisher to a mechanical royalty. In a few more years, this concept would become even more important, as we'll see when we deal with contracts and rights.

So music has meant money for millennia. As much as the phrase "music business" defines what has turned into a giant ruminant digestive system for sound, it also functions as an equation: music ≅ business. Even the artists who play only for themselves and friends get involved in musical commerce: they buy instruments, sheet music, and especially records. But even before Edison embedded sound on tinfoil, music and business had an uneasy partnership. Whether the music sucks or doesn't—a highly subjective and personal matter—a ton of money gets spent in the production, promotion, and ultimately the sale of all things musical. Where money goes, greed and all of greed's henchmen—avarice, bullshit, corruption, deceit—come out to play.

Which gets us to the meat of the matter—all ruminant digestive systems produce meat, after all. Because as much as the artist gets the music into the fan/consumer's hands and ears, the business creates the context for the commerce, and as it works today, it only builds on what has worked before. Throughout this book, I'll be picking points in history when certain practices became paradigms, showing how they became part of the popular music mindset. The precarious tightrope team of art and commerce play few more dangerous venues than popular music. For music to stay healthy, for musicians to both thrive and have the time to create, money must grease the wheels.

However, when the money becomes hidebound, can the other side of the equation avoid getting affected? Will the music business pull an ouroboros, swallowing its own tail and threatening to consume itself until it simply disappears? Or will it emulate the phoenix, growing old and burning itself out, only to arise, better and more beautiful, from the ashes?

Part I | **Playback and Payback**

*How the Record Business
Drowned in Its Own Success*

1

Who's in Charge Here? You're Kidding!

IN 1955, ENGLISH EMI purchased Capitol Records, a 12-year-old company that had been founded in the midst of World War II. Getting the raw materials for the manufacture of records had verged on impossible then, due to wartime restrictions on purchasing the lacquer used to hold the grooves on the 78 rpm record, and the copper used to cut the masters from which the glass-and-lacquer records were made. These obstacles didn't stop songwriter Johnny Mercer, lyricist–turned–movie mogul Buddy DeSylva, and some associates from forming the company, which they started with two major hits, Mercer's own "Strip Polka" and Ella Mae Morse's version of "Cow Cow Boogie." In the record business, the most successful businesspeople are often the most contrarian.

Yet a dozen years after starting, Capitol submitted to foreign domination.

Not that EMI was the first multinational record company—not by a long shot. In 1902, as the craze for sound recording spread beyond America, the Victor Talking Machine Company made the first international alliance, joining forces with British Gramophone Company. Victor had already pulled a contrarian move, switching from the wax cylinder sold by Edison and Columbia, and selling the new (at the time) glass-and-lacquer disc and the hardware to play it. British Gramophone became disc based, and Victor started to use British Gramophone's logo, a little terrier with its ear cocked toward the horn, listening to "His Master's Voice."

What EMI knew from experience dawned on the rest of the business world by observation: the record business, as it stood in

3

the early 1960s, lacked schooling. The people running the business possessed a lot of native smarts, but very few had formal business training—guys like Artie Ripp, who hadn't even finished high school, were running record companies and making a fortune. By 1967, record company revenues topped the billion-dollar mark, spiking that year on the crest of EMI's wave of Beatlemania and the subsequent invasion of the musical redcoats that segued into the Summer of Love—youth culture beginning to reach its full economic flower.

Now, by the tail end of the 1960s, the thinking in the corporate suites went something like this: if these uneducated guys, often working just this side of the law, could rake in all this big money, imagine what we, with our MBAs and JDs, could do if we brought some standard business practices to the party. It was pretty easy to see their point of view when you looked at some of the people in charge of many of the big hits of the mid-1960s:

Artie Ripp had ripped up the market with his own Kama Sutra label and his big act, the Loving Spoonful. Ripp had worked his way up after dropping out of high school:

> I started walking around Broadway and I'd see these kids who were making records and not getting paid. They could have a number one record on the charts and end up owing the record company a half a million dollars. . . . I thought, "This business has some system." . . . Every party was charged to the artist. "I've got a hundred hookers. Charge them to the artist."

Phil Spector, together with Lester Sill, ran the Philles label, home of the Righteous Brothers' "You've Lost That Lovin' Feelin'." Even before he left high school, Spector had enjoyed a rapid rise to chart success with his group the Teddy Bears and their hit "To Know Him Is to Love Him," which topped the charts, sold millions of copies, and earned the group about $3,000 in total. He had one year of college (working toward a degree as a court stenographer) before he headed to New York for a job as an interpreter. He never made the interview, falling in with a bunch of other musicians and doing studio work for songwriters Jerry Lieber and Mike Stoller. Having worked with Sill during his days as an artist, Spector rejoined him as a partner some four years later, after working his way up in the Lieber/Stoller organization to become a prodigious producer of hit records for artists like Ben E. King and Gene Pitney. With the Philles label, he and Sill helped introduce the world to the girl-group sound that dominated pop music before the British invasion took hold.

Simon Waronker had started out as a violin prodigy, a first-call violinist in Hollywood. He founded Liberty Records in 1955, at the age of 40, with the help of 20th Century Fox. Beginning with orchestral pop like Julie London, he moved into novelty records by Ross (Dave Seville) Bagdasarian, scion of the Chipmunks dynasty; rock and roll with Eddie Cochran; and R&B with Billy Ward and the Dominoes. He even signed a very young Willie Nelson.

Berry Gordy started Motown in 1958, and his story has come to be Horatio Alger–style folklore, especially in the African American community. After dropping out of high school to box, Gordy was drafted to fight in Korea. On his demobilization, he opened a record shop to support his songwriting. When neither made him enough money, he went to work on one of Detroit's many automobile assembly lines. His luck began to change when a family friend introduced him to Jackie Wilson, who took one of the songs Gordy wrote, "Reet Petite," into the *Billboard* Hot 100 Singles chart. Wilson recorded four more Gordy songs over the next few years. This gave Gordy the latitude to get off the assembly line and begin to produce music instead. He started a record label to put out the music he produced. He had early, influential hits like Barrett Strong's version of Gordy's song "Money" and Smokey Robinson and the Miracles' "Shop Around." The Temptations' "My Girl," the Supremes' "Stop in the Name of Love," and a number of other hits from Motown made Gordy a major force in the music business. At the height of the British invasion, he gave the English acts a run for the pop music dollar.

Ahmet Ertegun, son of a Turkish ambassador, formed Atlantic Records in 1947 with his friend Herb Abramson, funded by a loan from their dentist. "When I first started Atlantic Records," he said, "I intended to make good blues and jazz music, as well as some pop music. We did it for one main reason. We wanted to make the kind of records we wanted to buy."

Even some of the Beatles' biggest hits early in their career were not on Capitol in the United States but on the indies Vee-Jay, Tollie, and Swan. James Bracken and Vivian Carter Bracken had started Vee-Jay with a loan of $500 from a pawnbroker; Tollie was an imprint of Vee-Jay; Dick Clark co-owned Swan Records with Si Waronker. Clark was the only one in this crowd with a college degree. Similarly, Ertegun's Atco got into the act, reaching the Top 20 with an early Beatles recording of "Ain't She Sweet."

So, to the MBAs and JDs looking in, the record business seemed like it was just this side of gangland. They imagined what the business might look like if considerations like profit and loss statements entered into the equation.

What the corporations failed to account for was that the music business had been built on an often-entropic foundation that the assorted miscreants who grew up with the business understood and made peace with. The entropy worked on several levels.

The music business of the time (and much of it even now) would not do well in answering the key question of the Rotary: "Is it fair for all concerned?" Instead it operated on more of an everyone-for-themselves level. In many ways, it resembled (and perhaps continues to resemble) high-stakes gambling more than any particular business model. And like high-stakes gambling, the people who were the best at it knew how to stack the deck so that nobody noticed, had mastered the deadpan poker face in negotiations, and never, ever let anyone see them sweat.

Stacking the deck predominantly affected the way that artists were remunerated. Particularly in the early days of rock, as Ripp pointed out, musicians could sell millions of records and not make a penny from it, in fact owing the record company money. This went on until the lawyers began to take an interest in that end of the record business, representing artists to make sure that they got a relatively fair shake (and the lawyer got their percentage). Later on, we'll take a look at one of these chillingly one-sided contracts.

Independent blues and proto-rock-and-roll label Chess Records was notorious for this sort of behavior. "I got stranded in Chicago and Leonard Chess found me, picked me up, and put me on his label," recalled urban blues legend Etta James.

> He paid the balance of the money that [her previous record company] wanted. Chess had a check on his desk. He said, "I want you with Chess records. Let me show you what my artists get." Because I was kind of looking, I could see there was a check there. He lifted this check up to me and it was for 90-some thousand dollars, and it was made out to Chuck Berry and Alan Freed. I was about to faint, there were so many zeros there. And he said, "This is just for six months' payment for 'Maybelline.'" I had one hit record, "All I Do Is Cry," and then I had "Stop the Wedding" and then I had "My Dearest . . ."—they were going in layers. So, it was about a year later; when it would be time for me to receive some royalties, I went down there. I knew I was going to look down there and see a nice fat figure. I looked and I saw that it was written in red. And I said, "$14,000! All right!" And Leonard said, "Hold it, hold it." I just looked like, wow, that's really good for me. But he said, "Don't get all bent out of shape." And I was kind of confused, like "What is he saying that for?" And he says, "Look, Etta, don't worry about what that says. What do you need?" Now, I'm really confused. "Here's what I need, in big red numbers."

And that's when Etta James learned what red ink on a ledger meant. Between her housing expenses, recording expenses, and, most important, the money it took to buy her contract from the previous record company, even a year of hits couldn't get her into positive numbers the way the contract she signed was stacked up.

"Now, Leonard Chess did take care of quite a few things," she adds, "but those things could never add up to what my royalties were."

"Everybody that you talk to who came from Chess Records will tell you, almost like a broken record, the same thing," notes another Chess artist, Elias "Bo Diddley" McDaniels.

> We got ripped! It's bad, man. I appreciate Chess Records giving me the opportunity to become Bo Diddley and do all the great things I've done, but I don't appreciate being ripped off because I had to trust them with the money that comes in and they have to pay me. I ain't got shit. I've been waiting all these years like a good Samaritan, thinking that one day I'll look in the mailbox and say, "Oh wow! There's a check in here that will make my pockets look like footballs." It never happened. You dig what I'm saying? I'm very upset about it. They made a pit bull out of me, with an extra set of teeth. Is that bad enough? They poked at me and poked at me and made me an evil dude.

Beyond this, Ripp, Spector, Sill, Gordy, Chess, et al. all knew that they could, through no fault of their own, lose millions as easily as they could make them, and on occasion they did just that. Few of them got into the music business to get rich; it just happened that they did. Many, many others made a living, and some lost everything. "It was a labor of love," noted Bob Weinstock, who made a living with Prestige Records, in the process recording immortal sides by Miles Davis, Sonny Rollins, John Coltrane, and dozens of others.

> Most of the people involved in the business at the time—Orrin Keepnews [Riverside], Les Koenig [Contemporary], Alfred Lion [Blue Note]—were collectors and fans. We loved the music. For the musicians, too, it was no joke; they were very serious about what they were doing. It was a pleasure to work with them. Our shared goal was to make good music—which we did.

Of course, one of the ways Prestige Records made money was keeping recording costs down. It was notorious as the "junkie's label," paying off its addicted artists with a fix. It certainly had its pick of some of the finest: John Coltrane, Thelonious Monk, Miles Davis, Sonny Stitt, and Sonny Rollins were all addicted, all living in New York, and all recording for Prestige.

Another aspect of the record business on which the MBAs could not get a solid handle was the actual profits and losses. The losses, because the businesses were private, were private as well. The gains were visible for anyone to see (and hear). The winners were as obvious as the losers flew below the radar, so it was easy to believe, if you weren't inside it, that everything that came into a record store flew out to the tune of singing cash registers.

Beyond that, the "record guys" demonstrated, even with their failures, an innate knowledge of what people wanted to hear. It was an era when the perception of music largely selling itself was not as far fetched as it seems now, though the mechanics of how the music "sold itself" would appall the MBAs when they started to make their move to capitalize on the gold on vinyl that they saw in records.

2

Answering to the Stockholders, Not the Audience

PUBLIC LOSSES were not all that visible if the company didn't want them to be. Even the *gonifs* knew enough to hire clever accountants. The corporations had them on staff. For instance, carefully hidden in the Warner Bros.' film paperwork was the fact that in 1963, its five-year-old record division was losing about three million dollars a year.

Despite this, in the mid-1960s Seven Arts, a small distributor and producer, doing its best corporate approximation of a tiny mongoose eating an enormous cobra (or the same cobra eating a cow), swallowed Warner Bros.' film and record companies. This gave Seven Arts enormous amounts of debt. Unable to sustain it, in 1967 Seven Arts sold out the entire company, which at that point included Atlantic Records.

The buyer—the first major nonmusical company to take the plunge into the deep, cold, murky waters of the record business— was the Kinney Corporation. Kinney had built its business on limousines, parking lots, and chains of funeral parlors. The head of the business, Steve Ross, had a lot in common with the self-made music people he'd be working with, one of the reasons Warner Bros. would actually work well for nearly two decades after it became a public company in the early 1960s. A Brooklyn guy with a great head for figures, a disarming personality, and a mastery of the art of the deal, Ross had married well, but had proved his mettle in the way he ran his wife's family business, building it into a public company by 1962.

Earlier in 1967, he had acquired a small talent agency, and he enjoyed working in show business. When the Seven Arts deal came up, he saw no downside. "If you're not a risk taker," he said, "you should get the hell out of business."

Ross was not a musician, or even particularly musical. He had the dubious honor of pioneering the era in the record business in which business acumen meant more than musical acumen. For example, at the CBS Record group in the "Black Rock" building, the *2001*-like mock obsidian monolith at the corner of 52nd Street and Sixth Avenue that housed the company at the time, a similar change took place. Goddard Lieberson, the conservatory-educated president of Columbia Records, retired, turning over the record company president's office to one of the company's lawyers, Clive Davis. Davis recalled:

> It took several years to break down the barriers of suspicion that existed against lawyers and people who couldn't read music. . . .
> I was not a rock 'n' roller, by any means. I came to my position at CBS as someone who loved Broadway, someone who loved songs. I was a lawyer and I wore my suits and ties in New York and I never tried to be "with it."

Within a few years at Warner, Ross had sold off all the nonentertainment assets of his company and, 10 years after he took Kinney public, Ross renamed the company Warner Communications, Inc. For the first 10 years, Warner's record division was the envy of the music business, mostly because it was run as if it were a privately held company. Ross put experienced music businesspeople like Mo Ostin and Joe Smith in charge while keeping other music business legends like Atlantic Records honcho Ahmet Ertegun doing what they did best—finding music they liked and selling it. Business as usual put Warner on top of the music business heap and kept it there.

"Warner's Mo Ostin and Joe Smith had clout, but Steve Ross was the big boss," recalled Walter Yetnikoff, who replaced Davis as head of Columbia about the time Warners moved in across the street from Black Rock, into its new Rockefeller Center digs in 1975.

> With Warner movies and Warner music at his command, Ross was a smooth operator, a much beloved leader who, unlike CBS, paid his underlings well. With the Grateful Dead, Van Morrison, Black Sabbath and James Taylor, Warner was winning market shares left and right. Ross also had a selling tool that I lacked: Ross told artists he could put them in the movies. I had no movies to put them in.

"Steve Ross realized it was music, not film, that was the engine of growth," said Jac Holzman, who headed the Warner-owned label Elektra Records at the time. "We threw off so much cash that we were self-funding as we went along. Jerry Levin [the former Time Warner CEO who succeeded Ross] didn't have a clue about what the music business was about. He didn't respect it. He didn't care, and it showed."

Because of that disrespect, the record companies Time Warner held started falling into disrepair, suffering from their own success. The nature of publicly traded companies is inherently very different from that of privately held companies. Because a publicly traded company sells stock to the public, it has to publish financial information quarterly via the Securities and Exchange Commission (SEC), and provide a corporate report annually to all of the people who hold its stock. Before the record divisions became so visible and the profits became such a driving force within the web of corporate holdings for already public companies like RCA and CBS, the performance of those divisions flew largely under the radar.

By the 1980s, however, the music divisions accounted for a much larger percentage of their corporate parent's profits. As the people in charge went from old-line professional music people like Joe Smith to corporate appointees, accountants, and MBAs, the nature of the business began to change. Those quarterly reports became more and more important, and the method of generating the profits less and less essential.

In the 1950s, '60s, and '70s, before the corporate reports spotlighted the cash laid out for the practice, record companies had the leisure to develop artists. It took Bruce Springsteen three albums to develop a reputation beyond the Jersey Shore and his record company. Today he probably would never get the time he needed to make his breakout albums and become one of Columbia's biggest sources of income from 1975 onward.

However, even the more successful independent record companies, where this talent could develop, saw fit to sell out to the corporate interests. There were many reasons why the smaller, independent record companies succumbed to the siren song of the majors, but when boiled down to their essence it was all reduced to one: money. Independent distribution left a lot to be desired, especially when a company wanted to compete toe to toe against the big boys. "In 1967 or '68, we sold [Atlantic Records] to what was then Warner Seven Arts," recalled Ahmet Ertegun.

> When we first came, we didn't have any distribution. That was created after the group got together, after Warners and ourselves, and then Asylum and Elektra, solidified. Then we set up our own distribution. Then my brother set up our international distribution, which is now one of the most formidable in the world.

Companies that relied mostly on deep catalog often did well—Fantasy was independent for nearly half a century before being acquired by another, wealthier independent company, and then only after the company's owner decided he'd rather make movies. But for the most part, independent record companies capitulated to either the lure of incredible amounts of money—like the half a billion paid to Herb Alpert and Jerry Moss for their A&M Records—or overextension of their assets, which is how the Sony Music Group came into possession of the CTI catalog.

For those who are unfamiliar with the strange and somewhat melancholy tale of CTI: after leaving the ABC/Impulse Label that he founded, Creed Taylor started his own string of jazz labels in the late 1960s (CTI, Kudu, and Salvation), with moderate successes by George Benson, Milt Jackson, Chet Baker, Bob James, Freddy Hubbard, and dozens of others. With engineer par excellence Rudy Van Gelder behind the board and Taylor making the musical decisions, they managed to do quite well for about five years. Then they started to do even better.

"Deodato's *Prelude* was the start of the success of the label, and the failure," noted the label's former operations manager Didier Deutsch.

> The success of [Deodato's] "Also Sprach Zarathustra" created the drive that propelled the label to the forefront, and also was the cause for the label's eventual demise, because they overexpanded at that time. They tried, but with very few exceptions they did not succeed.

This is to say that they never again achieved the status of the Deodato single, which spent two weeks just shy of the top of the *Billboard* charts. Rather than accepting the single's success as the freak occurrence that it was, Taylor made the fatal error of thinking it was precedent.

Deutsch said:

> It's very nice to sell 250,000 albums, but for a small label, it's quite a burden to have that kind of money. They got too much money at one time, and they decided to expand and go independent. In nine months, they opened something like nine branches, and all the money was gone. They spent money they didn't have after a while. They were not able to sustain the success of Deodato's album with other albums.

Ultimately, the CTI catalog was absorbed into the vast CBS Records archives of recorded sound. There, it became further fodder for the reissue mills that helped grease the corporation's more successful distribution channels. As the profitability of these channels became more and more evident, more and more of the big boys came out to play.

Beyond corporate entities that got the entertainment bug, like Ross's Kinney, record companies had a certain appeal to companies that made the hardware for their music. Philips Electronics, for example, had long been in bed, corporately speaking, with the record business. It brought the technology to the relationship, manufacturing records and inventing the compact cassette and the CD. By 1980, along with its original holdings like Deutsche Grammophon, it owned Mercury Records, MGM Records, Verve Records, RSO Records, Casablanca Records, Decca Records, and London Records, all of which had become part of Philips's recording arm, PolyGram.

While a 1983 merger with Warner Bros. got thrown out by both the German Cartel Office and the U.S. Federal Trade Commission over fears that it would create a monopoly, 15 years later the standards seemed to relax. At that point, the sale of Philips's music software division to Seagram went through with much gnashing of music business teeth, but just a whisper at the FTC. Seagram, the liquor giant, had bought MCA—the entertainment conglomerate that had started in 1929 as a talent agency—in 1995. By that time, MCA had already bought out (or acquired the assets of) such noted indies as Def Jam Records, Motown Records, Uptown Records, Geffen Records, Chess Records, and Universal Pictures. PolyGram, in the interim, had made high-profile purchases of A&M and Island Records. Seagram acquired PolyGram for a bit over $10 billion, and its music labels were put under the umbrella of the Universal Music Group. Only two years later, all of Seagram was acquired by the French media conglomerate Vivendi.

"Everything that's wrong with the record industry today amplifies itself out of the hallways of Universal, and has since the company was glued together," said one West Coast media executive. Helping to explain why he left the record business, he ran down a list of the company's change-resistant key executives:

Zach Horowitz, Doug Morris, Jimmy Iovine, Jordon Schur, Polly Anthony, and L. A. Reid are all dopes that are hanging on to an outdated model delivered on a 20-year-old format, that most people could care less about, now sold in stores that worry more about selling tires and washing machines. . . . If you're a major label senior executive, why would you want anything to change, especially the perks and the salary?

Like Philips, Sony manufactured entertainment hardware and wanted a foothold in the software end of things, especially after the fall of its Betamax standard as a consumer format for video. One of the reasons it failed is that Sony's main competitor, Matsushita, owned film rights; Sony did not. "Sony wanted their own software," Walter Yetnikoff said of the company's 1988 purchase of the CBS Record group, in part to feed the burgeoning market Sony had recently cultivated with the Walkman. "In that department, CBS Records was a gold mine."

Two years earlier, the privately held German publishing and entertainment conglomerate Bertelsmann AG bought RCA Records and changed the company's name to BMG Music. The sale included RCA Video, the company's direct-marketing arm, and its custom pressing service, which would make CDs featuring mostly RCA acts for various companies (for example, songs about smoking for a tobacconist). The sale did not affect the joint-venture RCA Columbia Home Video club.

The video club, however, prefigured on a smaller scale the shape of things to come. On August 5, 2004, BMG and Sony announced the merger of their music divisions. "By pooling the resources of two of the most creative companies in the music industry we are perfectly positioned to help our artists realize their creative goals," the new hybrid company's CEO Andrew Lack (a television executive up until a couple of years earlier) said, "while at the same time providing greater value to music consumers around the world."

One of the reasons for the merger was, of course, to remain competitive with the Universal Music Group, which took over the

#1 record manufacturer position upon its merger. (Sony/BMG still fell short of pulling ahead by about half a billion dollars.) Another reason was to jettison about 2,000 employees, cut its payroll, and enjoy savings of about $350 million.

EMI remains unmerged as of this writing, though rumors of an EMI/Warner Bros. merger (just so they don't feel left out) keep flying. EMI owns or distributes the Virgin, Blue Note, and Capitol labels, to name a few. With EMI's recent successful years and a jump on the digital marketing of music (more on this later), however, a Warner/EMI merger may not be necessary, and in fact might be a drag on EMI. In 2004, it had something most of the other major global record companies did not: a profit.

All this corporate bedfellowing left Warner Bros. as the only U.S.-based major international record company, a distinction it maintains as of this writing. This is not to say that the company has not changed hands and corporate identities perhaps half a dozen times since Steve Ross passed on in 1992. Warner Entertainment became a part of the Time Warner empire, then part of the AOL Time Warner family, before getting sold to former Seagrams head Edgar Bronfman, who took the company public. As this is written, rumors swirl about Bronfman unloading his (and his investors) shares in the company.

So the "big six" that started the 1980s has dwindled down to the big four "major" record companies, record companies with global distribution and clout: Universal, Sony/BMG, EMI, and Warner. In terms of the economics of the new millennium, this is not unusual. "Like the major players in many industries," Patricia Seybold, author of *The Customer Revolution*, observed, "these companies are in the process of consolidating."

But even people in the record business agree this is not a great thing. "The consolidation has made the record business more about business," said record exec Tom Corson. "Before, it was more about records."

3

Who Does What to Whom
A Brief Tour of a Fictitious Record Company

WELCOME TO FUN with flowcharts. In this episode, we play Sherpa, following a piece of music from the artist's brain to the consumer and through all the steps in between. While this tour does not represent any specific record company, all of them work something like this, and have for eons. These are the broad strokes that help explain how music gets turned into a corporate commodity—and one reason the business has hit ebb tide.

Starting at the top, we have the artist. This may be one of the few instances in which the artist is at the top of the corporate structure, but for our purposes, it all starts here. The artist creates music and needs to communicate it. This is the kind of artist who would not be content for the work to get circulated only among friends and family—this artist wants the world to know and hear. Our artist can be a male or female or a group, making any kind of music and attempting to find an audience. In the process, an artist will often find an advocate and avatar, otherwise known as a personal manager.

The Team

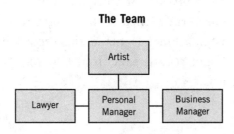

The Major Label Paradigm

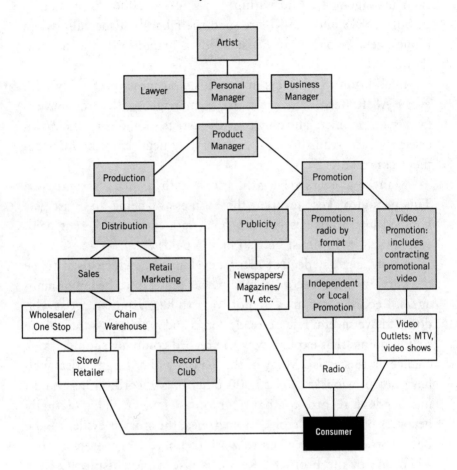

A word of warning—anyone can be a manager. Unlike, say, booking agents or automotive mechanics who in some states need licenses and must follow certain regulations to stay in business, artist managers need no license, no credentials, no experience, only a contract. No one regulates them. For you artists out there, it behooves you to make sure the manager can deliver, that the manager knows people in the music business who can help propel your music. (Keep in mind, artists from Christina Aguilera to Leonard Cohen to INXS have found it necessary to sue their management. And within one week in 2006 the managers of both INXS and the Killers sued their bands. Especially when money gets involved, an artist needs a manager they can trust. 'Nuff said.)

In addition to contacts in the music business (preferably with every A&R person in creation), a manager will often have a lawyer on retainer. The only time the artists should need their own attorney is to read through (and possibly negotiate) the management contract.

Many managers have affiliations with a *business manager*. This person makes sure that the business of being an artist gets handled like a business—taxes filed, money invested, rent paid, employees (if the artist gets so lucky) paid, etc.

Lately, a great deal of artist development, which used to be the purview of the record company, has fallen into the lap of managers. Record companies do not want to hear from an artist who doesn't have several release-ready songs and a "story"—the unique selling points that explain why the record company should take a chance on this artist. Many of the majors will not sign artists who have not previously sold 20,000 units of a record, either via an independent record company, or on their own. That actually becomes part of the "story." Sometimes, the story is evident—the Bacon Brothers didn't need to work too hard to generate a story when one of the brothers, Kevin, is also a movie star. (On the other hand, it doesn't help them sell earth-shattering numbers of records.)

For the sake of this chapter, we're going to assume our artist's sales and story are convincing, else our Sherpa won't have very much reason to guide. The manager gets the artist on the A&R radar and signed to a major label.

Getting Signed

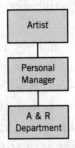

Occasionally, artists will get onto the A&R radar without benefit of a manager. If the artist gets signed, the first thing the A&R person in charge will do is find the artist a manager. The reason is pretty simple: in most cases, record companies would rather do business with a manager than have an artist running amok in their hallways. A manager ostensibly knows the "rules of the game." A good one knows how to play the rules as well as play by them. Managers will push to keep an artist in a record company's face rather than its rearview mirror. And believe it or not, that's what the record companies want—they realize that without someone holding a cattle prod there would be no motion at all.

All the little boys and girls intent on getting into the music business wanna do A&R. There is a certain amount of glamour and power there. Theoretically, the A&R department decides which artists get in. They are the gatekeepers, the maw of the digestive system of a record company. However, as we'll see later on, it ain't necessarily so. A&R people work insane hours, learning to live without sleep. Their day usually finds them at their office by 10 A.M., sifting through CDs and paperwork. Each CD generally gets about 30 seconds a track unless:

1. it has too many tracks—circular file and not even a note
2. the track is so unengaging the A&R person forgets to forward to the next track

3. the A&R person actually likes the track, in which case it goes into a pile for further review

The paperwork involves making sure all of the projects the A&R person currently has on tap are working properly—the producer the A&R person hooked up with the artist is working out, the artist is living up to contractual obligations, the company is living up to contractual obligations, negotiations with managers and the label brass are moving forward, and other issues involved in feeding the hungry maw of the record label are being handled.

Ultimately, an artist and manager who go the major label route sign a record deal offered through the A&R department. A major record company generally will pay the artist an advance against future royalties (usually between 10 and 20 percent of gross sales). The manager gets a 15–20 percent cut of this off the top. The rest of the advance will pay for making the record—studio time and hiring producers and engineers and the like—as well as giving the artist something to live on while the record is being made.

In the meantime, the A&R department will get busy.

The A&R person oversees the initial steps of the artist through the record company and recording process. If the artist did not come to the company by way of a production deal (a deal where a producer takes the artist into the studio initially and records three tracks; if those tracks land the artist a record deal, then the producer gets a piece of the action and produces all or part of the full album), the A&R person will suggest producers. If the artist or producer doesn't have a studio, the A&R person might help find the best one to suit the artist's needs. For artists who don't write their own material, the A&R person might also suggest songs.

Beyond that, though, the A&R person is the artist's champion within the record company. Often, if an A&R person leaves the company, that person's artists get divvied up among the people who are still there. These artists are called "orphans," and sometimes they get adopted by someone who loves their work and will continue to be their champion, and sometimes they wind up with the wicked stepparent of A&R.

This is not an atypical event, nor does it only happen to new artists, nor only in the record business. As Pete Townshend said, "When I was doing *The Iron Giant* with Warner Bros., the people in charge of the company and the line producers changed five times! Five times! So every time it was like a new group of people to deal with. The project remained, but the people changed."

Those poor orphaned artists frequently don't last long, unless they manage to rise above the neglect (usually with the aid of a good manager) and actually sell enough records to let them make demands of the record company.

The Handoff

Ultimately, all this activity by the A&R person, the artist, et al., will result in the producer and the artist delivering some form of digital recording medium to the A&R person. This master then makes the rounds of the record company. The heads of the company listen to it to make sure they want to sign off on it (whether or not they know a thing about music) and the promotion department listens to it to see if they hear a hit, something they can work with to get the recording some attention. It really doesn't matter, as the deck is stacked against everyone—conventional wisdom in the record business says that only about 5 percent of the records released actually recoup their advances eventually. Only perhaps 15 percent turn a profit for the record company. This is not for lack of trying, and more's the pity.

Once everyone has signed off on the recording, the A&R department hands it off to the product manager and the production department. At this step of the process, the recording goes from a raw tape to the package that you would find at your local record retailer.

Front Office and Back Office

The production process involves deciding what artwork will appear on the cover, how many pages the booklet inside the CD package will run, what kind of packaging it will use, what will be printed on the CD itself, etc. Beyond this, the production department will also come up with promotional copies of the CD, usually packaged in cardboard, paper, or plastic, as the record company has two systems through which the recording will pass— the "front office" promotion machine and the "back office" distribution machine.

Distribution

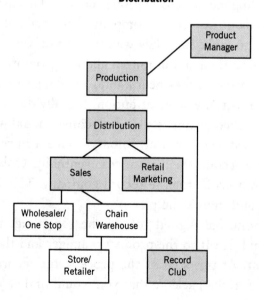

At its most basic, the distribution side gets the recording places where a consumer can buy it—a record club or catalog, a store, a Web site, anywhere a CD can be bought. At most record companies, distribution occupies a separate space from the front office functions of A&R, promotion, product management, legal, etc., although at the remote branches, sometimes the local sales and marketing force will share office space with the local promotion force. (The actual manufacturing of the CD takes place at a third location, separate from both the front office and the distribution team.)

The first thing that gets done is the sales department creates a "one sheet." This document will have the name of the artist, title of the record, order number, bar code, and the artist's "story." This might be the first exposure anyone, including the sales force, has to the artist's CD, which they will refer to as "the product." They go out to the chain warehouses and offices, determine how many copies of each CD the buyers want. Some recordings don't get ordered at all. After all, over 30,000 CDs have been released every year since the mid-1990s, many more than will fit in most stores, as we'll see.

In the meantime the marketing people prepare artwork and budgets for the displays at the base of each row of records, or "endcaps," counter displays, and other point-of-purchase techniques at retail. At the least, they make one-foot-square "slicks" of the product cover available for display by the retailers. If there is a budget for it, the department might sponsor a contest for retailers to create a display. The manager of the store with the best display selected by the marketing department wins an appropriate prize—usually a play on the artist's name or the title of the album. The marketing people's job is to make the product more visible, within budget constraints.

Slightly before the release date, the initial shipments go out to the stores or the wholesalers. Almost all CDs come out on Tuesdays, mainly because that allows them to report a full week of sales to the SoundScan sales-tracking service, which runs from

Tuesday to Tuesday. That way *Billboard*, the music industry's main trade magazine, can compile the charts based on the Sound-Scan information and go to print by Friday.

Promotion

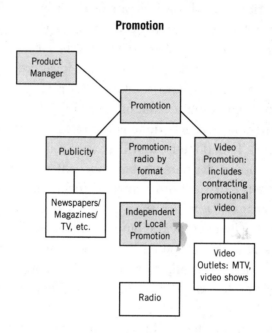

While all this is going on in the back office, the front office is cranking up the promotion machine to get the artist's "story" out to as many people as possible. The main source of exposure for music since the 1920s has been radio, but economic dynamics and the relationships between the record companies, consumers, and radio have changed radically over this last decade or so—so much so that an entire section of this book is dedicated to dealing with those particular dirty little secrets.

The entire promotion department at an indie might be one or two people, calling radio stations, writing press releases, going online to get their artists' names out there virally. At a major, it's a very different story. There is the senior vice president of promotion, who quarterbacks the promotional team. In the main office, there is a head of promotion for pretty much every genre and format of radio—the national head of classic rock promotion, national head of rhythmic Top 40 promotion, and so forth. They take care of business on a nationwide basis. In most of the branch offices, two or three local promotion people work the radio stations in their area under looser guidelines—in one office one person might handle Southwestern rock promotion—all the rock as opposed to the more specialized promotion people in the back office—while in another office someone else handles R&B promotion for New England. A record company might employ over 100 promotion people nationwide, working to get the company's records played by the local radio stations in their genre.

The publicity department tries to secure whatever media coverage on the artist it can garner—reviews of the artist's recording, news stories about the artist, etc.—again within constrictions of its budget. This is frequently where the buzz for an artist gets started. However, the publicity department is often the Rodney Dangerfield of the record company; it gets no respect at all. One publicist of my acquaintance recalled that the promotion department of the major record company for which he worked just usurped about half the publicity department's budget one year when promotion ran over.

With the rise of MTV in the 1980s, video promotion became a very important means of breaking an artist. Some artists that could never get a break on radio broke big at MTV. The network's influence started to ebb in the 1990s as it lost track of what the M in its name stood for and remade itself as a teen and young adult lifestyle channel.

Another promotional outlet that runs in waves of importance is the club scene. In the disco 1970s, the new wave '80s and the moshing '90s, club promotion broke artists on a regular basis.

All of this to get the consumers into the store to spend their $16 on a CD.

4

Q: How Many A&R Guys Does It Take to Screw in a Lightbulb? A: We Can't Screw Anymore— They Cut Off Our Balls!

VIC STEFFENS AND Mike Caplan sat in Caplan's office in the Sony Building on Madison Avenue one day in the early part of the 21st century. Caplan, at the time, was a respected A&R guy at Epic Records. His bands got love from the critics, but usually not the number of sales that it took to succeed at the "majors" level. That has never been too unusual—we'll see that such a small percentage of bands get the level of sales needed to succeed at the "majors" level, it's a wonder the "majors" level exists at all. But I'm getting ahead of myself.

One of the bands Caplan had signed, Moe, had at first seemed like a natural. They had a huge following nationwide, and were an integral part of what many touted as the "next big thing" in popular music, the jam band movement that had started to well up from what the major-record economy regarded as the underground. Like so many recordings at the major label level, Moe's potential outstripped the reality of their sales. The label brass found the number of units Moe shifted so disappointing that they dropped the band. However, Caplan's signing of Moe still inspired Steffens to set up the meeting.

Steffens has a well-earned reputation as a producer and engineer. His credits include recordings by Lita Ford, Blue Sarceno, Matt "Guitar" Murphy, Sly Stone, and dozens of other artists from blues to gospel to jam bands. He also owns his own studio, Horizon Music, and his own record company, Horizon Records, and manages several of the bands on Horizon as well (prototypical, as we'll see, of a possible future of the music biz). One of the bands with Steffen's company, the Mighty Purple, had similar roots and fans as Moe. Despite Moe's dismissal from the company roster, Caplan still apparently saw potential for the jam bands, and had some interest in signing the Mighty Purple to Epic.

Polly Anthony, at that time the president of Epic Records, came into Caplan's office. She said hello to Steffens and chatted for a few minutes. As she left, Anthony called to Caplan over her shoulder, almost as an afterthought, "Just so you're not signing another one of those jam bands."

At which point all Caplan could do was smile sheepishly. Even if he wanted to bring in the Mighty Purple, now he couldn't. He had just been overruled.

In A&R, nothing fails like failure, and nothing succeeds like success. When one band in a "movement" or "genre" fails to live up to the title of "next big thing," that genre and all artists painted with that genre's brush (or even those that just come in contact with the paint) will likely never get the opportunity to reach a vast audience suddenly. They'll have to build—or, even worse, rebuild—their audience more organically.

When an artist does catch the public's fancy, half a dozen nearly identical artists will spring up after. Those artists' stories are based on how much like the hit artist they are. (This appeals to radio, which has come to thrive on flavor-of-the-month sameness to keep its audience from switching stations.)

This situation is nothing new. From the "sweet bands" of the early 1940s to the "boy bands" of the late 1990s, when someone found a formula that worked, everyone tried to capitalize on it, and when a formula failed they dropped it with equal or greater rapidity. As 1950s record company owner Bob Marcucci recalled of the heady early days of rock and roll, "I just knew the idols were going to come in. Presley was very, very big. He and Ricky Nelson were really the two big artists, and I felt that if I could find kids like that and put them on my label, I could have some big stars, too."

He did, signing Fabian and Frankie Avalon to his label. With the help of *American Bandstand*, these became two of the most popular performers of the late 1950s and early 1960s, and laid a path for others just like them: Bobby Vee, Sal Mineo, even Bobby Darin, before he became one of the first adult contemporary swingers for the Baby Boomer era.

What has changed over the years is the role of the A&R department. In the early days, they still went out and found talent, but, as the acronym would have it, they took that talent— the A stands for Artist—and put it together with songs—the R stands for Repertoire. They even booked the studio time and hired the musicians and arrangers (although some of the era's A&R people, like Mitch Miller or Goddard Lieberson, were quite capable of writing the arrangements themselves, thanks).

"In the days of direct to disc," noted Miller, the renowned anti-rock head of A&R for Columbia Records during the waning heyday of the "great American songbook," "you went into the studio and people had to know their business. If you didn't get it on the take you were doing, you had to throw it all out and do it again."

Jerry Wexler, the legendary head of A&R for Atlantic Records a generation after Miller, concurred, tongue firmly in cheek: "Nobody really knew how to make a record when I started. You simply went into the studio, turned on the mic and said, 'Play.'"

Most of the people who said "Play" worked for the record company until rock and roll came along. Even after that, Sam Phillips owned Sun when he started producing Elvis. George Martin was an EMI employee when he went to work with the Beatles. Ahmet Ertegun and Tom Dowd were both on the Atlantic payroll (Ahmet, of course, as the boss) when they made all the great early Ray Charles sides. Maxwell Davis ran seminal L.A. blues and R&B companies Aladdin and Modern, in addition to bringing in most of the artists and making most of the records.

"Maxwell Davis is an unsung hero of early rhythm and blues," noted Mike Stoller. "He produced, in effect, all of the record sessions for Aladdin Records, Modern Records, all the local independent rhythm and blues companies in the early '50s, late '40s in Los Angeles."

Ertegun pretty much created the idea of the independent producer with his relationship with Jerry Leiber, Mike Stoller, and the Coasters. "They had this group who we later called the Coasters," said the Atlantic founder.

> They were called the Robins at the time they were recording for Jerry and Mike's label. We wanted to sign that group, and we also wanted them to continue producing them. So we signed the group, and we made a production deal with Lieber and Stoller. I guess they were the first so-called independent producers. We had a long series of hits with them.

"We figured we knew how to make records," adds Stoller, "because we had watched people make records, good people like Maxwell Davis, and so on. We learned a lot by watching him, because he was on a lot of the sessions where our songs were being done."

As record company owners during the 1950s who actually signed the artists and then went into the recording studio to make the actual records, Davis, and even to an extent Ertegun, expanded the definition of A&R even as they contracted the role. As respected "ears," if they didn't hear it, they didn't sign it. That was as true when they were the point men as it was later when they appointed other people to bring in the talent. Even as time went by, people they hired to do A&R often were little more than the boss's talent hounds and retrievers, bringing home the music for the boss's decision, a more postitive spin on what went on with Anthony and Caplan.

The Lieber and Stoller deal opened the floodgates to the point that today most recording is done by independent producers. Of course, the recording process has become much more involved; whereas Miller would record single takes onto a transcription disc, effectively recording a three-minute song in three minutes, now producers capture hundreds of digital tracks per recording in a process that might take weeks or months per song to finish. While we'll explore the economic upshot of that change in technology later, for our current purposes let's just say that, under these circumstances, if an A&R person had to produce records, that A&R person wouldn't be able to do anything but record.

Sometimes the contemporary A&R person does have studio chops. Some, like Paul Atkinson, did time in bands before they started signing them. But for the most part, major label A&R has become the domain of glorified, hamstrung talent scouts. Now more than ever, A&R people are limited largely to the flavor of the week. Sometimes, someone will get lucky, find an artist mining a new vein of the same old same old, and pique first radio and then the public's interest. Suddenly all the other groups on the scene, all the other artists that sound like this, have a chance of finding themselves and their managers in the crosshairs of at least one A&R department and embroiled in a strange, Byzantine courtship ritual with the record industry. While they have become fewer and further between, a bidding war between companies is what managers live for; being able to predict the next big thing is what keeps them in business.

Take, for example, when Nirvana broke, selling 10 million copies of their sophomore album. Suddenly, all you needed was to be from the Seattle area and play the guitar and you could at least get an audience with A&R people. Groups like Pearl Jam,

Soundgarden (who'd had some indie success even before Nirvana), and Stone Temple Pilots all scored on Nirvana's coattails.

Similarly, for a while there has been what amounts to a boy-band farm down in Orlando, which produced certain teen girl singers as well (more on them anon). Likewise, during the short reign of funk, George Clinton had placed variations on essentially the same band with every major record label. During the late 1950s, the Philly scene, thanks to *American Bandstand*, burgeoned. During the early 1960s, when *Bandstand* moved to Los Angeles, the show performed the same service for surf music.

The main thing that has changed is just how risk-averse record companies have become. Polly Anthony's distaste of jam bands was just the tip of the iceberg. The stakes have become so high, the stockholders so demanding, that there is no longer time to develop artists, cultivate sounds, or even create trends. It has all become very reactive. Between this and the regular personnel bloodbaths used to keep the bottom line down, the glamour of A&R has waned considerably.

A former A&R guy who moved on to better things put it this way:

> Budgets all over are much less than they've been in the past, which affects all areas of an A&R guy's life and work, meaning that the salaries are much lower (as much as 50+ percent) than they were five years ago, expense accounts have been massively scaled back (no perks like in the past), and bands aren't generally getting anything close to what they used to from labels in their contracts. It's only gotten worse since I left.

Yet the A&R department still performs a service, feeding the hungry maw of the record company with equally hungry artists ready to be eaten. They keep the distribution wheels greased, keep the records coming out. For the major record companies to retain that element that makes them "major," the ability to distribute their own product, they need to keep these channels open.

5

Charting the Course
How Changes in the Charts Changed the Biz

ONE OF MY early full-time professional experiences in the music business was an internship at the late, lamented trade periodical *Record World*. It came about because of a summer job I had at a radio production company in the same building. I went up the elevator at 1700 Broadway and introduced myself to the editor, Mike Sigman. After I explained the concept of an internship to him (basically "slave labor with an educational component, though you can pay my train fare and feed me"), we struck a deal. I'm proud to say that for as long as the magazine existed afterward, it had an intern from the journalism department at Rutgers.

I learned a hell of a lot about journalism, magazine production, and the mechanics of the music business during my time there. Some of it I learned the hard way (like by not quite twigging exactly where ASCAP got its money—it sounded like a protection racket to me at the time), some by observation, some by inference, and some by actually being told, "This is the way things work." (I also met Michael Zilkha through *Record World*, and wound up being signed as an artist to his Ze Records imprint about a year later, for my hot minute as a recording artist.)

As one of my main jobs at the magazine, I helped to gather information on the charts every week. The chart department in New York consisted of four people (including me). We also had our correspondents in the L.A. office. Every person in charge of a specific genre (the dance music columnist and R&B editor, for example) was responsible for compiling his or her department's chart information. I helped with the jazz and dance music charts and gathered information for the main sales chart as well. This involved calling various retailers, radio stations, and clubs and entering their sales information or playlists onto a graph, with the #1 song or record getting 10 points, #2 getting 9 and so on down the line. A similar method was used about a half mile down Broadway and across the street, where *Billboard* had its offices.

The department spent Monday and Tuesday compiling the charts. This often involved working until close to midnight every Tuesday. The heads of the chart department went into their offices and closed their doors and got on a conference call with the Los Angeles office until they had settled on the numbers. On Wednesday, we tallied up our information and created the actual charts. One of my jobs, every Wednesday afternoon, was to copy the charts and distribute them to everyone in the office. At 4 P.M., we sat down and fielded calls from consultants, record companies, managers, radio station groups, and other journalists requesting the coming week's chart numbers on specific albums ("Last week it was #4 on the pop chart. It was #1 on the dance chart?") or Top 10s.

What I inferred from the closed doors in the offices of the chart heads, especially after hearing all the indistinct arguing that seeped through, was that these charts, while mathematical, were also a process of compromise. Even the information-gathering process didn't strike me as thoroughly accurate. What if the retailer didn't give precise numbers? I would learn several years later, as a record-store manager for a fair-sized chain of stores in the New York metro area, that sometimes stores improvise their inventory counts. If the information was compromised even at that early stage of the gathering, how accurate could the final tally really be?

For example, there was great consternation and gnashing of teeth in the chart department the first week of October 1979, when the Eagles' *The Long Run*, their long-awaited follow-up to *Hotel California*, came out. All indications said that it should debut at #1, but that just didn't happen. The conventional wisdom at the music business trades said that albums needed a slow build, a climb up the charts. That's what made every week in the charts exciting. It was kind of like a horse race (a sport that a surprising number of music business people enjoyed—I know of one who told me about losing a publishing company at the track one sunny spring afternoon). In the end, the sales were too strong to ignore—the chart department felt they had no choice but to debut *The Long Run* on the chart at #1.

The era of compromise and deliberation over the chart numbers all changed on May 25, 1991. On that day, *Billboard* publisher Howard Lander wrote:

> For more than 30 years, our sales charts have relied on rankings of best-selling records obtained from stores, over the telephone or by messenger service. Until now, the only technological changes have been the introduction of computers to tally the data more quickly and the recent usage of fax machines—but the basic methodology has remained the same.
>
> In the last few years, the introduction of point-of-sale systems that scan bar codes at retail checkout counters has made possible a whole new degree of accuracy for measuring record sales: the ability to count precisely the number of units sold, rather than just ranking the titles. *Billboard* has worked diligently over the last two years to take advantage of this new technology to produce more accurate charts. With this issue, we are proud to begin using actual piece counts for two of our leading charts: Top Pop Albums and Top Country Albums.

The source of this information was a year-old company called SoundScan. The charts, however, were ancillary to the company's mission.

"We wanted to create a management information system," said company cofounder Michael Shallet, "a tool that would allow industry people—be they record executives, concert promoters, artists, managers, booking agents—to measure the cause and effect of the various marketing things that they did."

To do this, SoundScan hooked up its computers to the point-of-sale computers at retailers across the country, mostly the big chains that already had the point-of-sale computers to scan the bar codes of the recordings they sold. As the system rolled out, the company also started equipping independent stores with point-of-sale systems so it could monitor their sales as well. As far as the charts were concerned, this replaced preconceived notions of how records sold with solid, statistically significant sales figures. Said Shallet:

Before, you had a mentality as far as the chart was concerned that said sales should look like a bell curve—that the curve should start slowly, it should rise and the time frame would be different, how long it took to rise to its apex. Then, as gently as it rose, that's how gently it would fall off again. But that really was never the sales pattern of a record. They keep stores open until after midnight so they can sell after the street date, and you see people dying to get a hold of the product. That is the real sales pattern.

Chaos erupted in the record business. Not only had the gentle bell curve disappeared, but suddenly every assumption in the business disappeared as well. Hardly a month went by without one or another blockbuster album entering the charts at #1. Genres that the industry regarded as "marginal," like country, proved every bit as popular as pop. The mainstream record business seemed surprised by this, as if Nashville was another planet and the tastes in New York and Los Angeles totally reflected the tastes of the rest of the nation. (While they've gotten over the shock, they still don't seem to have let go of that notion.)

One executive at Time Warner described another upshot of SoundScan as "the multiplier effect," or, as in A&R, nothing succeeding like success. When a record hits the charts, many retailers routinely discount the price. Some put the top albums in a preferential display, which makes sense; when an album makes the Top 10, that means people *want* it. Therefore, until it reaches a saturation point, an album that reaches the top of the charts sells even more, and the charts are dominated by the same records week after week—i.e., the discounted ones. "Records slipped to the lowest common denominator," the executive noted. "The resulting market lock-ins led to mediocrity."

A Columbia University study backs up this observation with empirical evidence. A group of 14,000 people were given access to a Web site where they could download music and rate its "quality." The ratings, however, were rigged; for example, one band was ranked 26 out of 48 in terms of quality. But the study showed that when a lot of people downloaded a song, more people continued to download it, whereas when there were few initial downloads, the song became one of the least downloaded in the study. The study suggests, the sociology professors at Columbia concluded, that people make their musical choices based on popularity rather than "quality." "It turns out that when you let people know what other people think, the popular things become more popular," said Columbia sociology professor Duncan Watts.

SoundScan brought other changes. At a very basic level, it changed the "reporting day" from Wednesday to Tuesday, with all reports compiled on computer (we didn't have one back in the *Record World* days) and available Tuesday evening.

Other digital-age companies changed the process for compiling singles and tracks charts, which rely on information on radio play as well as sales. In the old days, compilers got the information from the program or music director of the radio station, and they trusted it (though as we'll see later, there was a lot on the line that would make one question its veracity). However, a company called Broadcast Data Systems (conveniently owned by the same parent company as *Billboard*) found a way to offer a far more accurate picture of the songs on the air. In a similar manner to the way SoundScan tracks the digital barcode of albums sold, BDS's computers monitor the songs played on radio stations and compare them to digital "thumbprints" of the second 30 seconds of every song release (stored in an enormous database). They check the second 30 seconds to avoid the chance of on-the-air talent talking over the record and fouling the sample. Similarly, a computer program called Selector, which most professional stations use to create their programming, can directly upload the playlist for the week to anyone authorized to view it. *Radio and Records* used this method to track spins until *Billboard* bought it and switched it to BDS. The songs that get the most spins chart higher.

Terri Rossi, *Billboard*'s director of operations, R&B music division, said, "The singles chart must be both an accurate measure of actual airplay and units sold, and also charted to the R&B music marketplace in such a way that a single can go to No. 1 on the R&B singles chart without necessarily crossing over to the general market."

These new methods led to trepidation over the removal of the "human element" of the charts, and further fear of homogeneity, since reporting might become "more of a science which will uniform the whole industry and take away from the individuality of markets."

Of course, as we will see when we explore radio, this worry might have more to do with "phantom spins"—radio stations reporting songs they didn't actually play—than any individuality, save how much certain individuals got to line their pockets. Nor was there any need to worry about radio becoming homogenous. That would happen, but it would come from a source far removed from the charts.

What SoundScan did do was exactly what Shallet and his partner, Michael Fine, set out to accomplish. "We still get calls," said Shallet. " 'Hey, what can I do to get my records up the charts?' The answer, of course, is sell records."

To which the Time Warner executive responded, "The Sound-Scan experience shows that businesspeople often settle for the least creative interpretation and manipulation of data."

This, of course, is a bind. Doubtless, SoundScan is a far more accurate measure of how records sell. It brings to mind something Churchill said about democracy: it's the worst system in the world, except for all the others.

6

Control Issues
Did Home Taping Kill Music?

"IT'S A GREAT scam if you think about it," wrote David Shamah, an economics reporter for the *Jerusalem Post*.

> You bought, say, *Goodbye Yellow Brick Road* by Elton John when it came out in 1973 (am I dating myself?) and you still like it. You even still have the album, although the record player is long gone and they don't make them anymore [actually, they do, but you have to look hard to find them]. You like the album so much you bought a cassette tape version to play in the car and later on a CD. Now you've got an iPod or similar MP3 player and you're considering buying the MP3 version. Hmmm. Shelling out four times for the same product?

From the time that Edison, Bell, and Berliner introduced recorded music as a consumable product until about the mid-1970s, the record business was in control. You wanted to own the music, you had to go through it.

That started to change, very slowly, around the end of World War II, with the advent of tape recording. The tape machine came to America from Germany with a Colonel Richard Ranger, who dismantled it, figured out how it worked, put it back together, and arranged for people to see it. "He showed it to me and Bing Crosby and [Hollywood sound engineer] Glen Glenn," recording pioneer (and inventor of the solid body electric guitar) Les Paul said. "He showed me the advantage of tape over disc and it immediately turned my head."

While the reel-to-reel tape machine became one of the music business's best friends, ushering in the complex multitrack recording studio—another Les Paul invention—very few of the machine's private owners were ever accused of trying to kill the music, though many committed music to their reels. Most of the owners of reel-to-reel tape machines tended to be either affluent adults, younger music makers, or students recording lectures (my dad had a huge, clunky Wollensak tape recorder, about the size of a piece of carry-on luggage and weighing 25 pounds if it weighed an ounce—what masqueraded as a "portable" back in the 1950s). They were few and far enough between that the music industry didn't pay much attention to reel-to-reel recorders.

The panic didn't even start when Philips introduced the cassette deck in 1963. While far easier to use than the reel-to-reel tapes, which often required Byzantine threading, the cassette couldn't get rid of the sonic hiss inherent in its design. Like the early Edison phonograph, it mostly found its way into offices as a dictation medium.

Then Ray Dolby's labs introduced a consumer noise-reduction system that got built into cassette decks starting in the mid-1970s. Now a cassette could make a serviceable copy of an album, and FM radio started to feed the frenzy with Midnight Album blocks, during which they would play a new album all the way through for the home-taping pleasure of their audience. By the early 1980s, the U.K. record industry trade group, the British Phonographic Industry, had become so alarmed that it created this logo:

But what was it really scared of? More than anything else, it was lack of control. For the first time since one of Edison's minions put a music cylinder on a phonograph for public consumption, the industry that controlled the music did not entirely control the medium on which people consumed the music (although we've already established that Philips, inventors of the cassette, owned several record companies, including classical music monolith Deutsche Grammophon). As the technology became better, the music business's paranoia escalated.

The palpable fear wasn't limited to the record industry, either. Home taping scared the publishing business as well, because without the mechanical royalties that came from the record companies, the publishers and songwriters were also out of business. When the digital tape recorder entered the picture in the early 1980s, it only got worse. As songwriter and publisher George David Weiss, whose credits include the Louis Armstrong hit "What a Wonderful World" and the Tokens' version of "The Lion Sleeps Tonight," saw it:

> When you tape something analog, with a home taping machine, you are degrading the original, because the head is being touched. The copy is not so hot. It's a copy. After you copy the first about six or seven times, you've got to go out and buy another tape. Another original. You have to buy one more so maybe we get out two, two and a half cents to take home. With copies, we're getting zero.
>
> But with the digital audio tape, forget it. You buy a compact disc, put it into this machine and nothing touches. It's all electronic information that is being sent from one side to the other. Nothing is being degraded, and the second one that is made is a clone, not a copy. It's exactly as good and as authentic and with as much fidelity as the original. Imagine what that means for us . . . this DAT machine is just going to devastate us: copy copy copy! Clone clone clone!

The music industry as a whole grew so frightened, it lobbied Congress and got the Audio Home Recording Act of 1992, which amounted to a levy on digital audiotape. It also pressured the manufacturers to include a serial copy-management system in the DAT recorders, which made it impossible for any one DAT recorder to make more than one copy of any given CD. The main DAT recorder manufacturers—Philips, Sony, and Panasonic—all had interests in the music business, so it wasn't that hard to convince them to do this, but it also made the medium all but useless as a consumer audio item, and limited the DAT market to the professional and semiprofessional music enthusiast. Once again, things were relatively under control.

So the record industry continued to exploit and benefit from the new digital medium of the compact disc. However, as we'll discover in the next chapter, less than 40 percent of the records sold in 2000 were new releases. If we can assume that it was more or less a "normal" year in the record business, that means that over 60 percent of the records sold are what the record business calls "catalog" albums. These albums were new once upon a time, and remain such consistent sellers that enough stores keep them in stock for the record companies to keep them in print. When they cease to sell, the record company will cut the record out of its catalog and take a band saw to the boxes of CDs left in its warehouse, cutting a small slit through the carton and into the jewel box of the CD—not so far that it damages the actual disc, but far enough that the cut is evident. Then it sells the boxes to a record liquidator, who puts them into stores for 99¢ or $1.99. For the most part, the artist will never see money on these CDs, as most contracts don't pay royalties for cut-rate and cutout albums. (But then most artists, more than likely, never saw money for their records beyond the advance anyway.)

So catalog is a very important part of the record business. Because of catalog, the CD essentially saved the industry.

Vinyl still ruled during the disco boom, which led to the disco debacle of 1980, sparked, in part, by the failure of the soundtrack to *Sgt. Pepper's Lonely Hearts Club Band*, a dog of a movie, a year and a half earlier. By the turn of the decade, the music business was in piss-poor shape. Record sales slipped by close to 20 percent. With pirated, counterfeit copies, some records got more returns than the company actually sold to the stores.

These things happen in waves. Artie Ripp, who had a label with Gulf and Western, recalled:

> Gulf and Western Records put out this soundtrack by Elton John from a movie called *Friends*. I think it was the first album that shipped platinum and came back double platinum. They took back that many returns with counterfeiters. They presented Jim Jones, the G&W president, with platinum and gold records and so on, and it was a total farce.

A year after the great disco deflation, Philips introduced the CD, first in Europe, then in America. It was a revelation to some. "We knew that CDs would become the dominant format when we first saw a CD player in 1982," said Don Rose, the founder of Rykodisc, the first CD-only record company. "We realized there was a potential for a lot of material to be reissued on compact disc, a lot of significant music that had more or less saturated its viability in the analog market."

Having recently mined the windfall of cassettes spawned by the advent of the Walkman, and having relied on dominance of LP for 35 years before that, the record business moved on from the "saturated . . . analog market" and took advantage of this opportunity to once again exploit their catalogs.

The allure of the CD was clear to both the consumer and the record companies. Since it was a laser-read digital format, nothing ever made contact with the actual recording. Unless you were very careful, most LPs developed scratches, attracted dust, and developed hisses, clicks, pops, skips, and all manner of surface noise. CDs, on the other hand, theoretically had none of these problems. The actual music, encoded digitally into pits encased in clear plastic, would supposedly last forever. The record companies sent interns and minor minions into the vaults to locate the master tapes of their bestselling recordings so they could digitize them and release their lucrative catalogs in the new format, once again capitalizing on recordings they had long ago paid for.

I worked in record retail when the CD first arrived in America, managing one of the first stores in New York City's Greenwich Village to stock them—as imports initially, costing upward of $30. People in the Village tended to be early adapters. They bought their players (which cost in the neighborhood of $1,000 in those early days) and needed the software to play on them. During the onset of stocking CDs at the store, I had lunch with my district manager, who asked me what I thought of this new format. I told him I thought it was great, but I wondered if I would ever see some of my favorite records, which tended toward the obscure, on the format. I needn't have worried. Nearly every record I ever owned on vinyl (with a few notable exceptions) came out on CD.

Doors producer Paul Rothchild didn't even know that Elektra had rereleased the Doors records on CD until he wandered into a record store and actually saw them. He bought the CDs and put one into his player. "It was abysmal," he said. "It had been taken from a minimum of fifth-generation master, perhaps even eighth-generation cassette-running master. It was noisy, distorted, obscene."

Rothchild was not alone in this experience. "The first few CDs of Elton that came out were dreadful," said Elton John producer Gus Dudgeon. "They were just terrible because [the people who made the digital transfers] basically didn't understand what they were doing." It took a few years, but finally they got this issue straightened out, largely through the efforts of people like Rothchild and Dudgeon.

The first decade and a half of the CD era were boom years for the record business. Indeed, even in the period from 1989 to 1998, CD sales doubled in dollar value from $6,579,400 to $13,723,500. Seemingly, music managed to survive home taping nicely.

7

Panic in the Suites
Napster, Grokster, and the Last Kazaa

STRANGELY, THE NEXT great panic attack came as sort of a delayed reaction, though one that Weiss foresaw, in terms of the ability to "clone" digital music, if not in the exact same medium. The cause of this panic was another new format that initially started in the music business's sister industry, the movie business.

The movie business loved the whole idea of digital audio, but they couldn't fit that much information onto the soundtrack of a film. German engineer Karlheinz Brandenburg came up with a solution, a digital audio compression protocol that basically trimmed some of the frequencies that were beyond the power of the human ear to perceive and most speakers to reproduce, and further compacted the musical data so that a song that might take up 30 megabytes of information on a CD (which generally could hold up to 700 megabytes of data) shrank down to about 3 megabytes of digital data. He brought this idea to the Motion Picture Experts Group, which adopted Brandenburg's Audio Layer 3 compression protocol—MPEG 3 for short, or MP3 for shorter, based on the file extension used for these pieces of compressed musical data—as the standard for digital audio compression for film.

Brandenburg's company decided to make the protocol "open source." Not that it mattered much in the early 1990s, when computers were comparatively puny and the code would have overtaxed them. Initially, it took a dedicated device to actually compress the files.

There is an axiom in the computer world, however, called Moore's Law, after Intel founder Gordon Moore. In 1965, Moore predicted that the number of transistors that would fit on a microprocessor chip would double every year, thereby doubling the power and speed of the computer. Moore's Law is a variation on this idea; it basically states that computing power doubles every one or two years. It took five years of this doubling before the higher-powered personal computer could deal with the algorithm for MP3, at which point (around 1995) high-end computer users had the digital muscle needed to "rip" digital CD audio into MP3 files on their own personal computers.

By this time, another development in computing became more and more commonplace. Started as a means for scientists to send data back and forth with relative rapidity, the Internet had been in use by the academic and military communities since the mid-1970s. When the graphical Web browser Mosaic was introduced in 1993, however, this potential wellspring of data became more accessible to the computer literate. This included college students, especially those studying the burgeoning fields of computer engineering and science (in order to perpetuate Moore's Law). These students discovered Brandenburg's open-source algorithm, and suddenly, between the high-speed connectivity available on college campuses and this new ability to compress a song encoded onto a CD down to a tenth of its original size, digital music zinged back and forth between students' computers over the campus networks.

While aware of the phenomenon, the record companies didn't care too much about it at first. After all, it was only a bunch of college kids, and they couldn't get the songs away from the computer.

People who don't learn from history are doomed to repeat it. In the 1920s, when radio started its ascendance, the record companies took the attitude, "Why would anyone want to listen to someone else playing records for them when they could play their own?" However, during the Depression if people had a radio, they didn't really need to spend 75¢ apiece on records. Radio provided enough entertainment to make them forget their troubles for a few minutes. In 1921, record sales had topped $100 million. By 1931, they slid to under $20 million, a fall caused, in part, by the record industry's own hubris in ignoring the appeal of radio.

The industry hadn't lost this hubris some 70 years later, which shouldn't surprise people. It ignored the digital transfer of music in 1995 just like it had the rise of radio in 1925—at its peril.

If the record companies had embraced this technology back in 1995, figured out the many ways it could be exploited and then exploited them, the music business might be a much healthier, happier place (in economic terms). Everyone could easily access music instantly anywhere, either by subscription or per piece. Music would have the same kinds of business precautions that prevent the average person from "ripping" a DVD—though new programs to circumvent these safeguards arise faster than the industry can retool to defeat them.

Even so, sound recordings would become far less expensive, because the physical packaging, warehousing, and real estate expenses would not exist. People would happily spend money on digital copies of record companies' catalogs once again. But that didn't happen. Unfortunately for the record business, several things prevented this.

For one thing, the open-source nature of the MP3 format put the computer literate way ahead of the curve. By the time the biz became aware that college computers overflowed with digital music files, the means of compressing music had become institutionalized.

Record companies also failed to recognize the Internet as a means of, once more, selling through their catalogs. Perhaps this was because they hadn't yet milked the CD for all they could. Remember, the glass-and-lacquer disk had served them for over 40 years. The vinyl disc reigned for 35. They had just finished the brief decade of the cassette when the CD fell into their laps. The CD had barely had 15 years in the recorded-medium throne when the challenge of the digital domain, of software that never actually needed a permanent container like a CD or a tape, challenged both the assumptions and the dominance of the record business.

The threat also came from outside the business (even the cassette had come from within—the invention of Philips), and it blindsided them. Worse, they had no control over it, or even any idea how to control it. Coming to grips with the change would take them a decade and a half, and by the time they did, the genie had long escaped its bottle and the music business landscape was forever altered.

The record business's first impulse was to try to use its lobbying muscle to control the digital domain. By 1993 cable TV and satellite systems were cablecasting digital music. Fearing that consumers' ability to tape this digital music would allow them to make near-digital-quality copies, the record companies began to lobby Congress for new laws and amendments to the copyright code.

So it's not like they totally did not see the possibility. Most people in the industry just ignored its ramifications. Some people didn't. Todd Rundgren was one of the first artists to put up his own Web site with the option to pay a membership fee and hear everything he did as soon as it was done. He began to see that actual record stores would become a thing of the past (an idea we'll deal with in more depth later on):

> It will be Tower Records and Blockbuster Video, except they won't have storefronts. They'll have big, faceless buildings with giant mainframe computers in them, waiting for you to call up. Then they'll download it to your house and they'll charge you for it, just as if you walked into the record store to buy it. The difference is that prerecorded media will disappear.

And actually, the CEO of Sony agreed, to an extent. "Retailers have to be proactive," said Michael Schulhof in 1995. "There are opportunities in the future that are not threats to retailers' business. Retailers have to do more to ensure their place in the future electronic marketplace."

By 1997, users of the Internet began to probe the music business—and copyright law in general—in some rather tender areas, and the record business began to slowly take notice. On college campuses around America and the world, students were posting copies of songs, along with "cracked" commercial software and images of naked women (most of the users were male computer students). Anyone with Web access could find the song files, find a player for the files, and voilà! Instant music collection.

Indeed, to the record business the World Wide Web had come to resemble the Spanish Main of the 18th century: it was a haven for pirates. The reaction of the record business was to load cannons and engage in battle. "Until the appropriate balance between free-flowing information and intellectual property is struck," said then-RIAA president Hilary Rosen, "the Internet will never achieve its potential to become a viable medium for the sale of music. We must not let a pirate market on the Internet get established before the legitimate one is ready."

She would sound this theme over and over again for nearly a decade. However, the industry she was representing seemed less than interested in turning the Internet into "a viable medium for the sale of music." And by the time she'd said this, it was already too late.

Some tentative steps were taken. Oasis asked fan sites to please take down unauthorized music and videos from their sites. Geffen Records sent polite letters to the deans, provosts, presidents, and heads of IT of the various colleges with some of the biggest and most visible bulletin boards, making them aware that by hosting these bulletin boards, they were in violation of the copyright laws of the United States. "The Internet's threat to the control of music has caused the handful of interlocked global monopolies which dominate the music industry to reveal their naked greed," said *Rock and Rap Confidential* editor and social and music critic Dave Marsh. "This new technology offers the potential to make all the music available to all the people all the time."

However, since this potential didn't fit in with any of the record business's current paradigms of distribution, it didn't see the possibilities. For example, Oasis's management, while it might have not wanted a downloadable version of the group's current album on the fan sites, might have actually thought twice. After all, *fans* of the band tended to visit these sites, and wouldn't fans be apt to buy a CD, especially after they heard it? Beyond that, if the management didn't want unauthorized music on the site, wouldn't it have been in Oasis's best interest to, perhaps, authorize some non-LP B-sides, live tracks, or rarities? This offers a win-win situation: The fans have music—indeed, music that no one else would get if they didn't visit the fan sites. Oasis earns the goodwill of its fans and gets its music out to people who might not otherwise hear it.

Of course, as it turned out, this all became a moot point. Now, pretty much anyone with a computer can download nearly anything Oasis ever recorded, either legally by paying between 80¢ and a dollar, or in the legally gray to blatantly illegal area of P2P downloads. At the time, however, the record companies had big issues with digital music.

But the record companies' anxiety stayed on a back burner at the time. More general sites for MP3 files had found their way onto the Net, like MP3.com, and search engines like Lycos found the still-more-common bulletin boards, but CD burners had not yet become widespread. As of 1996, the only way to get music files off the computer was to put them on a cassette: home taping strikes again.

Over the course of the next year, the record business got a one-two punch worthy of Lennox Lewis.

From the consumer's viewpoint, chip technology once again provided the answer to immobile music files. Korean computer hardware manufacturer Saehan announced its newest innovation, the MPMan, in 1997. The product, in a limited way (it could only hold about an hour of music), liberated the MP3 file from the computer and put it into the pockets of early adapters. Suddenly, the music business sounded the alarm.

At just around the same time that alarm sounded, a first-year student at Northeastern got into trading music files via Internet Relay Chat (IRC). He saw a way to extend IRC's capabilities so not only could the files be passed, but people could also search one another's computers for music and download it. He gave the program his IRC handle, and before long anyone with a music jones and a modem had downloaded Napster and was using it to access music files, person to person, peer to peer.

"It was rooted out of frustration not only with MP3.com, Lycos, and Scour.net, but also to create a music community," former Northeastern student Sean Fanning said of his innovation. "There really was nothing like it at the time."

Peer to peer remains a strange and troubling business model. Not only was Napster (and all the programs that followed in its wake) making music an essentially free commodity, but the programs themselves were also free. While nearly all of the high-profile P2P software and Internet music sites of the late 1990s managed to find investors, none had a really clear idea how to make money from their digital creations.

So, while the conversation continued around the record business, *within* the record business, the new notion of file sharing earned hushed whispers at best. "I think the [record] industry has basically ignored the warning signs that were on the wall," said Warner Bros. chief information officer Tsvi Gal. "We, as an industry, by and large ignored piracy in the hopes that it wouldn't be widely accepted. Of course, it's not going to go away so easily."

The record business's ostrichlike procrastination made possible a future in which music became a free good rather than a commodity, via a means of distribution over which it had no control, and indeed one it had ignored for the previous decade. Now, hundreds of thousands of people could and did share songs online—and not just college students, either. Accountants, writers, grade-schoolers, attorneys, people from all walks of life tested the digital waters of file sharing on Napster. Any mainstream song they could think of, they could find, and even a few oddities.

The word *Napster* became a curse word on the order of *payola* in the halls of the major record companies. In fear, the record companies and their business and lobbying trade group, the RIAA, started a campaign of terror directed at Internet Web sites, fans, and even the artists themselves. Toward the end of 1998, Universal made rap group Public Enemy take a downloadable track from its new album off its Web site. Capital Records then forced both the Beastie Boys and Billy Idol to remove music files from the Web, the Beastie from their own Web site, Billy Idol from the MP3.com site that eventually bore the brunt of a nine-figure settlement for copyright infringement. In Idol's case, a source close to the singer's inner business circle said, "Billy thought it was important to get some music out to his fans."

The RIAA denied that its members had anything against MP3 files as such. "There is no music industry campaign against the use of MP3 files," claimed Rosen. "Our concern is with the rampant posting of files without the copyright owners' or artists' authorization, free for the taking of their recordings online in the MP3 or any other format."

By 1999, with the dot-com boom booming and the Internet bubble still swelling, the battle lines were drawn. In the far corner weighing 800 pounds was the gorilla called the record industry. In the near corner, weighing about three pounds, with a cute kitty cat face and headphones was Napster. Again, rather than trying to do anything constructive on its own, the record business seemed to spend most of its time either trying to crush the Napster or saying terrible things about it when Napster managed to avoid getting crushed.

By fall 2000, the gorilla and its assistants, the weasels, had gotten a toehold on Napster, bringing Fanning and his associates to court. At the same time, all the major labels, scattershot, put up some form of Internet music service that they either bought out or created out of whole cloth. In either case, the companies' self-confident miscalculations became quickly apparent. "The problem is twofold," noted an anonymous Sony executive.

> First, everyone has their own proprietary technology and their own ideas of how it should be done, which is just confusing to consumers. Then there's the idea that people are interested in only Sony or only Warner product. That might have been the case back in the fifties when you knew that Atlantic records pretty much had all the really cool R&B acts, but all these companies now cross genres and have no single, definable identity for customers.

So the majors' early efforts on the Web were once again doomed by hubris. It was also still much easier to download from Gnutella, Kazaa, Grokster, or any of the other peer-to-peer programs on the Web (which the industry referred to as "pirate-to-pirate"). "It's a complicated process," admitted the RIAA's Doug Curry. "It's much easier for someone to upload thousands of CDs and put them online for free as opposed to changing 60 years of a large industry's practices overnight."

Market research analyst Mike McGuire from the Gartner Group agreed. The record companies, he said, "have a 100-year-old business model that's based on controlling distribution by controlling a physical thing. They can't do that anymore, or they can't rely on that entirely."

By 2001, the Copyright Control Services reported that music fans had downloaded a quarter of a billion tracks the previous year. Another study found that during one 30-day period, over 50 percent of the 12- to 24-year-olds surveyed had downloaded a P2P MP3 file, not only in the United States but in Canada, Sweden, Taiwan, Italy, the Netherlands, South Korea, and even urban areas of Mexico.

Then came the one-two punch of the early 2001 dot-bomb and the terrorist attacks of September 11, 2001. The former found that most of the for-profit Internet music sites (along with about 80 percent of the other new Internet-based companies) had burned through their public capital, sending their stock values plunging. At MCY, one of the vice presidents had to get a "bonus" from the company because the stock options he had to exercise after a year would cost him more in taxes than the stocks were worth. Fortunately, it was a loan he would never have to pay off, as the company burned through its assets, instituted massive layoffs, and eventually shuttered. It was hardly an isolated case.

Another reason that the record industry had trouble getting it together online was its control issues. These date back quite some time, as we've seen; the record business simply does not play nice with others. For example, in the 1980s I worked with a company called Personics. For around a dollar a track, it would make you a custom, high-quality cassette with any songs in its catalog of thousands. Unfortunately, very few of these songs came from major labels and virtually none of them were hits. The major labels just didn't trust these valuable properties to outsiders and thought that allowing them to be used in this manner would devalue them.

However, by 2001, the Web had become a free-for-all Personics, squared. People downloaded virtually any song they wanted and could then burn their favorite mixes onto CDs or download an hour's worth of music to their portable MP3 players, which had proliferated in penetration and grown in capacity over the previous two years. The record companies' worst nightmares were coming true: chased by the interconnected monster of the Internet, they jumped off a cliff of revenues and kept falling and falling, only they didn't wake up. The Pew Internet and American Life Project drove this home. In a survey of people who downloaded music, 80 percent of them didn't consider it stealing, and 60 percent didn't care about copyright, nor did they even want to think about paying for music over the Internet.

The record companies were in the middle of a period of marked decline that would last through this writing, with a brief respite in 2004. They saw CD sales dip from a 1999 high of 942.5 million units to a 2003 low of 745.9 million units. Once again the record business started wringing its collective hands and claiming that the downloading activity would put them out of business—what University of Texas economics professor Stan Liebowitz calls "Annihilation Theory."

Despite this, companies did actually try to sell songs over the Internet. MCY.com, before it crashed and burned, offered downloads that could be bought and played on most portable file players, although it used its own proprietary compression protocol. Former GRP Records president Larry Rosen and Grammy-winning producer Phil Ramone started N2K Encoded Music and the Music Boulevard Web site, offering both hard goods and downloads. Rather than use MP3, they opted for the easier-to-control (for them) Liquid Audio compression. Both sites offered limited access to music, however, as the major record companies were still suspicious of the Internet. They would not trust what they regarded as their major asset, their catalogs, to this wired devil. Ever the visionary, Ramone saw it differently: "We're standing on the precipice of a new generation of technology and work."

"Traditional music distribution has grown over-burdened and outdated," said Tony Stonefield, the CEO of another pioneer Internet music distributor, the General Music Outlet and Electronic Records. "Electronic distribution is clearly the next step for the industry."

That next step, that precipice, loomed nearer with alarming speed. Not only were music consumers defecting to the Internet in droves, but so were artists. Prince, in the midst of major disagreements with his longtime record company, Warners, gave up on record companies altogether. He began using Rundgren's model, making his music available online both as soft and hard goods. Perhaps if a record company asked nicely and gave him a lot of money, he might make some of the music available via more conventional outlets.

Who guitarist Pete Townshend, who made much of his solo output available as hard goods via his own site, concurred: "For new artists, it's a direct line to the general mass of the population so they can get some early response to their finished work."

"Record companies stand between artists and their fans," said Courtney Love. "We signed terrible deals with them because they controlled our access to the public. But in a world of total connectivity, record companies lose that control."

Not every artist felt this way about the new technology. Metallica, a band that encouraged the trading of live concert tapes among its fans, felt threatened by its commercially recorded output being available for peer-to-peer trading online, and submitted a list of the e-mail addresses belonging to a third of a million of its fans who had downloaded album tracks off Napster to the RIAA.

"Why does Metallica, like so many other musicians, focus on control?" asked the editors of *Rock and Rap Confidential*.

> When a band starts out, it owns all its own music, but that music is virtually worthless. The record industry alone has the capacity to turn it into something worth millions. But the price for this alchemy involves an assault on the ownership of the music, on its representation to the public, on the money that it generates, on every single aspect of its postproduction circulation. Famous musicians do not become rich except by continually battling the system that wants to keep everything for itself and give the actual creators barely enough for subsistence.

"Artists standing up and saying, 'Don't download our music,'" said Wharton School of Business professor David Fader, "is really the same as movie stars saying 'Don't watch our previews.'"

Between the high-visibility campaigns of the RIAA, Metallica, and others, the case against Napster went to appeals court, where, in summer 2002, the gorilla's full weight landed on the Napster kitty and flattened it totally—the central hub of the Napster network would not permit certain "unauthorized" songs to pass through, essentially removing the core of the music people were downloading. As the major record companies' music suddenly vanished from the service, Napster faced the same problem as Music Boulevard and MCY.com—it offered music with a limited audience. Ultimately, it closed up shop and sold what assets it could. However, before its first iteration was shuttered, users had downloaded 1.72 billion songs over the course of a month.

Of course, this didn't matter much to anyone but Fanning and the RIAA. In Napster's wake, dozens of "hubless" P2P networks took its places. Unlike Napster, which had a central nexus through which the music had to flow, the hubless P2P software accessed the users' computers via tens of thousands of shifting "nodes" on the Web. Most really didn't have "owners" per se—Gnutella, for example, had been set free on the world by a small team at AOL's Spinner radio. Only available for about 18 minutes before AOL realized what it was, the company removed it, but Frankenstein's monster was already at large and amok. The program spread virally.

The RIAA aggressively pursued its anti-MP3 course. Not content to just shut down sites that trafficked in MP3s, it started to seek legal relief from sites that directed people to MP3s, including a self-described "pioneer in the indexing, searching and linking of music-related sites and files on the Internet," MP3Board. The MP3Board position was that it served as merely a guide to where any MP3, legal or "pirated," could be found. It did not distribute any actual music. If most of the sites it pointed to happened to house "illegal" files, well, whose fault was that? The site pointed right back at the RIAA and its client companies for not getting with the program online. Beyond that, the MP3Board attorneys suggested that rather than going after the pathfinder, maybe the RIAA should follow the path and go after the actual infringers.

These infringers proliferated at a rate the record industry found alarming. Whereas a high-traffic evening on Napster had featured a quarter of a million users, some five years after the service got ridden out of Dodge on a rail it was not unusual to see five million users at a time logged in to the hubless P2P sites. This phenomenon was due partly to the fact that music fans felt entitled to their newfound ability to get music online, and partly to the growing penetration of broadband Internet in homes via cable modems, fiber optics, and DSL. Where even the fastest dial-up modem might take 15 minutes to download a song, a really fast broadband connection might finish in less than a minute. By 2004, of the more than 75 percent of Americans connected to the Internet, over half of them took advantage of access to broadband connections, and that number continues to grow.

By summer 2002, the RIAA had become desperate. It began to get aggressive not just with the companies putting out the P2P software, but also with the users of that software—looking into legal action against individual downloaders. It subpoenaed over 250 music fans, accusing them of getting MP3 files from one of the hubless services, Kazaa, and claiming that the downloaders could be found to owe up to $150,000 per song. As of this writing, over 16,000 people have been subject to these lawsuits.

"The end result of this," noted Phil Leigh of the research firm Digital Media, "is that you've sued your customers and you've deterred peer-to-peer activity, but you haven't improved sales. What have you accomplished other than frightening your customers and angering them?"

"The music industry is estranging an entire generation of music listeners," added Jerry Del Colliano of AudioRevolution. "Gen X and Y feel it is their right to download music despite copyright infringement laws. The RIAA killing off Napster was a failed experiment because new peer-to-peer networks like Gnutella rage on with files being swapped by the millions."

Leigh and Del Colliano were not alone in expressing these sentiments. Lawyer Fred Goldring urged the record business to "abandon the 'Shock and Awe' tactics. . . . The strategy of suing customers (thieves) and building ever-better locks for CDs and digital singles simply was not working and . . . everything we had done thus far had in fact made the problem worse." Since many in the industry had become familiar with the 12-step programs that dare not speak their names, Goldring suggested a six-step recovery program for the record business:

1. Admit you're powerless. File sharing is not going away. Downloading is already more popular than the CD.
2. Give up on anti-piracy technologies—they don't work.
3. Stop attacking your own customers (bad PR; worse business).
4. Focus less on finger-pointing and more on immediate, practical, fair solutions.
5. Give the people what they want, even if it requires that laws be changed.
6. Support initiatives that will allow unlimited access to every piece of music in the MP3 format, whenever and wherever someone wants it, with no conditions or restrictions, in an easy-to-use interface. People will pay for this.

"Here's the social reason that [Digital Rights Management] fails," concurred the Electronic Frontier Foundation's Cory Doctorow. "Keeping an honest user honest is like keeping a tall user tall. . . . At the end of the day, the user DRM is meant to defend against is the most unsophisticated and least capable among us."

"Lawsuits against file sharers are not going to save the music business," *PC Magazine* gadfly John Dvorak added.

In fact, the opposite is true. I'm convinced that the shuttering of the original, wide-open Napster . . . was the beginning of the end for the recording industry. This is because Napster was not just an alternative distribution network; it was an alternative sampling system. . . . On Napster, people were not just trading songs by engaging in mutual discovery. . . . You'd begin downloading songs A, B, and C—your favorite songs ever—and you'd see that one other trader had all three of these songs in his or her library. You could then peruse that person's entire collections. You'd notice the two of you had very similar taste! But wait, you'd find some unknown bands in his or her collection, so you'd download a few new songs and discover another band you liked.

Another area of concern in the early 2000s became a rising global gray market in MP3s that began to emerge, taking advantage of one of the Web's chief benefits, the often-dropped first part of its name—it is world wide. The Russian site allofmp3.com offered the same downloads that iTunes offered, but for about 3¢ each. The Future of Music Organization's Brian Zisk observed:

My understanding is that allofmp3.com might very well be legal in Russia, and though the IFPI [International Federation of the Phonographic Industry] exerted extreme influence on the Moscow City Police Computer Crimes Division to recommend to prosecutors that criminal charges be filed against this service, it was decided that no charges should or would be filed. While allofmp3.com might be liable in civil suits if they pay royalties incorrectly, this is no different than what U.S. labels and Web sites face if they pay royalties incorrectly, and while it is unknown if they are paying correctly, it is reported that rates in Russia are minuscule compared to those in the U.S.

So folks might be violating laws in the U.S. by using this service, and it's possible that allofmp3.com might be liable under U.S. law as shown by the recent legal victories against unauthorized imports, but my hunch is that if it were as clearly illegal as the IFPI is claiming (allofmp3.com has been doing this since 2000) that charges or lawsuits would have been filed long ago.

Foreign jurisdiction is a quite tricky area, and while it's easy to state that they should be nailed under U.S. laws, I don't think we'd want our Internet publishers held to the laws of all foreign countries—say, Saudi Arabia, for example.

While 2001 saw the beginning of legal sites with legitimate, licensed major label songs on them, with Apples iTunes leading the way (more on this in chapter 23), more people got songs from Kazaa, by a conservative ratio of 5:1 (though some peg it at 20:1 or more). Indeed, the University of Texas's Stan Liebowitz cites evidence that people download 300 million CDs worth of songs per month, while U.S. national sales run about 80 million CDs per month, a ratio of 3.75:1.

On the other hand, there may actually be evidence that the P2P protocols *help* album sales. A 2005 Australian study from the University of Western Sydney indicates that while nearly 40 percent of respondents copped to downloading music from one of the P2P services, nearly 70 percent of them still went out and bought the CDs. Said researcher Geoffrey Lee:

> The main reasons for downloading included: being able to listen to the song on their PC, being able to burn songs to a CD because it's cheaper than the original CD, and being able to sample the song before purchasing. . . . Sixty-eight percent of both generations surveyed [Baby Boomers and Generation Y] continued to buy albums through traditional retailers because they prefer the original copy, like being able to look at other CDs while shopping, or like being able to listen to new CDs.

Similarly, the Organisation for Economic Co-operation and Development published a report stating, "It is very difficult to establish a basis to prove a causal relationship between the size of the drop in music sales and the rise of file sharing." The study points to quality of the music, the growing number of entertainment choices, and physical (as opposed to digital) piracy as much bigger culprits.

A joint study by professors from Harvard Business School and the University of North Carolina at Chapel Hill came to a similar conclusion. When they really dug into the statistics, they could not find any evidence that file sharing had an effect on people buying CDs. Beyond that, they found that any effect it *might* have would be extremely small compared to the precipitous drop in CD sales.

A few folks in the record business agreed. While they would certainly prefer collecting money on all their intellectual property, they saw the alienation of their customers as foolish and destructive. Some even acted on these principles. Terry McBride, the president of Canada's Nettwerk Records, picked up the legal tab for one of the file sharers targeted by the RIAA. "These same file sharers are great music fans and are breaking new artists with little or no mainstream media support."

Stepping back a bit, again this reflects the cassette controversy. Through my teen years, my buddies and I exchanged cassettes all the time, turning friends on to favorite music, songs we wanted to do with our bands, etc. Almost universally, we would ultimately buy most of the music we liked from these compilations.

In Jamaica, a tourist with two blank cassettes (and perhaps a U.S. dollar) would often get one mix tape full of the latest hits on the island in exchange. When I went, I came armed with a bunch of blanks and wound up with a handful of great mix tapes that, again, sent me off to a local record store pretty quickly.

However, Liebowitz looked at the problem from the viewpoint of a market economist and disagreed, concluding, "MP3 downloads are causing significant harm to the record industry. It is not clear, however, whether such downloading in our current legal environment will cause a mortal blow to the industry. I suspect the worst damage to the industry is behind us."

In 2005, the U.S. Supreme Court ruled that the file sharing service Grokster could be held responsible for the illegal activities of its users. This led to the hope in the corridors of the record business that the long years of strife would soon end. "We will no longer have to compete with thieves in the night whose businesses are built on larceny," proclaimed the then-chief executive of Sony/BMG Music Andrew Lack.

Even so, by the middle of 2006, the digital music tracking company Big Champagne reported that at any given time 9.7 million file-sharers were on line, 6.7 million of them in the U.S. alone. This figure represented an 11 percent annual rise internationally and a 7 percent rise domestically.

To the record business, the issue still boils down to control. When John Lennon's widow, Yoko Ono, made Lennon's work available for sale digitally, Paul McCartney was asked whether the Beatles catalog would ever be available for download. He said he was sure it would happen, but that with all the parties involved, it was bound to be difficult. "I get involved in stuff I can actually control and do something about," he said. "There's a lot of strangeness in those areas, and I tend to keep out of them."

In a way, this is typical of many in the record business, who continue to run around, looking up and saying "the sky is falling," despite an upturn in sales in 2004 (the first year that the RIAA took digital downloads *sold* into account, coincidentally—or is it?). They look everywhere but within. "It's nothing new to say the recording companies are scared," said Professor Steven E. Schoenherr from the University of San Diego. "They've always been scared."

8

150 Records = 50 Percent of Revenue

EVERY NOW AND again, *Billboard* columnist Ed Christman sits down with his SoundScan figures and a calculator and crunches the numbers, determining what percentage of music released is really selling, and what actually makes a profit in the record business. These often alarming numbers offer a great insight into the business's woes. And while the numbers seem to distress him, they don't seem to surprise him. In fact, they surprise him less every year.

Christman determined that in 2000, 35,516 new titles (including reissues) hit the stores. The major record companies released 6,188 of them, and 29,328 came from independent labels. These new releases accounted for 37.8 percent of the records sold that year, just less than 300 million scans. Of those titles, 24,585, or not quite 70 percent, sold less than 1,000 copies.

In terms of per-unit sales, the figures look a little better, but still pretty bleak in terms of the overall picture. The average major label release in 2000 scanned 41,109 copies, while the average independent release garnered 1,438.

As we'll discover later on, much of this has to do with the way music is promoted. After all, how can we know we want to purchase a record if we don't know it exists? The traditional means of promoting recordings, for nearly a century, has been radio. The following cycle has made the recording world go 'round since the 1920s:

1. the consumer (that's us, folks) hears something on the radio
2. the consumer likes it
3. the consumer goes to the store and buys it

But as radio stations tighten playlists, follow formats, and generally concentrate their programming centrally rather than locally, they become less and less willing to take a chance on anything new. The stakes are just too high. Unfortunately, the record companies have only slowly woken up to this reality and started to try to revise the promotion-equals-radio equation.

Christman also analyzed the sales of all records in print for the year. During 2000, SoundScan tracked 288,591 albums, which sold 784 million units. Now simple division tells us that the average release, therefore, sold 2,717 copies.

Of those nearly 300,000 albums SoundScan tracked:

➤ 88 sold in excess of one million units
➤ 114 had sales between 500,000 and 999,999
➤ 204 raked in sales of 250,000–499,999 units
➤ 818 other albums sold over 100,000 units

Added up, 1,224 albums accounted for 440.6 million sales. That means that, if SoundScan provides a statistically accurate sample (which it does, by all reckoning), 0.42 percent of all albums sold accounted for 56 percent of album sales.

For a long time, the conventional wisdom in the music business has stated that most albums don't pull their weight. "We estimate that 80 percent of the 45 rpm singles do not recover their production costs, and 75 percent of popular LPs don't recover their costs," former RIAA chief Stanley Gortikov said in the 1970s. "That leaves a very small percentage of albums and artists to pay for the records that don't make it."

Conventional wisdom in the music business also states that for the average major label album to break even, it needs to sell between 250,000 and 500,000 copies. Albums that sell less than this don't even make back their money for the record company, let alone bring the artist anything like *royalties*. Therefore, only 406 albums (assuming that all or most of the CDs under discussion as selling over that 250,000 figure were part of a major label's active catalog) broke even. The major labels in the year 2000 operated on profits generated by about 0.14 percent of the records they released.

Granted, tracking the albums released in a calendar year includes some released in November and even December (though December releases are generally rare), leaving little time for them to hit the break-even mark. The November releases, however, are some of the strongest of the year, the ones *designed* to feed the vast holiday buying frenzy. These are the releases the record companies are *counting on* to get people into the stores before the end of the year.

Independent record companies, meanwhile, operate with far less overhead than the majors (more on this presently). The accepted independent average break-even range is 10,000–24,999 sales, depending on the recording cost and overhead of the indie. But even this lower threshold is rarely met; only 3 percent of the titles released in 2000 sold over 10,000 albums, accounting for just less than 83 percent of CD sales that year. That's less than 5 percent of product accounting for nearly 85 percent of total sales.

Five years later, Christman did these calculations again for new releases. In 2005, over 60,000 albums came out, including reissues with new bar codes and digital-only releases. These new releases accounted for 243.1 million of the 618 million albums sold in 2005. Of those recordings, only 32 garnered sales of over a million units, accounting for 57.2 million copies, which means those 32 albums, 0.05 percent of the releases, accounted for more than 10 percent of the record business. Another 62 albums went gold, selling between 500,000 and 999,999 copies; 103 sold between 250,000 and 499,999; and 213 others scanned between 100,000 and 249,999. So a total of 410 albums sold a total of 169.2 million copies—about 0.7 percent of the new records put out that year accounted for 70 percent of all new-release sales and 27 percent of total sales that year.

While these figures account for "legal" digital downloads via iTunes, eMusic, and the like, digital sales still seem more a curiosity than numbers of any consequence. The total number of digital album sales ran to 410,863, which accounts for 0.067 percent of all album sales. Of the 16,580 digital-only albums released in 2005, the majors issued 2,935 while 13,645 came from the independents. The majors' digital-only releases sold an average of 155 copies each, with the bestselling digital-only album selling about 12,000. Independent digital-only releases scanned an average of about 30 sales per title.

However, these digital releases may well become part of record retailing's "long tail." The long tail theory, proposed by *Wired* magazine's editor-in-chief Chris Anderson, basically states that if you have unlimited space for an unlimited number of products, some will sell very well, and some might sell poorly but consistently. If you plot them on a graph, you get something that looks a lot like a sleeping rat with a long, long tail representing those items that sell very few copies. However, taken in aggregate, this long tail accounts for half of all sales, sort of the flip side of the fact that 0.35 percent of all albums represent over 50 percent of all sales. The long tail, so the theory says, over time might just make these marginal recordings financially viable.

Between 1995 and 2005, that potential long tail grew substantially. The number of major-record new releases jumped from around 6,500 to over 11,000, and independent releases more than doubled from 22,000 releases to nearly 50,000, bringing the indies' share of releases from 75 percent to 81 percent.

So what's the point? Well a few spring immediately to mind. Since the charts are gauged by sales, those 0.14 percent of albums that broke even are the ones that made the charts, got onto the radio, and got all the publicity. These are the albums from that year that everyone knows. And indeed, like the little girl with the curl, when the record business was good that year, it was very, very good. In 2000, five albums sold over a million copies in their first week in release, naturally zooming and booming to the top of the charts, bringing musical immortality and uncounted riches to such culturally important (and I'm only being half sarcastic here) artists as the Backstreet Boys, *NSYNC, Britney Spears, Limp Bizkit, and Eminem.

This leaves over a quarter of a million albums fighting for a little less than half of the recorded-sound portion of the nation's disposable income—a shrinking figure, as we'll discover. These albums, many on independents with little promotional budget and little hope in the traditional avenues of promotion, generally have to count on press or word of mouth for exposure—certainly, for reasons we'll get into later, they cannot count on the radio. Not even records from major companies with huge promotion budgets can count on that anymore.

More important, of those 35,000 or so albums released in 2000, the average person probably could only hear music from about 150 or so of them from generally available media, even music a person would never actively listen to, heard walking down the street, coming out of stores, via airport sound-systems, behind commercials . . . there's music everywhere! In the meantime, the record companies have consistently released in excess of 30,000 recordings onto the market each year for over a decade and twice that much in 2005 alone. What do you think are the chances that one of those tens of thousands of records might become your new favorite of all time, if only you got the chance to hear it? And can a business in which 5 percent of its product supports the other 95 percent afford not to figure out a way to get that music heard and bought?

"In the pop-prism mentality of success in today's world we are inundated with numbers, numbers, numbers," Little Feat pianist Bill Payne said, "as if that is representative of any kind of quality."

That's important to keep in mind. The charts have nothing to do with quality—chart numbers denote quantity, the number of units of a particular product sold versus all the other products of that type, in this case compact discs. As we saw, the old saying that nothing succeeds like success takes on whole new dimensions in a peer-driven, familiarity-motivated arena like music, where charting means more sales on any number of levels. This leaves the vast majority of the music produced and recorded in any given year virtually unheard. When I tell my friends that they can hear more good music today than at any time in history, I'm talking about these CDs, these bands, and this music that falls through the cracks.

9

The Fable of the Elephant and the Rabbit

How the Indies Are Eating the Majors' Lunch

CONSIDER THE infrastructure of a major record company, as laid out in chapter 3. On the profits from less than 7 percent of its releases, a major record company needs to support its front office operations—officers, promotion people, A&R people, in-house counsel, publicists, etc., not to mention the space to house them in New York, Los Angeles, and Nashville as well. Then there are the back office operations, the sales and distribution nodes (and local promotion people) located all across the country. A major record company will employ thousands of people, all supported by less than 7 percent of the titles on which they work.

The owner of an independent label and I sat down with a group of potential students interested in the music business program at a New York City college, where he and I both taught. The evening had gone from an introduction of the courses to a seminar on the music business. The company president taught the class about running an independent label. His own label would sign artists, often ones who had toiled and boiled on the roster of major labels only to fall into the 93 percent that did not sell enough copies to break even, perhaps moving between 50,000 and 125,000 CDs. The exposure garnered by the labels, however, expanded the fan bases these artists enjoyed. So the president of this indie label would sign them, agreeing to split all profits 50/50.

How does this arrangement compare to the royalty system used by the major labels? Let's do the math. Suppose that at a major label, an artist receives a $125,000 advance against royalties with which to record an album. That artist sells around 125,000 copies at, perhaps, a "15 percent of 90 percent" royalty rate (many labels still figure in the pre-1950s glass-and-lacquer disk breakage allowance in their contracts). The company figures the royalty based on a price of nine dollars:

➤ 125,000 CDs at $9 each = $1,125,000 (the gross income from the CD)

➤ $1,125,000 gross income on the CD multiplied by the royalty rate of (0.15 * 0.9) = $151,875 (the gross income of the CD multiplied by the royalty rate multiplied by the breakage allowance)

Now, this doesn't look too bad. The artist got an advance of $125,000 and seems to have recouped it and made $26,875 in royalties. But that's only part of the story. As producer Steve Albini outlined it:

Advance	$125,000
Manager's cut	$18,750
Legal fees	$10,000
Recording Budget	
Producer's advance	$35,000
Studio fee	$22,500
Drum, amp, mic, and phase "doctors"	$3,000
Recording tape	$5,000
Equipment rental	$3,000
Cartage and transportation	$2,000

continued on next page

Catering $3,000
Mastering...$7,500
Tape copies, reference CDs, shipping tapes,
misc. expenses..$2,000
TOTAL COST...$75,000
Video Budget
Cameras $4,000
Crew $2,500
Processing and transfers $1,000
Off-line $1,000
On-line editing...$1,000
Catering $500
Stage and construction $1,000
Copies, couriers, transportation $1,000
Director's fee..$3,000
TOTAL COST..$15,000
Album artwork..$2,000
Promo photo shoot and duplication...................$2,000
Band fund...$5,000
New fancy professional drum kit.......................$5,000
New fancy pro guitars (2) $3,000
New fancy pro guitar amp rigs (2) $4,000
New fancy potato-shaped bass guitar $1,000
New fancy rack of lights and bass amp $1,000
Rehearsal space rental $500
TOTAL COSTS $132,250

So the artist pulled in $151,875. Subtract both the advance of $125,000 and the budget overage of $7,250 (i.e., $132,250), and the band actually realized $19,625—not too bad—in fact far better than most.

For example, if the band had sold 25,000 pieces less (and remember, as we established in the previous chapter, only one album in about 15 to 30, depending on the year, achieve those kinds of sales) and the figures look very different:

➤ 100,000 CDs at $9 each = $900,000 (the gross income from the CD)

➤ $900,000 gross income on the CD multiplied by the royalty rate of (0.15 * 0.9) = $121,500 (the gross income of the CD multiplied by the royalty rate multiplied by the breakage allowance)

For the sake of argument, we'll assume the band had roughly the same expenses. If the artist netted $121,500, and we take away both the advance of $125,000 and the budget overage of $7,250 (i.e., $132,250), the band still owes the record company $10,750 before it can collect one dollar of royalties. Nor does that take into account contractual withholdings like a percentage for reserves against returned CDs and other items. It may take years for the artist to actually see the royalties on that money.

This also does not cover other costs that might get written off against the artist's royalties according to the contract while the company "works" the record: in many cases promotional items and publicity junkets, not to mention the artist's limousine, all need to be recouped before the artist sees that first dollar of royalties (more on this later). Chances are, even the net income attributed to the artist in this exercise is high, and many of the other figures cited are low—many albums, especially major label albums, cost a lot more than that to produce, though as the budgets have shrunk so have the costs (with devastating effect on the recording industry, as we'll later see). Needless to say, very few make their money back, and even fewer generate royalties for the artist.

Now, by selling 125,000 copies of the CD, the record company grossed $1,125,000. Which means after paying the advance, taking care of the extra $7,250 in production expenses, and even putting the additional $19,625 in the reserve account, the record company grossed $973,125. Out of this, all the front office expenses, salaries, warehousing, back office expenses, record pressing, production, etc., etc., need to get paid. A little bit down the line, we'll find out that to mount a successful promotional campaign to radio stations can cost between $250,000 and $1 million *per song*. Remember, only about 1,000 albums of the 60,000 released actually sell as many copies as this one during the course of any given year. This might have been one of the few CDs that almost pulled its weight, at least as far as the record company is concerned.

Now let's look at the model that some of the indie labels espouse. The artist does not get an advance, or gets a fairly small one. The recording is done at the label's own studio, and is billed nominally to the artist against royalties—figure a cost of $14,000 to pay for the engineer, the rent, the wear and tear on the equipment, and the cost of the media used in the recording. So, between these recording fees, legal fees in the contract negotiations (since these negotiations tend to be much simpler than the major label kind, figure about half the price, or $5,000), and the cost of actually pressing the CD (figure another $7,500 for an initial run of 10,000 CDs), the artist would seem to be down about $26,500 from the get-go. But now things start to get interesting—the indie label sells the CDs to retail. If it goes through the first run of CDs, the numbers look something like this:

➤ 10,000 CDs at $9 each = $90,000
➤ $90,000 minus $26,500 production costs = $43,500 profit
➤ Split that $43,500 50/50 (e.g., a 50 percent royalty) and the record company and the band both come away with $21,750
➤ $21,750 minus management's 15 percent cut, $3,262.50, leaves the artist with $18,487.50

And that's only from the first run of records. With an artist that has already had the major label development, the indie president estimates he can sell, conservatively, 60,000 CDs. So on the next 50,000, artist and record company still split the manufacturing costs of $37,500:

➤ 50,000 CDs at $9 each = $450,000
➤ $450,000 minus $37,500 to press up 50,000 CDs = $412,500
➤ Split that $412,500 50/50 and each party comes out with $206,250
➤ $206,250 minus the manager's 15 percent, $30,937.50, and the artist realizes $175,312.50!

That's over 10 times what the artist made at the major. Of course, the major already did the heavy lifting, giving the artist the exposure needed to build a fan base that could support sales of 60,000 independent CDs. But, as Todd Rundgren put it:

> Record companies still have a function. They have to underwrite artists until they build a core audience. That's what record companies used to be. They used to be artist development. It was not a hits machine all the time, everybody in the company oriented toward that one blockbuster that makes the bottom line. It used to be that you were trying to get artists to a point that they would generate a dependable level of income in sales of what they did. That's what record companies can still do in this environment, underwrite and promote artists until they do have a core audience. . . . Branding is a very powerful thing. You will buy a shitty product with a good brand name on it. The record business is driven a lot by that.

"You don't need the major record companies," said Barry Bergman, president of the Music Managers Forum U.S., "for anything but mass media."

Indeed, for a "name brand" artist, the indie route could be the best, perhaps the only way to go. Stu Cook, former bassist for Creedence Clearwater Revival, now plays with his old buddy Doug Clifford in Creedence Clearwater Revisited. While it started as just a way to play the old songs to an audience, they released a record via major-distributed independent record company Fuel 2000. This represents the best of both worlds—an independent with the distribution spank of a major. It works for the major, as well. After all, it has a lot of people on the payroll at those distribution branches, and it needs to keep pushing product through that pipeline. And it's a good deal for the artist, who participates in the profits with a 25–50 percent royalty—that 50/50 split at the high end. "We're already into royalties," said Cook. "Our break-even point was $10,000. We get the same royalty rate as Michael Jackson. That's the way to do business."

"These are great times for independent labels," said David Sanger of Austin, Texas, indie Lazy SOB Recordings. "The reason is that manufacturing costs are within reach of anybody who wants to make a record."

Of course, the role indies play more often is as the farm club for the majors, doing the initial development that the major label then seeks to exploit and build on. Sometimes it works, as it did for Nirvana, which got bought out of its contract with Seattle-based indie Sub-Pop Records. More often it doesn't, but in most cases the major will help expand the indie band's following. Or so goes the conventional wisdom. Of course conventional wisdom often fails in an unconventional environment like the record business. The emo band Thursday sold 357,000 copies of its debut album on independent Victory Records. Universal Music Group imprint Island Def Jam Records bought the band out of its Victory contract. The IDJ record sold only 349,000 copies.

Then consider the case of another Victory band, Hawthorne Heights. The Ohio-based hard rock band, with minimal radio support, managed to sell over 750,000 copies of its debut (still on *Billboard*'s Top 200 at this writing) and saw its sophomore effort move more than 100,000 in its first week, debuting at #3 on the *Billboard* Top 200 Album chart. The band built its community of fans by pursuing an incessant, grueling touring schedule and working the Internet, particularly the online music-oriented social networking Web communities.

So by keeping lean and mean, by using promotion outside of the mainstream, and by making sure the artists they sign have the determination to work to make it, independent labels might become a growth industry and perhaps even remind the major labels what the record business is all about: selling music that reaches people. With an entire staff that would be small for a major imprint's promotion department, Victory Records managed to beat the majors at their own game, getting into that rarified 200 or so records out of 40,000 that sell gold or better. And while a percentage of Victory's sales go to the independent distributor, this way it only pays indirectly for all the sales and distribution nodes as opposed to the majors, which need to keep the product flowing to maintain the nodes. The majors have twigged this, opening up their own "independent" distribution companies, giving the indies access to their distribution nodes (thereby adding product to their flow), channeling the distribution fees into their corporate bottom lines, and occasionally striking "upstreaming" deals that again use the indie as a farm club—when an album sells a certain amount, the indie sells the contract to the major that owns the distribution company. So Sony/BMG controls the independent distributor RED, EMI bought independent distributor Caroline to serve this purpose, Universal revived their Fontana name as their independent distributor, and Warner has several, most notably the Alternative Distribution Aliance (ADA) and Rykodisc. Beyond these, there are still several totally independent distributors, such as New Jersey–based Big Daddy. As in so many things, each has its advantages and disadvantages to the indie company.

When we sat with the students, the indie record company president had an interesting metaphor for the way he worked versus the way a major label worked. He said that major labels were like elephants. Elephants are very large, very willful animals. They tend to be difficult to turn once they're heading in a particular direction, and it takes a lot to bring one down. Independent labels are more like rabbits. Rabbits are small and fast. They can respond to circumstances and change direction quickly, and run circles around elephants. They just have to take care not to get caught under the elephant's foot. Cunning rabbits, however, can do very well.

The former head of Tommy Boy Records, Tom Silverman, sold his company to Warner Bros. and found himself starting his business from scratch once again. In response to the insanity of having to sell millions to maintain a major label relationship, he said something to the effect of: "Great. If they want to send me all the acts that will sell 250,000 copies, we'll all make a mint."

Part II | **The Messy Suicide of Commercial Radio**

10

Airwaves of the People, for the People . . . Yeah, Sure

WHO OWNS THE airwaves? Who actually has the ultimate rights to all those broadcast frequencies?

The airwaves in America (and indeed, in most of the world) are theoretically public property. As mandated by the Radio Act of 1927 (HR 9971), which established the Federal Communications Commission, Congress empowered that commission to:

> from time to time, as public convenience, interest or necessity requires . . .
> a. classify radio stations,
> b. prescribe the nature of the service rendered by each class of licensed station . . .
> c. assign bands of frequencies or wave lengths . . .

It also delineated a variety of other responsibilities, some of which have been obviated by the passage of time. The primary one, however, involved assigning frequencies for various functions and licensing them. The FCC reminds us this doesn't just pertain to commercial broadcasting on the AM, FM, and television frequencies. Toy cars run on radio control and those frequencies need to be licensed. Your car remote is a small radio transmitter. Even microwave ovens use radio frequencies (micro wavelengths, if you will) and need to be licensed. Look at the back of your microwave and you should see an FCC compliance statement.

And, when you think of it, this is all good. Without someone watching out for these things, you might turn on your television and the popcorn would start popping, use your wireless modem and cause interference on all the car radios in your neighborhood, or broadcast your wireless phone calls to everyone's FM stereo (now *that's* entertainment!).

Before the creation of the FCC, things like that happened all the time. Many of the property squabbles over frequencies were due to the idea that the frequencies were, in fact, up for grabs. According to attorney Krystilyn Corbett:

> After broadcast, or "wireless," communication was first developed, rights to use a particular frequency of the electromagnetic spectrum were allocated through a "first-in-time" principle, as were many private rights. . . . One who wanted to broadcast simply appropriated a suitable frequency; one who came later found another, unused frequency. Rights established through the first-in-time principle were not, however, recognized and enforced consistently, and so many conflicts arose.

On the one hand, the courts wouldn't allow broadcasting to be regulated under the purview of the secretary of commerce. On the other hand, without regulation, there was nothing to say that one broadcaster could not use the frequency another broadcaster had used first, stepping all over it with a more powerful transmitter. By the mid-1920s, things became so confused on the airwaves that President Coolidge went to Congress and asked it to take some action.

The Radio Act in part proclaimed "that the air waves belonged to the people of the United States and were to be used by individuals only with the authority of short term licenses granted by the government." Back then, as opposed to now, "the government" still equated itself with "the people."

The next step in the process, the revised Communications Act of 1934, reaffirmed public ownership of the airwaves, stating that radio stations were required to operate in the "public interest, convenience, and necessity." The act also turned the FCC into a permanent body and prohibited anyone from "owning" the radio spectrum:

It is the purpose of this chapter, among other things, to maintain the control of the United States over all the channels of radio transmission, and to provide for the use of such channels, *but not ownership thereof* [italics mine], by persons for limited periods of time, under licenses granted by Federal authority, and no such license shall be construed to create any such right beyond the terms, conditions, and periods of the license.

However, the University of Chicago's Richard Posner described a broadcast license as, "for all practical purposes, perpetual." And by making that license transferable, Congress and the FCC essentially turned the radio spectrum into a frequency auction. Since the people who possess licenses are able to sell them, the broadcast spectrum has become, in essence, the property of those who can purchase a piece of it. As it became harder to revoke a broadcaster's license, that broadcasting license could stay in the owner's hands until such time as they somehow transferred it, leaving the owners of the airwaves—us—out of the transaction completely.

To try to prevent this situation from concentrating media access in the hands of the few and the wealthy, who could then ensure that only their own opinions were exposed to the public, some heavy restrictions were placed on media ownership. For example, rules were established:

➤ in 1941, so one company could reach only 35 percent of the nation's households
➤ in 1964, to prohibit a broadcaster from owning more than one station in a single market, except in very large markets
➤ in 1970, to prevent ownership of both a radio station and a television station in the same market
➤ in 1975, to prevent cross ownership of newspapers and television in the same market

The public was also given the ability to challenge a station that they felt didn't serve the "public convenience, interest, or necessity," and prevent the renewal of that station's license. The FCC codified these policies in 1946, and again in 1960, when it established 14 criteria for maintaining a broadcast license. By 1965, the effort it took to vet the criteria for each renewal had turned into a real drag on the FCC's time. Then the courts got involved, and several rulings began the process of handcuffing the FCC to the standards required to confirm the renewal of a license. From these cases came a flood of challenges to renewals, especially after the FCC denied WHDH a renewal in 1970, citing public demand. In 1970, the FCC streamlined the process, stating it would renew licenses if the station could show at least "substantial performance free of serious deficiencies." Somewhere in there, the pendulum began to swing away from public ownership of the airwaves and more toward a model of private ownership.

Theoretically, the airwaves have stayed in our hands. The sad fact is, somewhere toward the start of the 1980s, they slipped through our fingers.

11

Regulations? We Don't Need No Steenking Regulations

STARTING IN THE Reagan administration, regulations that had held media ownership in check for five decades began to get stripped away. By the mid-1990s, any company could own pretty near all the media outlets it could afford.

One of the planks on the platform that brought Ronald Reagan to office was getting as much government as possible out of people's lives and businesses. One of the first major policy initiatives to reach fruition, in 1981, was the official beginning of the deregulation of media. Gone were some of the more stringent rules of ownership and cross ownership. Rather than have the government dictate the rules, the FCC had decided to let the market govern. According to an FCC report, "Given the status of broadcasting today, the marketplace and competitive forces are more likely to obtain these public interest objectives than are regulatory guidelines."

Some of the rules that went by the board in the shakeup included:

➤ Radio stations no longer had to keep detailed program logs—though, as we'll see in the next chapter, that didn't really matter, as radio stations were beginning to be programmed effectively *from* the logs.
➤ There was no longer any limit on the amount of advertising a station could air, whereas previously the limit was 18

minutes (30 percent) per hour. If a station thought it could maintain listeners broadcasting nothing but commercials, nothing could stop it from doing so.

➤ The regulations requiring a certain amount of local interest news and "public service" programming—a prime means for challenging licenses—no longer applied.

➤ The broadcast ownership rules became far more relaxed.

By 1984, the number of radio stations any one entity could own had nearly doubled, from seven FM and seven AM stations (limits set in the mid-1950s) to 12 FM and 12 AM stations. The numbers had risen to 20 each by 1994. (However, owners were still limited to one station per band in any one market.) The courts got into the act, for example overturning the "fairness doctrine," requiring stations to give equal time to opposing viewpoints, in 1987.

The trend came to a head with the Telecommunications Act, which Bill Clinton signed into law in 1996. Suddenly, it became open season on radio stations. The national cap on the number of stations a company could own disappeared altogether.

In a market with:	A single entity can control:
45 or more stations	up to 8 stations, no more than 5 in the same band
30–44 stations	up to 7 stations, no more than 4 in the same band
15–29 stations	up to 6 stations, no more than 4 in the same band
14 or fewer stations	up to 5 stations, no more than 3 in the same band

The floodgates opened. In particular, radio and entertainment impresario Robert Sillerman began buying stations as if they were Monopoly properties. Said Sillerman:

The recent passage of the Telecommunications Act, in substantially the form which we anticipated . . . opens up significant opportunities for us, not only in our existing markets but in other areas throughout the country. In Greenville-Spartanburg, we will be operating a triopoly, three FM Stations and one AM station, and in Jackson we will have three FMs and two AMs. This high level of radio station ownership within a market has never before been possible and we anticipate much greater operating efficiencies and excellent results as a benefit of deregulation.

Throughout 1996 and 1997, rarely did a month go buy without the announcement of some Sillerman acquisition. Then he sold off all his radio stations to the AM/FM chain and went off to corner the market on concert promotions and venues.

About two years later, another huge radio chain, Clear Channel, bought Sillerman's former stations in a deal for the 443-station AM/FM chain, creating the largest radio broadcasting company in the United States. Then in March 2001, about five years after deregulation began, Clear Channel bought out Sillerman's concert promotion and venue business for $2.7 billion in stock. When the sale was announced, David Lieberman proposed the following scenario in *USA Today*:

Consider what could happen when a big act such as KISS, Britney Spears, Backstreet Boys, Marc Anthony, or Cher comes to your town.

Their songs will be virtually unavoidable, particularly on the radio station sponsoring the concert. If the radio's off, or on a different station you won't miss all the billboards [Clear Channel's original business and still a big one] advertising the event.

The radio sponsor's Web site will be one of the easiest places to buy tickets to the performance. Fans will probably go there anyway when it hosts a cybercast or chat with the artist.

Then, at the arena, you'll find yourself surrounded by merchandise and ads—many of them for the radio station and upcoming concerts.

In short, there'll be no escape.

Or, as one record company head summed it up, "You cannot have a hit record without Clear Channel."

The most astonishing part of all this is that Clear Channel had to have a fire sale to bring itself within even the lenient ownership regulations. It sold off around 25 percent of all its stations. But even now, Clear Channel owns six stations in New York City and nine in L.A., respectively the #1 and #2 markets in the United States, and over 1,200 stations total.

A few other major players also took advantage of deregulation, including:

➤ ABC Radio, with three stations in New York and three in L.A., and over 60 total U.S. stations
➤ Emmis Broadcasting, which owns three stations in New York and two in L.A., and 25 total U.S. stations
➤ CBS Radio, which owns six stations in New York and seven in L.A., and over 180 in the United States

These are only four of the bigger players as of this writing. In 2002, 21 companies owned over 40 stations each. Clear Channel has as many as all 20 of these other chains combined.

This centralized concentration of media and money has had a chilling effect on music. With the high financial stakes of keeping dozens or hundreds of radio stations solvent, radio needs to guarantee profits. The music is flypaper and the listeners the flies, and the owners want to catch as many flies on a strip as they can by programming to the lowest turn-off rate possible.

"Radio stations are becoming more and more homogenized," Patricia Seybold observed, "so they are less interested in new or niche music."

This had led to disposable pop, regurgitated rock, and repetitive rap; everything on the radio sounds the same, a seamless stream of sonic syrup. Anything with a modicum of personality or potential to offend has to develop somewhere outside the broadcast frequencies.

"In the next five or 10 years," artist Todd Rundgren predicted in 1992, "I think that radio stations are going to continue this downward slide. What they'll be good for is what they initially were good for, which is bringing live events, events that are not part of the database, but being created extemporaneously."

He proved prescient, right down to referring to the recorded content on radio as "the database."

12

The Death of the DJ
The Curse of Selector

BACK IN THE 1970s, radio meant the world to me. An avid fan of album rock station WNEW-FM, I learned more about music from its disc jockeys than I had as a musician. They didn't call the program director and afternoon DJ Scott Muni "the Professor" for nothing. One could hear a WNEW DJ, on a whim, play a set of Tom Lehrer, just because it was germane to something he or she had said. Morning man Dave Herman could play something as starkly not-rock as Claude Bolling and Jean-Pierre Rampal's *Suite for Flute and Jazz Piano* every morning. They made radio spontaneous, interesting, and fun.

During fall 1977, as a Rutgers freshman in my first media and journalism class and already one of the main DJs on the campus radio station, I came upon an article in one of the music business trades about WYNY-FM in New York, formerly WNBC-FM. The station had recently changed format to what it then called "adult pop." I found the format more troubling than fascinating, but the method of delivery rocked my world. NBC had decided to automate the station. Computers would run the whole thing, even cuing the DJ, who would be known thereafter as an "announcer," and later as "on-air talent." The innovation became the topic of my first major college paper.

A dearth of available literature on the subject meant that most of the paper would have to rely on firsthand observation. So I went to the station, talked to the station's GM (a very young—though not as young as I was—Bob Pittman), and sat for an hour with the announcer. The announcer's booth and the control room both showed signs of the recent construction. On one wall was the announcer's booth, with just a 12-inch-wide, square Plexiglass window as its link to the outside. The booth looked like someone had just put it up; no one had even primed or painted the raw wallboard. Through the double pane, one could see the opposite wall, where about 20 feet of then-state-of-the-art radio automation machinery stretched from one end of the room to the other. Two floor-to-ceiling apparatuses held about 200 tape cartridges each. Every few minutes one of them would rotate a tape cartridge into the "play" position. I recognized the tape cartridges from the college radio station—we used these tapes for the songs that the program director deemed "in rotation." This mechanism gave new meaning to the terms "in rotation"—the songs literally rotated.

In the center of all this was another device I recognized, a circa-1977 computer, complete with a half-inch drive transporting a reel of tape from spool to spool. It stood about six feet tall, and controlled the whole thing. It primarily operated a new program, created specially for automated stations, called Selector.

In the booth, the announcer, who until several weeks earlier had actually had a hands-on relationship with the music he played, sat with a dot-matrix-printed list of the songs that would play during his shift. Also listed were the commercials and breaks during which he had to back-announce the earlier tracks, read an advertisement, and then preannounce the next song.

In his book *FM: The Rise and Fall of Rock Radio*, Richard Neer recalls when Selector came to WNEW:

> Computers were just beginning to be used to program stations. The knee-jerk reaction is that this represents a bad trend, and certainly, given the direction radio has taken in the last decade there is justification for that viewpoint. But the computer saves the jocks and programmers a lot of work by replacing . . . paperwork with a mouse click. . . . Despite some initial bugs, Selector works at most radio stations where the music director simply feeds songs into it and the computer spits them out at random.

The music could then be perfectly balanced according to the factors the PD views as important.

Nearly 30 years later, both Selector and automation have taken over radio. Between 85 and 90 percent of all radio stations use this program to create their playlists. Some maverick stations remain free-form; some use other programs. The automation has gone from a wall worth of equipment to a desktop PC with the music on a hard drive. But it has changed the entire gestalt of commercial radio.

As Neer notes, the program itself is not inherently evil. For six years I worked with Selector in what may well be the purpose for which it is best suited, programming an automated, 24/7/365 music service with no advertising or "on-air talent."

At its heart, Selector is a database program. The director of programming or music at the radio station inputs information for each song programmed, along with "rules" about how that song fits into the format of the radio station.

This can be as complex or simple as it needs to be. As you can see, there are a lot of options. The most important one is the category ("Cat"). This is the song's basic classification, the role it plays in the station's hierarchy.

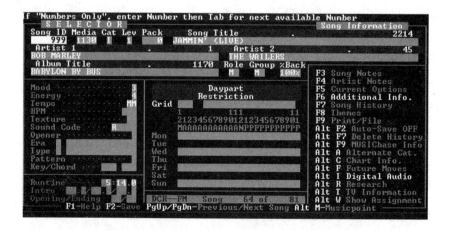

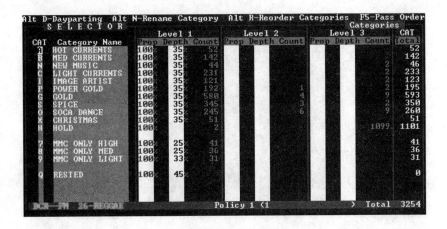

Other rules could include whether the performance is by a group, male vocalist, or female vocalist, or if it's an instrumental.

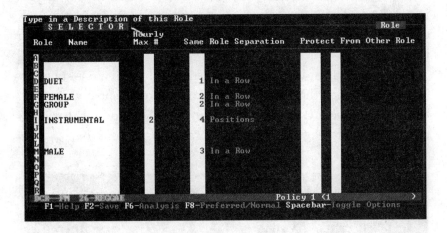

Notice how the rules are set, so that there can't be more than one duet in a row or two female vocalists in a row, and there must be at least four songs between every instrumental.

Then the music director or program director can set the rules for the sound of each song.

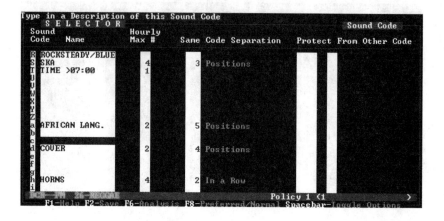

In this case, the station could only play four ska tracks over the course of an hour with at least three tracks between them; only two African language tracks with five songs between them, and no more than two cover songs with a minimum of four tracks in between. There are a variety of other rules under the sound code as well—the system can handle as many as 52, twice through the alphabet.

When the PD or MD finishes entering the information—putting new records into the playlist and taking records out or recoding them—he or she presses a couple of keys and Selector goes through the database of songs and rules, programming the station.

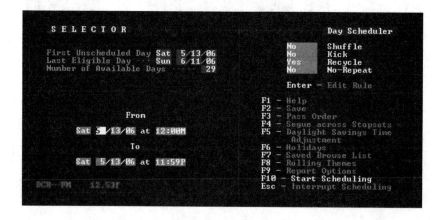

Once the program completes this task, it generates a list of songs in the order that the automated system will play them:

```
File: 4BF13N0I.PRN                                    RCS File View Utility
*STEPPING RAZOR                        PETER TOSH
*EQUAL RIGHTS                          J.HIGGS
*
*
*RS                                    COLUMBIA/7037    WB47-13
*03:30:26  3:48 H          026   3024
*COULDN'T BE THE PLACE                 JULIAN MARLEY
*A TIME AND PLACE
*
*
*RS                                    TUFF GONG/546102ATIMEANDPLACE-12
*03:34:14  3:19 H          026   2457                                    Y
*CALL MI SISTER CAROL                  SISTER CAROL
*DIRECT HIT: SISTER CAROL LIVE         C.EAST
*
*
*RS                                    CATAPULT/026     WB145-13
*03:37:33  2:51 H          026   2834
*WHERE I'M FROM                        T.O.K.
*THREAT                                C. THOMPSON/R. CLARKE/A. MCCALLA
*
*
*DH                                    GREENSLEEVES/732THREAT-05
                                            Press <F1> Key for Help
```

On a station with "on-air talent," that person gets a copy of the list. Unlike during the heyday of progressive rock stations some 25 years ago, rarely does the talent actually touch any recorded media on the air. It has all been preprogrammed. The term "disc jockey" has become a nostalgic anachronism in contemporary radio. The on-air talent has little or no say over what goes over the air anymore.

So how do requests get on the air? Well, as a person listening to the station, the requester probably wants to hear a song that's on the playlist anyway. The talent knows when a song is going to come up, and announces the request when it does. The talent might even record the person making the request, to make it seem like it's happening at that moment. But the days of "You say it, I'll play it" are long gone.

13

The Process

How Songs Really Get on the Radio

THIS SCENE TAKES place in a radio station programming department.

Ring! Ring!

"WHNK programming. Hank here."

"Hey, this is Beth from PoMo Promotions."

"What's on your mind?"

"Oh, you know. Our records. Dave and the Marshes been lighting up your nights and your phones?"

"You know it. Got that spinning 14 times a week."

"Wow, that much? You report it to *Hits*?"

"Of course. *R&R* will verify it off my Selector feed, and so will BDS."

"Now how about that baby band, the Booyahs?"

"We're not going there again. That turd wouldn't float."

"C'mon. WTMI across town is on it."

"That must be why our listenership is up."

"Listen, the Booyahs are going to be on the road with Dave. I've got to give the banner to either you or 'TMI."

"Well, you know we've been on Dave since the first album. We broke him in this region."

"Yeah, but this is now. 'TMI is spinning both. They're giving the Booyahs seven a week."

"I'll bet. Do the owls and bats enjoy it?"

"Okay, it is moonlight, but at least it's on the air."

"C'mon, Beth, I'm playing fair with you. I always have. But I need to keep the gig, and spinning stuff like the Booyahs will land me on my ass pretty quick."

"Well, who was it who told you about the 'HNK gig to begin with?"

"Yeah, I know. I owe you that. But the Booyahs? We did call-out on that record and people started snoring."

"Hey, I'm getting a lot of pressure from upstairs. The chairman's grandson plays the drums in the band. Can you do a smash or trash with them? Anything? Listen, we're going to be doing co-op with the concert promoter, but we can't give an ad to a station that isn't playing the record, right?"

"How much co-op?"

"Haven't decided yet."

Sigh. "Tell you what: I'll give it two moonlight spins, and if it gets any phones at all, I'll up it to three and do a smash or trash."

"Great. Talk to you next week."

"Oh, before I let you go. Those iPods we gave away last week. The contest was for 10. You sent us a dozen. Should I ship them back?"

"Nah, too much paperwork to put them back in inventory. It's easier if you keep 'em."

"OK."

"OK."

Click.

Variations on this theme go on over the phone every week between program directors and people promoting records to radio, everywhere commercial radio exists. To clarify some of the jargon:

➤ When Beth asks if an album has been "lighting up his phones," she refers to both requests and people actually complaining about a song. Programmers like it either way. It means that people are actually *listening*. Although songs people hate may lead them to tune out the station, most won't unless the station plays two or three songs they can't stand in a row. The opposite of love, after all, isn't hate; it's indifference. What a programmer would find worse is a song that zones people out so they're not listening, because that means that they will zone out the advertisers' messages as well. Even worse is a record that causes the audience to—*gasp!*—switch stations. If that happens, a program director will have to send out a lot of résumés to find a new job. Is it any wonder that a radio programmer makes such an effort to test songs before they go on the air? Or that proven artists take precedent over even the most talented unknowns? People like familiar things, so that's what radio gives them, especially when losing a ratings point means potentially having to cut advertising rates or lose advertisers. "As much as people say, 'We'd love to hear new music and local music,' " said WWDC's Joe Bevilacqua, "whenever anybody's attempted that in the past couple of years we've fallen flat on our faces in the ratings."

➤ *Hits* and *R&R* (aka *Radio and Records)* are two trade magazines that publish charts of airplay in various musical formats and genres. *R&R* uses BDS, the technology that "hears" the second 30 seconds of a song (see chapter 5) to determine its airplay charts. *Hits* lets the station simply report adds and spins.

➤ "Moonlight" is moonlight rotation, scheduling a record so that it will play only between the hours of midnight and 5 A.M., when losing listeners matters least.

➤ The relationship between promoters and programmers is such that the promoters willingly provide a wide variety of favors (more on this anon), not the least of which is keeping track of job openings. Radio is a very transitory and fickle business.

➤ "Call-out" is call-out research, in which the station calls people in their listening audience, plays snippets of songs for them over the phone, and gets an opinion on those songs. Then often ignores the opinions. "Call-out has become dominant," noted J Records head of promotion Richard Palmese. "Very few program directors rotate records by gut."

➤ "Smash or trash" is a contest run by some radio stations to get the phones lit up and get the listeners involved in helping to "program" a station. Listeners vote whether a song is "a smash" or if it should be "trashed."

➤ "Co-op" is short for cooperative advertising, which is advertising the record company "splits" with other partners like record retailers and concert promoters. Since radio sells ads on commission, the program director will take home a percentage, often between 20 and 25 percent.

➤ The bit with the iPods is self-explanatory, but not uncommon. Often promoters send items for contests that never happen. The general manager of a Midwestern Top 40 station cut a promotion deal and suddenly managed to take several vacations a year. "Theoretically, those trips were for promotional purposes at the station," said a radio professional, "but the GM decides to take his family instead."

The bottom line is that radio and records have become big business, and as the business gets bigger, the players seem to become more conservative, as will anyone who has a lot to lose. Thus, getting anything added to a playlist, particularly anything new, causes problems at every level of promotion, even the major label level. "The real problem is that, as record labels and radio stations become more averse to risk, they shrink the number of artists they invest in (in terms of both money and time)," said author James Surowiecki. "That may be rational in the short term, but it's bad for the culture, and interestingly I'm not really convinced it's good for business, either."

These conversations are preludes to the Maalox moment of any promotion person's week, the conference call. Usually held right after *Billboard* releases the chart numbers for the coming week's issue, it serves the legitimate purpose of shoring up weak areas and dealing with problem records. The record company's senior vice president of promotion gets all the heads of the programming departments, all the local promotion people, and even some of the independent promotion people on the phone together. These calls can last upwards of six hours and become abusive, and have led to firings, raises, promotions, ulcers, and perhaps drug addiction and suicide.

"Okay, how are we doing with that Booyah's record in your area, Beth? I'm not seeing as many spins on that as I'd like."

"I know, boss. It's a tough sell out here. I'm getting it added to WHNK, though. The street team is going to be staying up late listening for it, calling and e-mailing. Hank wants phones, and damned if he's not going to get them."

"Good. How much is he giving?"

"Couple of spins this week."

"What will it take to get him to up it?"

"Well, we've got the banner when they open for Dave and the Marshes at the Bumphouque Arena. Then there's the co-op for the shows. How much can I offer?"

"I think we can do seven large for a month of ads in anticipation of the show."

"That should put us over."

"Glad to hear it."

And Beth puts the phone on mute for a moment and lets out a long sigh of relief. She's dodged the bullet for another week. The VP is happy, too. As stressful as he makes this call on his team, the call he has to make next, to report adds to superiors in the company, makes the pressure he puts on his staff seem mild, because he has to give the folks running the company the big picture, and that picture had better include a lot of airplay.

Both Beth and her boss know the radio truism Richard Neer stated:

> One always had to be wary of stations that were too malleable to record company inducements. Heavy airplay may accompany a promotion, based on a large schedule of advertising and free concerts that may have nothing to do with a record's potential. No smaller-market programmer was immune to such enticements because revenue is so critical.

"Getting on the radio is like mounting a military campaign," said promotion head Palmese. "We try to identify who our 'heroes' are, the program directors who like the song enough to step out and add it to their rotation."

Ring! Ring!

"WHNK programming. Hank here."

"Beth from PoMo. Now, what about those Booyahs?"

"Man, those college students do stay up late. Got a dozen calls from the campus at three in the morning on Tuesday and about four in the morning on Friday. Three were from the same number. You've got your three spins and a Thursday drive time smash or trash."

"Very cool." She writes a note to herself to warn her street teams to use their damn cell phones. "By the way, I got the co-op budget. We're going to want about $7,000."

"Great! Can I write you up on that?"

"That's why I mentioned it."

"Excellent."

"Still on Dave and the Marshes?"

"Holding steady at 14 spins a week. We may actually up it or start playing another song from the album as the show gets closer, especially if we get the banner, the announce, and Dave comes up here for an interview and to do some bumpers."

"Well, I know the last one is no problem. I'll see about the other two."

"Cool."

"Well, that's all for this week. Talk to you next week."

"Always a pleasure."

And why is it always a pleasure? Well, PoMo just bought $7,000 worth of advertising. If Hank's commission is 20 percent, he just pocketed $1,400.

So why do major labels dominate commercial radio? Because the major labels have the deep pockets to employ street teams, buy co-op advertising, and build their acts' profiles. Is any of this illegal? Well, maybe the iPods fall into a gray area, but nothing here in this chapter is really actionable. But that's not to say that record companies and labels don't engage in actionable behavior.

14

Payola Isn't Dead. It Always Smelled Like That

AT THE TURN of the 20th century, phonograph records were not the only game in town. As America became more affluent, every well-heeled home had to have a piano, and generally someone in the house could play and read music. It became a sign of refinement, a major status symbol in parlors and living rooms, not unlike a good stereo system toward the tail end of the century.

So while the record business took its first baby steps, sheet music, established back in the day of Gutenberg, also turned into a major commodity. In 1892, for example, Stephen Foster's "After the Ball" sold one million copies of sheet music—just in the course of the year.

Nothing sells that well in a vacuum. The selling of songs fell to a new form of music businessman, the "song plugger."

The precursor of the record company promotion department, a song plugger earned his keep by enticing people to buy sheet music. He accomplished this in several ways. The most basic way involved going from large sheet music retailer to large sheet music retailer around a prescribed territory, sitting down at a piano, and playing both the music that potential customers handed him (so they could hear it before they bought it) and his company's songs. This required the publishing companies to have regional offices all across the country. A more profitable way to entice buyers involved getting performers to sing the publisher's songs on stage. By the late 19th century, various areas of the country had show circuits that presented minstrel shows, early vaudeville, and even burlesque.

In places where there was segregation, there were segregated vaudeville circuits. The late boogie-woogie piano legend Sammy Price recalled his early years as a performer on one of these black-only circuits:

> The TOBA was a theatrical circuit that was organized in the '20s and they had about 26 cities where black artists could travel, like the Plantation Circuit and the other circuits. It started in St. Louis, from St. Louis to Kansas City, Kansas City to Dallas, Dallas to Houston, Houston to Shreveport, Louisiana, Jacksonville, Florida, all around to Baltimore, which is where they would discontinue that show.

These traveling shows enjoyed across-the-board popularity wherever a theater could support them. A song performed by a vaudeville headliner nearly guaranteed a publisher a hit. So paying the headliner to perform a song was not uncommon. The roots of this practice were deep, and even respected to an extent. Gilbert and Sullivan did it. The performance of "subsidized" songs helped many a vaudevillian make ends meet.

Of course, other factors than subsidization influenced a vaudevillian's decision to perform or not perform a song, just as other factors influence a radio programmer's decision to spin or not to spin. A radio programmer wants to avoid losing listeners and a job. The vaudevillian wanted to avoid getting pelted with overripe vegetables and other projectiles.

As time went on, people continued to pay for play. They tell some great stories about artists who beat the system this way. Dave Cousins got his British progressive rock band the Strawbs on the radio in England by finding out which stores reported to the BBC. He gave the price of the single to all of his friends and family and their friends and family and sent them to those shops. Noting the rise in sales, the BBC started playing the song, and suddenly it began to sell without Cousins having to underwrite it.

The story is great because it is so rare. Throughout the rock era, getting a record on radio has been a major, and often dirty, chore.

As former Columbia head Walter Yetnikoff put it, "The music business—and especially the cutthroat business of generating hits—has always had its shady side. What else is new?"

For the better part of a century, the equation in the record business has read "S = R + P," where "S" represents sales, "R" stands for radio and "P" means promotion—or the other "P" word. While once in a blue moon record companies *do* manage to sell records that don't get radio play—the soundtrack to *O Brother Where Art Thou?* or bands like Anthrax, Hawthorne Heights, and Mannheim Steamroller sell considerable numbers without benefit of a hit—generally the path of least resistance to getting a hit involves getting a song on the radio (if you can call that least resistance).

The symbiosis between radio and the music business began very nearly with the introduction of radio to a popular audience. In 1924, the *New York Times* trumpeted:

QUESTIONNAIRE REVEALS RADIO BENEFICIAL TO MUSIC INDUSTRY. Broadcasting has in many instances created a desire on the part of listeners to buy records. This is clearly shown in the case of Wendell Hall, an instrumentalist and singer, who visited many of the large broadcasting stations. When singing from WEAF, he rendered some songs that were more than three years old and for which there had been no recent demand in record form. Several music stores in Brooklyn reported a sudden demand for records of these songs, and upon questioning, it was found that the renewed popularity was caused by the broadcasting of the selections.

This led to a rapid change in the role of the song pluggers. Suddenly they didn't need to bring their music directly to the people. They could reach the people with much more ease by just getting a song on the radio.

"I was a song plugger 50 years ago," said Juggy Gayles, one of the people who invented and developed the idea of promoting music to the radio as a means of selling records back in the days when it involved getting the big bands to play it on their regular broadcasts. "In those days we looked to get our songs played on radio. Today, we look to get our records played on radio."

By 1955, *Billboard* was reporting that 2,700 radio stations nationwide accounted for 300,000 songs played per day:

> The cry that radio "killed" music—shortened the life of songs—was already being heard in the late 1930s. Network radio, the system of "remote" broadcasts by bands coupled with the virtual death of vaudeville (once the chief source of song promotion) had already worked a major change in the business. . . . In this remarkable statistic lies the answer to what has happened to the music-record business, the answer why it has grown rougher and more competitive than ever before on all levels.
>
> Several developments point up the fact that the deejay's role has increased in stature over the past few years. First of these is the fact that station management tend more than ever to give the jockey complete freedom of selection of records.

The power of the DJ led to some of the more interesting courtship rituals in corporate America. The record companies catered to vices the DJs didn't even know they had. "I had to get the broads to the hotel," said Artie Ripp of his early days in the record business, "and then make sure the disc jockey who had just finished with the redhead knew that the blonde was down the hall."

Joe Smith, who was a DJ in Boston before rising to the presidency of Elektra Records, knows about this practice from both ends:

> A guy who will go unnamed was the music director up at WINS when Alan Freed was there. It was a hot radio station. The guy was making $125 a week as the music director. And he was living over on Sutton Place, wearing fancy suits, driving a fancy car, going off to Europe, on his $125 a week. The station manager, oblivious to all this, said, "You're doing a great job. We're

going to promote you to the news department and give you $200 a week." He begged him, "Please! Don't do that to me!"

Payola was a modus operandi, a way of life in the golden age of rock and roll, in the '50s. In 95 percent of the cases, the best disc jockeys didn't play records for money. They played records and they got money. A distributor or a label would give a disc jockey $500 a month or $1,000 a month, and you would pick from their records. If there was nothing there, you didn't play it. Everyone was in such fierce competition for ratings and business that you couldn't make up a program of stiffs, just because you got paid.

"Guys at the radio stations got money, of course," Ripp agreed, "but the interesting thing was that most of them were taking money to play records they would play anyway."

In its own way, this might represent capitalism at its finest, a study in supply and demand that even Adam Smith would admire. On the one hand, the disc jockeys and music directors wanted to keep that $1,000 a month coming in. At a time when a good salary in radio was $125 a week, that $1,000 nearly doubled what most made. However, to keep that money coming in, you had to keep the audience listening, and audiences know when a song sucks as well as the DJ, and probably even better. So it involved a delicate balance, and more than likely Smith and Ripp's rose-colored version of the bad old days of radio on the take has a smack of truth.

In the late 1950s, however, the U.S. Congress took an interest in leveling the media playing fields. It started with hearings on "the TV game show scandal," wherein a major winner revealed he had received the answers in advance of the show. When the congressmen saw the kind of media play this got them, they looked for another high-profile target, and found a way to kill two birds (or more) with one stone.

Neither the mainstream record industry or the performance royalty organizations, companies that collected money for the song owners and payed them (theoretically) every time a song was played, particularly liked rock and roll at its outset—especially

ASCAP, which was still pretty snooty about who it let join (the reason one of the other performance royalty companies, BMI, represents so much early rock and roll). Since the major record companies had yet to finish milking the careers of the Doris Days and Frankie Laines, they let the independent companies break rock and roll, and these independents made a fortune.

Both ASCAP and the RIAA had been lobbying Congress about rock and roll. By convening hearings about radio taking bribes to play music, congressmen could answer these lobbyists and maintain their high profiles in the media at the same time.

It takes money to make money, and some feel that—especially at this juncture in the rise of popular music and rock and roll—payola actually *helped* level the playing field for the new performers. "Black artists got far more exposure than ever before," author James Surowiecki noted, "and small labels put out records that everyone was listening to. I'm not convinced that would have happened without payola."

The records that "had a beat and you could dance to" came out largely via the indies, and payola almost served to vet them. After all, a record company must have had the funds to get a record distributed if it had the funds to grease the DJs.

The major companies missed the point in a lot of ways, ignoring the emerging baby boom generation and the idea that these kids didn't want to listen to the same music as their parents, that Patti Page and Perez Prado and Perry Como didn't appeal to the kids who listened to their portable radios, bought the Coca-Cola the stations sold via advertising, and went to the dances and concerts the radio stations sponsored. They failed by not targeting the kids, the same way they would fail by *only* targeting the kids 50 years later—the further irony of this being that it was largely the same audience being ignored!

But subpoenas were dispatched and the radio and rock and roll record industries were summoned to Washington to testify. "I was out with Jimmy Van Heusen and Dick Clark was out with his wife," Juggy Gayles recalled of the days before the hearings. "Clark and Van Heusen were impressed with each other. Clark told us that his lawyers told him to keep his cool. If they ask you a question they already know the answer."

He watched the hearings and followed them. He saw Dick Clark handle the congressional hot seat with aplomb, basically telling the hearing that, as the owner of several record companies himself, if such a thing as payola existed, he would probably pay more than he would ever receive. One of Juggy's bittersweet memories involved his subpoena to appear before the payola hearings. It was issued for George Resnick, Juggy's given name. No one knew George Resnick, so the summons didn't get served, sparing Juggy the agony of testifying against friends and associates, like Alan Freed, who shot off his mouth like a bottle rocket in front of the committee.

"Alan could be his own worst enemy," Juggy said of the late dean of disk jockeys, whom he helped lure from Cleveland to bring his inimitable style to New York.

> George Furness and me, we got him brought to New York. When the payola thing happened, he was taken. He saw what Dick Clark did and thought, 'I'll show him headlines.' He blew his cool and shot off his mouth. He didn't want to hurt anyone. He was a beautiful guy, a genius. He got taken by a lot of people. I never gave Alan Freed a dime in my life. He used to pick up the tabs when we went out.

As a result of the hearings, Clark was forced to divest himself of many of his side businesses, ancillary to his hit television show *American Bandstand*. He sold off several record and music publishing companies that were deemed a conflict of interest with his main business. Alan Freed, one of the most powerful DJs on the air, got the brunt of the committee's ire. Although the fines didn't amount to much, he could no longer find work. His testimony made him an industry pariah. Within seven years, he had drunk himself to death.

After the hearings, the government quickly passed a law against payola. The 86th Congress voted in the Communications Act Amendments on September 13, 1960, with the stated purpose of

> [promoting] the public interest by amending the Communications Act of 1934...to impose limitations on payoffs between applicants; to require disclosure of payments made for the broadcasting of certain matter; to grant authority to impose forfeitures in the broadcast service, and to prohibit deceptive practices in contests of intellectual knowledge, skill, or chance; and for other purposes.

At the level of the individual radio station, this legislation had a chilling effect on the DJs. Since the individual DJs were the recipients of the payola, they no longer got to pick their own music to prevent even the appearance of influence on the individual shows. The era of the powerful DJ ebbed for about a decade, until free-form FM became a popular format (after which that fell by the wayside due to Selector). Instead, the responsibility fell to the program director and outside consultants. This actually made the record promoter's job easier. Instead of taking care of six disc jockeys, the payoffs just went to the program director, actually cutting the payola budgets for a while. In addition, the methods become somewhat more subtle.

Into the 1960s, when he joined Atlantic Records' promotion team, Juggy Gayles continued to give out money for airplay. "They all took and everybody paid!" he said. "They used to give me money to go on the road and 'take care of the guys.' Some of the [program directors] would say, 'I don't want money from you.' I told them they gave it to me to give to you. Take it."

How deeply ingrained was payola? Consider the reaction of Coed Records when its own payoffs were discovered. Through the late 1950s and early 1960s, Coed had a slew of hits with modified doo-wop songs like the Crests' "16 Candles," "You Belong to Me" by the Duprees, and "The Last Dance" by the Harptones. When it came to light in U.S. Tax Court in 1967 that the label had deducted almost $19,000 from its taxes in the two years before the Communications Act Amendments were passed, money it had paid "to disk jockeys and other employees of various radio stations for the purpose of influencing such individuals to give preference to the playing" of its singles, the label argued that "the practice of payola was common in the industry for many years. It said a company that failed to make these payments would not have its records played."

This view of the relationship between radio and record sales persisted as the conventional wisdom of the record industry. "We have become, year by year, so dependent on radio exposure of our records that without that play, we're cooked," said Warner Bros. VP of creative services Stan Cronyn in 1973. "In the last 10 years, and dramatically in the last five, the record business has sold only what it could get played."

Payola remained like a boil under the skin of the entertainment business. You couldn't help but be aware of it if you were in the business, but it wasn't evident to anyone outside. As one FTC official had predicted at the end of the 1959 investigations, "It may not be exactly payola, but it'll be something else, something subsurface."

In the 1970s, it erupted again in a series of angry pustules. A Newark federal court began to investigate the industry's mob connections, pay for play, sex for play, and a new variation on the theme, drugs for play, which was dubbed "drugola."

One of the investigation's chief sources from within the record business was a former vice president of Columbia Records named David Wynshaw. Wynshaw had been the right-hand man for former company president Clive Davis, whom the company had dismissed under a cloud of financial malfeasance that involved misappropriation of nearly $100,000 of Columbia money for home decorating and his son's bar mitzvah. Within the company, Wynshaw had a number of unflattering nicknames, like "the Royal Procurer," but he loved his job. "I took all the artists around town

when they came in. I'm known at the Copa and the Waldorf. . . .
I liked the action."

Wynshaw claimed that Columbia spent at least a quarter of a
million dollars a year just on payola to R&B stations, which it
distributed through the promotion company run by Kal Rudman,
who also published the highly influential tip sheet *The Friday
Morning Quarterback.*

Wynshaw allegedly also had ties to a reputed member of the
Gambino crime family, Pasquale Falcone, who worked as a talent
manager and was accused of trafficking heroin on the side.

Once again, the airplay the company purchased primarily ben-
efitted African American performers, as the scandal centered
around the Columbia-distributed custom label Philadelphia International Records, purveyors of records by the O'Jays and dance
hits like "The Hustle."

In the wake of these investigations, the Los Angeles district
attorney's office began to look into allegations that record companies in the city used cocaine to promote their records. "It's a
nice way to make headlines," observed MCA Records president
Mike Maitland.

David Geffen, president of Asylum Records, had more prosaic
concerns than just headlines. He feared a chilling effect, that even
the whiff of a hint of "cokeola" would cause radio stations to cut
back their playlists, and hurt the chances of getting new talent on
the air. "If Joni Mitchell were just starting out today," he said,
"she'd have trouble getting radio air play in this climate. Radio
stations are afraid to take a chance on new artists unless they have
huge hits because they're afraid they'll be questioned about
whether they were paid off to play them."

THROUGH 2005 and 2006, coincidental with announcing his aspi-
rations to run for governor of New York, the state's attorney general, Eliot Spitzer, launched several high-visibility, sound-bite-
friendly campaigns, the most ballyhooed one an investigation into

that old standard of the music business: payola. Instead of investigating the receivers of payola, as Congress had in the 1950s and '60s when it targeted Dick Clark and Alan Freed—Spitzer went after the record companies. He caught Sony/BMG, Warner Music Group, EMI, and Universal Music Group like kids with their hands stuck in a cookie jar, unable to get loose because that would mean letting go of some cookies.

Spitzer characterized the practice of payola as:

> corrosive to the integrity of competition. It is corrosive to the music industry. It is corrosive to the radio industry. . . . It is essentially the same scam where instead of airing music based upon the quality, based upon artistic competition, based upon aesthetic judgments or other judgments that are being made at radio stations—radio stations are airing music because they have been paid to do so in a way that has not been disclosed to the public. This is wrong and it is illegal.

During that investigation, several Sony/BMG promotion department memos became public:

➤ "Please be advised that in this week's Jennifer Lopez Top 40 Spin Increase of 236 we bought approximately 63 spins at a cost of $3,600."

➤ "Please be advised that in this week's Good Charlotte Top 40 Spin Increase of 61, we bought approximately 250 spins at a cost of $17K."

➤ "We ordered a laptop for Donnie Michaels at WFLY in Albany. He has since moved to WYHI in Miami. We need to change the shipping address. . . . Can you work with Donnie to see what kind of digital camera he wants us to order?"

➤ Michaels proved to be a problem for Sony/BMG promotion in general. In addition to the computer, apparently they booked him on a junket to Las Vegas. The Sony exec planning the trip sent a memo warning, "Make sure Donnie is not staying in a room too high; he has a fear of heights."

Sony agreed to stop paying for play, hire a compliance officer, and pay a $10 million fine, which the attorney general's office turned over to the Rockefeller Philanthropy Advisers for distribution among New York nonprofit organizations. It also paid the attorney general's office $100,000 toward the cost of Spitzer's investigation. In an internal memo, it announced the "promotion" of company attorney Gil Aronow to the post of compliance officer.

It further warned all employees against:

➤ Misrepresenting "their identities in order to influence the selection of music on radio or television programming, and that includes, of course, calling a radio station posing as a member of the general public to request airplay for Sony/BMG tracks." This would, effectively, defeat the purpose of street teams, however.

➤ Providing radio stations with CDs, DVDs, concert tickets, or "other product" if you didn't work in the promotions department.

Not long afterward, the Warner Music Group paid a $5 million "fine" and made similar concessions to settle the investigation into its radio payoffs. EMI settled for $3.75 million, while the largest major record company, the Universal Music Group, got hit for $12 million. Certainly these are semiserious fines, but they were levied against corporations. No one, to this date, has done real time for payola violations, despite the federal statute that provided penalties of up to $10,000 and/or incarceration for up to a year.

One way to get around any legal prohibitions is to simply think of the song as an advertisement. Some promoters bought three-minute blocks of airtime to get certain songs on the radio. The radio stations preceded those songs with an announcement that they were brought to the listener by whoever paid to have them played. And, of course, the PD—as salesperson for the ad—pocketed the commission. "The difference between what's legal and illegal mostly boils down to disclosure," noted Surowiecki.

> If a radio station announces that it's been paid to play a song—which it can do by saying something like "This song is sponsored by Arista"—then it can take the money. If it doesn't, then it can't. But, although this rule is hard and fast, there are all sorts of loopholes in determining whether there's been a quid pro quo, and independent promoters take advantage of them.

Even paying for play in this manner doesn't guarantee a hit. All the promotion in the world, all the payola in the world, and all the airplay in the world will not turn a terrible record that no one wants to hear into a hit. As Dick Clark said:

> I ran a test once to prove that you couldn't break a record by playing it if the record just didn't have it. I played a record every day for seven months. It was a record by Tommy Sands, I've forgotten the title. It had all the earmarks of a hit. . . . I wrote a letter to myself and sealed it. It's still sealed, I never opened it. I enclosed a copy of the record and I wrote, "Capitol Records, one of the largest companies in the world, is promoting this record by this young singer who has several hits, the writers are good, the promotion behind the record is good, there is every indication that the record could be a hit except it stinks. It will not be a hit. However, I will play it every day . . . to prove that you can not make a record by exposure alone." And it never was a hit. I ran into Tommy Sands years later and he said, "I always wondered why you played [that song] every day." I told him the story. The letter still resides in a briefcase I've got sealed up for posterity. But the important part is that you can't make a record a hit by playing the hell out of it.

Surowiecki agreed. "A well-worn truism in the music industry is that you can't buy a hit, and I still believe that, for the most part, is true. People can't really be fooled or bludgeoned into liking something they don't."

But beyond that, during the heyday of the 1950s payola scandal, it would seem that Spitzer's criteria of "quality . . . artistic competition" and "aesthetic judgments" were more in play than they were when he went after the record companies. As we've seen, broadcasting had already become pretty homogenized. The only quality radio seems to value currently is sameness, familiarity. Spitzer's stated quest for eliminating payola in the hope of a level artistic playing field didn't necessarily correspond to the criteria radio programmers looked for in the music they put on the air. They just wanted better flypaper for attracting more flies.

So the latest payola "scandal" boiled down to some slapped wrists, some bitten sound, and a lot of publicity putting the candidate for governor on a national stage.

15

We Don't Do Payola. We Let the Independent Promotion Companies Handle It

A COUPLE FRIENDS of mine promote records independently. They use their contacts and experience in specialized markets to get music released by their clients in those markets in front of as many people as possible. Not long ago, some major record companies hired them to work certain recordings. They received an annual contract that set down the rules of conduct the companies expect promoters they hire to follow. My friends both called me laughing at one of the paragraphs, which basically read, the promoter is not to pay for play, and if the promoter *does* pay for play, the record company knows nothing about it. In Washington, D.C., they call this "plausible deniability."

Every record company has a promotion department (even if it's one of the hats worn by the president and sole proprietor of an artist-run indie). Even the most skilled promoters, however, find markets they can't crack. Often they'll get help from specialists, independent promotion people who can get the right record to the right person to get a buzz started. After Juggy Gayles left Atlantic, whenever record companies reached an impasse in New York, he became one of these go-to guys:

I worked for Epic; I worked for Columbia; I worked for Atlantic; I worked for Warner. All they wanted from me was New York City. As long as I knew what the winners were, and

I wasn't picking losers, I could get it played. I had some credibility around the stations here.

By the late 1970s and early 1980s, it took more than credibility to get records played. A network of independent promoters, appropriately called the Network, controlled radio promotion. "I know what radio wants," one of the Network heads, Joe Isgro, told Columbia Records president Walter Yetnikoff. "Radio is hit with so much product they need to weed. Radio knows I can weed. Radio respects me. Radio listens to me. What I bring them, they play. I'm the maitre d' who decides who gets in the restaurant. Give me a hit record, I'll make sure it's played."

The main difference between Isgro and your average maitre d' was that Isgro gave out the tips in order to receive the best (turn)tables. And these were not the "$50 handshakes" that Joe Smith or Alan Freed might have accepted during the "bad old days" of payola. Isgro dealt in serious money. One radio general manager claimed that Isgro paid him in excess of $100,000 a year for four years. The estimates for the independent promotion budgets at the major record companies at the time range from $10 million to $80 million a year for each company (there were six majors then). It seemed as if only the independent promoters could get a record on any station on which it was worth getting airplay.

At the time the stakes in the record business were extraordinarily high. The bottom had started to fall out of the business with the ignominious death of disco as a "popular" music. The majors were either owned or had been acquired by public parent organizations (until GE sold RCA Records to privately held Bertelsmann in 1986) that demanded upward trends in sales every quarter. By $S = R + P$, getting the music on the radio by any means necessary was essential. So if it took $10 million a quarter to keep cash flow high and the books looking good, that's what they spent. And if it took having bands that sounded like everything else so that the promoters would handle them, well, so be it.

When the record company revenues went into freefall in the early 1980s, however, someone in the corporate suite at Warner Communications began to look at the budgets. The item that stood out on the left side of the expense column was those tens of millions going to the independent promoters. The guys in corporate paid the in-house promotion department's *salaries* to get records on the radio. Why should they also have to pay independent promoters? In a rare (at the time) edict to the record companies, Warner Corporate told its three record labels to stop using independent promotion. This seemed like a good idea to the folks at CBS Corporate as well, so Columbia and all the CBS-affiliated labels declared a boycott on independent promoters, too.

It turned out to be a boycott in name only. Yetnikoff recalled:

> The artists were furious when they learned that indies would be eliminated. Artists hunger for hits with as much, if not more, desperation than the labels. To get around the ban, the labels, including our own, would give extra money to the artists or their managers so that they, and not us, would hire the indies. Any way you looked at it, independent promoters were in the game.

So it didn't turn the spigot off, just reallocated the money to a different budget line, but it seemed to appease the corporate offices, at least for a minute or two. However, the game didn't last long for Isgro and the Network. In the dead of winter 1986, NBC News aired a segment on what it called "The New Payola"—interestingly, only months after NBC's parent company GE divested itself of RCA Records. The segment showed pictures of Isgro and his associate Fred Disipio attending the Rock and Roll Hall of Fame inauguration ceremony. It also showed Isgro with a reputed associate of the Gambino crime family, Joseph Armone, whom wiretaps revealed was on Isgro's speed dial and whom Isgro referred to as "his partner." Up at the Columbia Records offices at Black Rock, Walter Yetnikoff fumed and sputtered with a mixture of fear, loathing, and white-hot fury:

When I saw a tape of the show the next day, I dropped everything and stormed up to [CBS president Thomas] Wyman's
office. I was enraged. "It's bullshit," I said. "Not a shred of
proof. No substantiation. They film these guys getting out of
their cars like they're convicted killers. As president of CBS you
gotta do something. You gotta put out a press release and call it
what it is—a journalistic scandal worse than the scandal it pur-
ports to expose. You need to defend Columbia Records and you
need to defend me."

Meanwhile, the industry ran for the hills. Disipio and Isgro
were dropped by every label, including ours. I had no choice.
[CBS chairman William] Paley gave the order.

If NBC had wanted to shut down the Network, it couldn't have
succeeded more thoroughly. If it had wanted to wipe out payola and
corruption in the record business, it couldn't have done worse. As
it turned out, Yetnikoff was right. It took three years for the U.S.
attorney's office to deliver any sort of indictment, after a long and
arduous investigation. Isgro, former CBS VP Ray Anderson, and
Isgro's associate Jeffery Monka faced 57 counts, including violations
of the Racketeering Influenced and Corrupt Organizations (RICO)
Act, defrauding the record companies, payola, money laundering,
and kickbacks. However, after a trial that presented a parade of
witnesses talking about payola, drugs, threats, and other illicit
incentives to play certain records; nearly 10 years of legal wran-
gling that involved three appeals; spectacular legal gaffes by the government prosecutors; and God knows how much taxpayer money,
the cases against Isgro, Anderson, and Monka were dismissed.

Charges were never brought against Disipio, and in 1993,
while Isgro et al. were still caught up in the legal morass of
appeals and dismissals, EMI president Charles Koppelman hired
him as a consultant to teach his promotion department promotion strategy. Koppelman likened it to hiring Joe DiMaggio as a
hitting coach.

Still, for all intents and purposes, their credibility and useful-
ness as promoters evaporated. Their careers went on. Anderson
became president of independent R&B label Dr. Dream. Isgro

went into movies, producing the film *Hoffa*. He also started another label, Private I, and consulted through a company called Raging Bull Productions. Private I and Dr. Dream were among the first labels to start signing artists dropped by the majors and capitalizing on their followings. Isgro signed Rick James, Bootsy Collins, and the Gap Band to Private I, while Anderson's label featured Dash Rip Rock, Rich Little, and Paul Kelly.

And musically, what did the end of the Network era augur? Well consider the #1 records in 1985, the year before the Network hit the fan. That year Phil Collins topped the charts three times and Wham! twice, and John Parr and A-ha had their only real hits. By buying music onto the air, the Network ushered in sonic homogeneity, a musical malaise that still afflicts popular music. As most of the music the Network worked tended toward the middle of the road, radio started to regard rock as a niche format, and the height of R&B was Whitney Houston and the Commodores. The Network disappeared, but it branded popular music, and the scars remain.

While the Network was finished, independent promotion didn't go away. It did, however, mutate. At the height of the influence of the Network, and just before it came crashing down, a young promoter in Chicago, who had worked independent promotion in New York and toiled in various Midwestern cities as an employee of CBS, came up with his own idea. "In 1983 or '84, I went to an FCC attorney and laid out this promotional assistance/revenue sharing opportunity," said Jeff McClusky.

> The idea was to take a portion of our income and go to one of the two or three Top-40 stations in various medium and small markets and supply that station with promotional assistance, if they would work with us and not other independents. That's where it started, and it's the standard [as I speak]. By the time other companies caught on to this way of doing business, we'd become the dominant company in our area.

The basic model for promotion that McClusky invented worked like this:

1. He signed up a station as a McClusky station.
2. The station agreed not to work with any other independent promoters.
3. He provided the station with a promotional budget, which it used for things like the station van, because the more the station could increase its profile, the more value it would hold for McClusky and his clients. And if the budget offered a few more dollars than the van cost, no one was the wiser.
4. Every week, McClusky sent the records he wanted "his" stations to add. Usually there'd be around 10. Of the records the station added that week, a certain percentage had to be McClusky's.
5. McClusky charged the record companies a relatively small weekly fee, and bonus fees for:
   ➤ getting the record on the chart
   ➤ getting into the Top 20
   ➤ getting into the Top 10
   ➤ getting into the Top 5
   ➤ topping the chart
   ➤ reaching gold status
   ➤ reaching platinum status
   ➤ and, of course, each level of multiplatinum

Ironically, this method proved, in its own twisted sort of way, to be more democratic than the Network. It aided the first commercial wave of rap music, as the independent companies that put out rap could afford dealing with McClusky, while the members of the Network were far pricier. If McClusky didn't bring home the bacon, the record company had to pay only the relatively small retainer, and if he did, the company was likely making enough money that it was happy to give McClusky his share. While the Network built from the top down, McClusky's method could build from the middle up. As the Network began to crumble,

McClusky's power began to accrue, and many other companies started to use his method.

For one thing, McClusky didn't have to count on stations reporting one thing and playing another. He offered enough music that most McClusky stations could find sufficient McClusky records to add every week that fit their formats. This proved useful a few years down the line when, as we've seen, the chart methodology became more sophisticated and publications such as *Billboard* and *Radio and Records* stopped relying on station reports.

"There is a greater reliance on verifiable information," noted independent promoter, radio consultant, and talent advisor Jerry Lembo. "Today's benchmarks are monitored airplay (Mediabase and BDS), Soundscan, and call-out research."

As all this was building, Joe Isgro ran into trouble again—outside of the record business. On March 30, 2000, a federal grand jury indicted him on charges of loan sharking. They must have caught him red-handed, as he pleaded guilty to two counts and was sentenced to 50 months in prison. No longer the dapper, tan, successful music businessman of his Network days, Joe Isgro faced the judge in shackles. He wore a prison windbreaker and blue chinos. His hairpiece was gone, and what was left of his natural hair was a sparse gray.

In the meantime, Isgro's successor as the 800-pound gorilla of national promotion, Jeff McClusky and Associates, grew more and more powerful. In 2001, *Billboard* celebrated McClusky's more-or-less-20th anniversary with an advertising supplement that ran nearly 40 pages, most of them ads paid for by the major record companies and many of the larger indies, film companies, local press, service providers McClusky did business with—like travel agencies, florists, and limousine services—lawyers, managers, other radio-specific trades and tip sheets, and even some artists themselves.

Once again, the scourge of independent promotion became a watchword around the industry, the only way to get anything played. The indies had all the major radio stations contracted to work with them, to the exclusion of even the record company promotion staff. Once again the infection began threatening to break through the surface in a nasty rash of boils. "Record companies that want to suggest music to radio stations have to now go through the independent promoter that has been hired by the radio station to be the exclusive source of access to the radio station," said Carey Sherman, president of the RIAA. "And independent promoters pay the radio stations large amounts of money in order to have that exclusive relationship."

Unlike Isgro, however, McClusky maintained at least the appearance of propriety. He had none of the alleged mob ties. His methods were a lot slicker than any previous indie promotions companies, and his paper trail tended to at least look aboveboard. He had legal contracts with the radio stations. He invoiced the record companies like any other service business. The company maintained an efficient, businesslike demeanor.

Things began to change, however, when another 800-pound gorilla, in this case the recently coalesced 1,200-station-strong Clear Channel chain, began to question the need for McClusky. It had enough spank on its own and could afford the vans and other perks that McClusky brought to the table. "We now recognize that these relationships [with independent promoters] may appear to be something they're not," said Clear Channel president and COO Mark Mays. "We have zero tolerance for 'pay for play,' but want to avoid even the suggestion that such a practice takes place within our company."

When Clear Channel's contracts with the indies ran out, they were not renewed. Clear Channel began using the clout of over 1,200 stations to go directly to the labels for contests, promotions, and marketing. "Strong relationships with artists and record labels are a priority for our business," said Clear Channel CEO John Hogan. "Eliminating these relationships with middlemen should . . . provide opportunities for us to create better ways to market and promote music for all concerned." Suddenly, the services of McClusky became far less valuable to the record companies.

And when New York attorney general Spitzer unveiled the results of his payola investigations, he targeted McClusky, describing his business model as an effort to "dodge the payola laws" and a means to "perpetuate the fiction" that stations were not receiving money or gifts from record companies in exchange for airplay. The investigation found that the independent promotion companies like McClusky allowed the record companies to continue to pay radio to play their songs, keeping the price of a hit high. Instead of the record company's own employees making the payoffs, they could filter the money through the independents.

For the major record companies, keeping the price of a hit high was part of the idea. It allowed them to maintain a lock on most commercial radio by dint of their deep corporate pockets. While a series of $50 handshakes might have vetted the indies, giving them the appearance of enough prosperity to get a record to the public in the 1950s and '60s, the price of independent promotion kept them pretty well out of the game through the late 1980s, '90s, and beyond, as McClusky and his peers priced themselves ever higher. Anyone who couldn't afford it got shut out of the upper echelons of the charts, except in those rare instances when public demand outranked corporate money. Hits by independent record companies became as scarce as *foie gras* at McDonald's.

In 2005 McClusky saw his promotion business go from 175 stations that were his to 30. Having lost most of his business to Clear Channel's withdrawal, he shuttered that portion of his company, calling the remaining 30 client stations and telling them that he would not renew their contracts or fund their annual promotional budgets as he had in the past. He did hope that they would continue to use him, however, as a "valuable source of information and advice about new music." He had diversified his interests in the music business. He claimed that the other areas of JMA had become even more lucrative than his promotion business, saying he made more money, for example, by consulting for publishers and merchandising companies looking for new talent, and venture capital firms who wanted to buy some glamour by investing in the music business. Nor did he plan to totally stop working with the record companies on promoting their records; he would go back to the old way of doing it and work for a flat fee rather than the multi-tiered bonus system.

Indie promoter Lembo reflected on promotion post-McClusky:

> Some things we think about now when promoting a record . . . is there marketing support, Internet activity, video (MTV, VH1, BET, Fuse, CMT, etc.), print media, touring, television appearances, satellite radio play (Sirius and XM), Music Choice [the digital music channels on certain cable systems], motion picture soundtracks, use of a song in a television show or advertising campaign? Is the artist top of mind when it comes to popular culture (e.g., *American Idol*)?

As Clear Channel ascended and McClusky fell, the record business scrambled. On the one hand, the broadcast frequencies remained as monolithic, homogenous, and monotonous as ever. In reaction to this, new choices like those outlined by Lembo sprang up.

So, did Eliot Spitzer succeed where the Isgro trial failed? Did he wash away the "corrosive" influence on "the integrity of competition . . . the music industry . . ." and "the radio industry" allowing "artistic competition, based upon aesthetic judgments or other judgments that are being made at radio stations"? Or did the infection of independent promotion and payola just once again go subcutaneous? One thing is likely, and that is that the half-century-old (or older) rules for getting a hit record won't change any time soon. "A song without significant record company support," noted the *New York Times*'s Jon Pareles, "stands about as much chance as a congressional candidate without campaign funds."

16

Arbitron Rated #1 in Symphonic-Punk-Country-Disco

Fragging the Format

IT BEARS REPEATING: in commercial radio the format is flypaper, and all of us are the flies. To extend the metaphor a bit, the format is specialized flypaper, and it targets specific flies. The stations you listen to know (generally) who you are and are set up to keep you listening and sell you their advertisers' products.

Where television has Nielsen tracking viewers, radio has Arbitron tracking its listeners. Up until very recently (and still in some markets), both Nielsen and Arbitron accomplished this feat through fairly similar means. Both solicited people randomly and asked if, for a small stipend, they would be willing to have their viewing or listening habits tracked.

"When you agree to keep a diary, you pretty much open your life to Arbitron," said radio and television columnist Larry Bonko.

> There is a page of "quick questions" to answer: What is your age? Where do you live? Thinking back six months, what radio station did you listen to most of the time? Arbitron asks about your income, the amount of schooling you've had and the zip codes of the places where you live and work. . . . Upon being selected, you are promised by Arbitron that the survey is easy and fun. Easy? Yep. Fun? That's a stretch. It's work. Arbitron paid me $5 to listen to the radio, fill in the diaries with the bright blue covers and mail them back in a postage-paid envelope.

Arbitron then collects this information and creates an elaborate demographic breakdown of who listens to what when and where. However, in other markets, Arbitron has started to use "people meters." These devices are worn by the consumer and register inaudible signals broadcast as part of the radio station signals. When the devices are turned in, the data in them is put into a computer. The consumers still have to fill in the demographic information, but the meters make the listeners' diary entries for them.

While it makes general information available to the public, like the overall radio station ratings—what the company calls "topline" ratings—the big news gets collected in what radio and advertisers refer to as "the book." The book not only shows how one station compares to another overall, but also breaks it down by the part of day and the listener's age, income, sex, and race. So a station might be rated #6 overall and have a full point and a half fewer ratings than the #1 station in the market, but still demand more per minute in advertising because that #6 station's minute reaches a much more affluent listener than the #1 station's minute.

How detailed does Arbitron research get? A recent report revealed such fascinating nuggets as:

➤ 82.5 percent of Chinese-speaking Asian Americans in New York and Los Angeles ages 12 and over listen to the radio for an average of 16 hours a week.
➤ 56.2 percent of that listening was done to the Chinese-language stations. The English-language formats Chinese-speaking Americans listened to were:
  ➤ adult contemporary (6.4 percent)
  ➤ news (6.2 percent)
  ➤ pop CHR [contemporary hit radio] (5.2 percent)
➤ 53.6 percent of them attended some college.
➤ 23.1 percent live in households with income greater than $75,000.

There was much more, but you get the general drift: Arbitron knows a lot about the people who take its surveys.

One of the things this report points out is that different formats reach different people. For example, in New York City, as of this writing, Clear Channel Entertainment owns adult contemporary station WLTW, urban station WWPR, CHR station WHTZ, classic rock station WQCD, rhythmic CHR station WKTU, and adult contemporary station WALK (actually a suburban station, but tracked with the NYC stations). These formats are *designed*, via their Selector databases, to reach different listeners.

Joe Smith noted:

> What has happened is that radio has fragmented so much, to deal with special audiences, girls 15–19 who are left-handed. I could, on the radio [in the 1950s]—as could any disc jockey in the country—play a range of Bo Diddley to Doris Day, without ever considering that you were crossing unknown lines. You were programming hit records, and hit records seemed to have a commonality of interest. I was not looking to a black audience or a girls' audience or an older audience.

Consider that the fast-diminishing oldies formats are the only stations that would dare segue from James Brown to Creedence Clearwater Revival to the Ronettes with no one thinking twice about it, because radio during the era they try to recapture sounded like that. Today, when formats tend to run all R&B or all contemporary hits, that sounds astonishingly egalitarian—and try finding a non-oldies station that plays the Ronettes or James Brown at all. Programmers would have you believe that older hits have neither relevance nor resonance outside of specific formats geared toward older music.

Beyond that, if a station's Arbitron ratings fall below a certain area, or it doesn't seem to reach the demographic it craves, it will flip formats. Often this causes such an outcry from fans of the "failed" format that they write to the FCC for relief. However, the FCC's stand on the issue is as follows:

The Commission is authorized by law—the Communications Act of 1934, as amended—to license broadcast stations and to regulate their operations in some respects, but the act prohibits the Commission from censoring broadcast matter and from taking any action that would interfere with free speech in broadcasting, a freedom also guaranteed in our Constitution's First Amendment. [I wonder what pre-Sirius Howard Stern and CBS would say about that.] Therefore, although there are limited statutory exceptions, in general neither the FCC nor any other governmental agency has the authority to direct broadcasters in the selection and presentation of programming. . . . No federal law or regulation requires that the Commission's permission be obtained for a change in a radio station's entertainment format.

A 2000 report found that there are about 10,000 commercial radio stations in the U.S. Although, as just noted, formats can change at the drop of an Arbitron point, at the time the popular music formats on radio (excluding news, talk, classical, and sports radio) broke down like this:

Format	# of Stations
Rock and modern rock (formerly known as album-oriented rock)	1,990
Adult contemporary (contemporary without hard rock or hip-hop)	692
Rhythmic Top 40 (pop, R&B, and hip-hop)	495
Contemporary (all new)	376
Hot adult contemporary ("soft rock" with a beat)	335
Contemporary hit radio [CHR] (Top 40 with a 20-song playlist; all [the same] hits, all the time)	306
Adult album alternative (music for former album-rock fans who still wanna rawk; modern rock without the synthesizers)	176
Urban (modern R&B and hip-hop)	103
Spanish (actually a bunch of different genres, from tropical to Tejano, but the survey didn't subdivide)	103

Alternative (the breeding ground for rock and [especially] modern rock, but edgier, with fewer sythesizers)	85
Country (another variegated species of radio that didn't get subdivided)	80
Soft adult contemporary (all-new so-soft-it's-squishy music)	75
Urban adult (modern R&B without the hip-hop)	61
Modern adult ("soft rock without the oldies")	59
Smooth jazz (aka instrumental pop)	36
Jazz	32

Smith lamented this new fragmentation:

> Now there are people who do a lot of research, phone-outs, phone-ins, and again, narrow banding in terms of their outreach to what they play. It's ludicrous to me that a record doesn't make it into the AOR [album-oriented rock, what is now called modern rock] world. What is the AOR world? Have we invented a group of people who won't listen to this hit record by Kenny Rogers? That's awful. Kenny Rogers makes some wonderful records that last a long time; people dance to them and hear them. If the guy's got a #1 record of "Lady," why couldn't that be played on a radio station? But the narrowcasting, and the perceptions that programmers have of putting people in bags, is what's different from where it was back in the radio of the '50s.

Of course, this is all powered by advertising. If a format like adult contemporary appeals predominantly to women—and Arbitron consistently reports that it does—where do you want to advertise tampons? If a format consistently appeals to men 25–54, where do you want to advertise beer? If your medium is radio, Arbitron tells you which flypaper attracts which flies, how many of them, and how often.

"It's a tool," said one station owner, "that we use in our business every day."

17

Are You Sirius?
Can Satellite Radio, Webcasting, and Podcasting Save Broadcasting (or Even Themselves)?

WHEN I TOLD one of my former students the subtitle of this book, he said, "Radio! Radio, radio, radio sucks!"

We now have a pretty good idea why standard terrestrial broadcasting has this reputation. With the broadcast frequency spectrum full in many urban areas, the keen competition really doesn't help; it has a homogenizing effect, and very few stations take the leap to sound different. The stakes are just too high.

One of the adages of business has it that the way to get rich is to fill a niche. Find a problem and solve it. Build the proverbial "better mousetrap." In radio, these solutions have taken three specific shapes: satellite radio, webcasting, and webcasting's kissing cousin, podcasting. Unfortunately, as of this writing, none of them have proven financially viable, though all are getting close.

While a relatively recent development in the broadcast world, the idea for satellite radio has been brewing for over a decade, since the FCC decided to allocate the 2.3-gigahertz band of frequencies to satellite-based audio broadcasting. The set price for a license to broadcast on these bands was $80 million, and the FCC had four takers. So far, three companies are in the sky and on the air: Sirius Satellite Radio, XM Satellite Radio, and WorldSpace. WorldSpace operates in Asia, Africa, and Europe, while XM and Sirius compete for the North American market.

Where "terrestrial" radio stations (i.e.; the AM and FM stations we're *not* discussing in this chapter) broadcast analog signals on their carriers, the satellite broadcasters use a digital signal, similar to the encoding on a CD. (Recently, to combat the competition from the satellite providers, many terrestrial stations started piggybacking a digital "high-definition" version of their programming. As of this writing, the jury still has not come in on whether the new format will capture consumers' cash.)

Each of the satellite systems has its own proprietary chip to decode the digital signal coming down from its orbiting transmitter. XM and WorldSpace each have two satellites in geostationary orbit over the equator. WorldSpace's satellites are called AfriStar and AsiaStar, while XM's are named Rock and Roll. As long as you have a view of the southern sky (and you have a receiver with the proper chipset) you can generally get the digital signal from these two stations.

This works well for WorldSpace, which is aimed mostly at stationary objects such as houses, offices, and the like. The service makes information, education, and entertainment available to places that, heretofore, had no available radio programming—hard to imagine for Westerners, but many places in Africa and Asia don't have local broadcasters. WorldSpace sees itself as a means of empowerment, bringing the communications age where it never went before.

Sirius took a slightly different tactic, launching three satellites in higher, elliptical orbits. This cuts down on—but does not eliminate—one of XM's prime problems. XM and Sirius design hardware to move with the listener. They make home/office sets, sets for the car, and even sets that can be carried around like a personal stereo. However, if the XM listeners lose sight of the southern sky, they potentially lose their signal. So XM and—to the lesser extent that it's necessary—Sirius both use strategically placed antennae called repeaters to get the signal where the satellite won't reach. Like conventional radio, the satellite sets tend to be useless in tunnels and other underground places like garages where the signal can't penetrate.

As of this writing, XM offers 150 channels; Sirius offers 130. In an area where all the terrestrial frequencies were taken, a non-satellite radio listener would theoretically have about the same number of choices (based on 100 active frequencies on each spectrum, but some out of reach of certain parts of every listening area). But, as we've seen, many terrestrial stations would overlap and compete, and be programmed to the lowest common denominator.

Both XM and Sirius have the advantage of diversity, albeit narrowcast diversity. They have stations that broadcast just 1970s rock or '70s pop; stations that broadcast classic country, contemporary country, or bluegrass; stations for Afropop, reggae, and Asian music. XM has every Major League Baseball game while Sirius broadcasts the NFL, NHL, and NBA. All of XM and most of Sirius's stations are commercial free. Both charge (as of this writing) about $13 a month for the service. Only 6.2 million people actually subscribe to the satellite services, accounting for an approximately 4 percent penetration of U.S. households—spit in the ocean compared to terrestrial radio. XM also offers some of its service to subscribers of satellite television broadcasters DirecTV, for people who want to listen to radio on their televisions.

Both feature the human element of announcers. When they have a guest programmer, like Sirius's Underground Garage channel, "produced by Little Steven," the producer creates his or her own Selector database of songs. The stations sound quite a bit like terrestrial stations, complete with bumpers—the little spots between songs that identify the station and offer some hint as to what it plays. The satellite-casts bring local-hero jocks like Mark Coppola to a national audience, and give rinsed-out (as opposed to washed-out) personalities like original MTV VJ Mark Goodman a home. Some of the personalities on satellite are downright surprising—Bob Dylan did a show. Rolling Stones producer Andrew Loog Oldham and rocker Joan Jett have regular slots.

Like cable television, satellite radio is only censored by the end user, the listener, by the time-honored method of changing the station. This appeals to personalities like shock jocks Opie and Anthony (XM) and Howard Stern (Sirius). Stern made the jump to satellite radio after getting the boot from CBS/Infinity Radio's broadcast stations; Sirius offered him a reported half a billion dollar contract. The service was counting on at least a million of Stern's 12 million listeners to make the jump with him, the number of new subscribers it claimed it would need to cover Stern's payday. In the end it got 2.7 million. Some cite Stern's presence on Sirius as the element that could turn the satellite service into a viable brand.

The wealth of choices is satellite radio's key selling point, though the digital clarity doesn't hurt either. However, with the rise in cellular Web access and widespread Wi-Fi, within a few years satellite radio could have a run for its money from more than just the terrestrial stations. While the satellite stations offer perhaps 300 programming choices, mobile access to Internet radio offers tens of thousands, with about 100 new ones going live every month.

Web or Internet radio is nothing new. In 1999, I got a message from my friend Sam Pocker saying that he'd just tried out the audio-streaming software SHOUTcast and "I'm still shaking." Sam has been a webcaster ever since; he currently creates podcasts (more on that anon) for bargain hunters.

For hobbyists and even college stations, webcasting avoids the most expensive and hardest-to-maintain aspects of broadcasting: the actual license, purchase, and upkeep of the broadcasting equipment that sends the signal through the air. A professional, commercial radio transmitter can cost in excess of $10,000 (if you can find a frequency for it), and getting a license is a difficult, and in some areas impossible, process in itself. Beyond that, transmitters tend to be temperamental technology. Web radio obviates all that overhead.

Arbitron reported that 37 million Americans listened to radio on the Web in June 2005 (six times the number of satellite radio subscribers), up from 11 million four years previous. "The growth potential is huge," said John Potter of the Digital Media Association, "but there are still significant challenges. The record industry is doing their best to keep Internet radio in a box."

By law, webcasters have to follow far more rules than either terrestrial or satellite broadcasters owing to the record industry's ongoing fear of the online space as a place for their product to get pirated. These rules came to the table as part of the Digital Millennium Copyright Act of 1998. For example, Internet radio stations cannot play more than four songs by any one artist over the course of three hours. They are prohibited from mentioning the idea of recording their content.

A Web radio station can find itself with requests from Baltimore, Bangkok, Boston, and Baghdad. Location becomes irrelevant, although some stations like to keep things local. One Connecticut station will let anyone with Web access listen, but only people with in-state telephone exchanges can actually register for membership. And what does the membership get you? The ability to make requests and use the interactive elements of the station, like weather, traffic, concerts, and the like, all geared to a local audience.

Infinity Radio's vice president of streaming media, Matt Timothy, noted that Internet radio needs to use the Web's interactivity. "To win," he said, "we have to give as much control to the user as possible."

Webcasting allows KEXP, a 4,700-watt FM station in Seattle funded by former Microsoft honcho Paul Allen's Experience Music Project, to reach well beyond the 10 or 15 miles its transmitter would allow. A throwback to the days when DJs roamed the earth, before the takeover of Selector, the art of the segue continues to be practiced at KEXP. "It's all about creating context for the music," said Kevin Cole, one of the DJs. "Take Clap Your

Hands Say Yeah—if you can mix that into some early Talking Heads, you can see, 'Oh, yeah, that's what's going on here.' "

One of the services KEXP provides to its listeners in Cyberia is hour-long podcasts—broadcasts recorded and saved as MP3 files to be downloaded to computers and portable listening devices, predominantly the iPod (more on the iPod later). A growing segment of webcasters have opted for this method. Podcasts range from shows like Sam's to National Public Radio broadcasts; podcasters range from amateur DJs to the pros at KEXP.

According to Potter, most webcasters continue to operate at a loss, however. Unlike KEXP, they don't have Paul Allen to subsidize them (though KEXP expects to be completely donor-sponsored by the end of 2006).

Commercial radio is now looking at the phenomenon. In a study, Bridge Media polled 4,000 radio listeners in six markets who also listened to podcasts from their favorite station. According to Bridge president Dave Van Dyke:

> It's apparent that a regular schedule of podcast listening is a key element in order for a radio station to receive the benefits of increased listening.

The study revealed that people listening to two or more podcasts a month increased the frequency of regular listening.

On the other hand, like webcasters, as of this writing very few podcasters make a profit.

Another technological innovation at KEXP is a low-bandwidth stream for Web-enabled cell phones and pocket computers. Some KEXP personalities have gotten calls and e-mails from people streaming their Internet signal from their phones to their car stereos. This points to the next step in webcasting—widespread availability of Internet radio. And as I write this, the first steps toward remote-access Web radio have already started. The entire cities of Philadelphia and San Francisco, and entire counties in Michigan (Muskegon) and Arizona (Cruz) plan on becoming digital hotspots. The first generations of cell phones and receivers utilizing Wi-Fi will have hit the street by the time this book does. "Once Internet radio's available everywhere and you'll have 'Internet Walkmen,' it will be a watershed moment," said Bryan Miller from WOXY, a former terrestrial radio station that made the switch to the Internet. At least, that's his commercial hope.

Certain hardware manufacturers have the same vision. Motorola announced a technology initiative called iRadio that would do essentially what the KEXP fans did: play Internet radio over a car radio.

Ford and Microsoft announced a pickup truck with similar technology built into it. While the main reason is to give contractors who work out of their trucks more than their offices the ability to use a computer and the Internet while at work sites, both companies stress the broadcasting implications. "The Ford mobile office system," they claim, "is also an entertainment unit to play MP3 files or listen to Internet radio over the vehicle's stereo system."

So before long, a person might be able to program several hundred URLs for favorite webcasts into a device he or she plugs into the dashboard or steering wheel, giving access to the sites at the touch of a dial or button (or voice command). In the mood for zouk? A URL such as www.radioantilles.com might have nonstop zouk online. Gotta hear some Mozart? Someone might set up the domain www.stolzvonwien.com to fill that Mozart jones. The hardware could even Web crawl to find a particular piece you want to hear—call it out to the voice recognition element in the car and the Google Songsearch software built into the car will find it and put it onto the car stereo, in nanoseconds. None of this technology exists now, but don't bet against it.

The rise of Web radio could have one of two ramifications for the record business. On the one hand, it could totally obviate it— the artists get their music directly to the Web stations and get royalties every time the song gets played on line. Or it could offer a new opportunity for record companies to profit. As radio spreads out and gets far wider but thinner audiences, more of the artists making music will get a chance for exposure, the $S = R + P$ equation on both steroids and a diet—longer, stronger, and way, way leaner, the long tail comes to radio.

The sheer abundance of Web stations and the ease in creating them might turn into a goldmine for aggregators, who put the station into an easier-to-use format than just millions and millions of choices. Companies like Live365 have actually done this for years, attracting advertisers and sharing the wealth.

That wealth is a key issue here. Terrestrial radio and satellite radio have a lot of heavy backers. For terrestrial radio, there's nearly a century of history, and public companies that own hundreds of (or in the case of Clear Channel, over a thousand) stations. Billions have already been spent to launch the hard goods of satellite radio—not to mention the people required to program, staff, maintain, and actually DJ. By contrast, pretty nearly anyone can put together an Internet radio station. And live Internet radio on the verge of broad penetration is just the kind of thing that scares the debentures off the companies with big money invested in high-overhead technology.

Part III | **Retailing Records**

18

Rock and the Hard Place
Records Become a Commodity and Face Real Estate Prices and Profit Margins

ONE OF THE biggest problems the record business faces, besides letting people know that their product exists at all, is actually getting that product to the people who might want to buy it. The quandaries facing record retailers get more difficult daily. As with so many of the problems within the music business, "doing things the way we always did it" creates far more static than it clears up. Change never comes easily, but failure to change can cause disaster. While retail uses a more recent business model than, say, the record companies, the model has remained largely the same for over half a century.

In the early part of the 1950s, the main buyers for sound recordings weren't stores. Record salesmen made the bulk of their money servicing the owners of jukeboxes. There were over 300,000 of them, each held 50–100 singles, and the machines went through the popular discs pretty quickly.

In those days, before big stores carried large inventories of music, people would buy their records at variety stores, musical instrument stores, appliance stores, and the like. The records would sit in racks—at the appliance store, they'd put them next to the phonographs. This gave the salesmen who serviced these stores their appellation—"rack jobbers."

Sam Gutowitz didn't even get serviced by a rack jobber. In the years prior to World War II, he ran a novelty and magic shop in downtown Manhattan's financial district. In the 1930s, as radio began its ascendancy as the entertainment medium of choice and the Depression had the world in a choke hold, the record business took a dive just like the bankers in the area surrounding Gutowitz's store—falling from a high of $105.6 million gross sales in 1921 to $5.5 million in 1933. So when a customer walked into the store and asked whether Gutowitz had any records, Gutowitz was surprised. "I thought [records] had gone out with the dodo birds," he would later recall.

He remembered actually stepping on a glass-and-lacquer 78 in the basement of his Washington Heights apartment building, so he told the guy to come back in a couple of days. He negotiated a deal with the building superintendent—the pile of records for either a can of beer or three cigars (the story would change with the telling)—cleaned them up, and resold the stack for $25. Like so many before him, Gutowitz realized the joys of music. "I said to myself, this is a beautiful business. What am I doing wasting time with toys and novelties?"

Seeing that records were a hot commodity, he got a good deal on some singles that had previously done time in jukeboxes, so he started stocking and selling them. These recordings did so well that he moved his shop to Midtown, settled on 49th Street, and opened a store using a nickname he'd acquired as a kid, Sam Goody.

Goody's name now hangs over the front doors of hundreds of record stores around the world. His adventures in record retailing make a good study, as he led the way in discount record retailing and came to epitomize the business. He lived the ups and downs of record retail and the music business in general, as he represented the business's ultimate goal—selling records.

Goody began selling records using merchandising techniques common to the novelty market but heretofore unheard of in record retailing. In the late 1940s, he saw the future in vinyl LPs. One of the staunchest advocates of the LP in retail, he once gave away 40,000 turntables that operated at the new microgroove speeds—33⅓ and 45 rpm—one to anyone who bought $25 worth of LPs. He lost money in the short run, but recognized it meant he had 40,000 new customers.

For his next major merchandizing maneuver he marked all his new LPs down 30 percent off retail list price. He could sell a 10-inch long-playing disk that listed for $3.98 at $2.80. Since he bought disks for $1.85, he still made nearly a dollar on everything that he sold. By keeping his overhead to 15 percent, and carrying 300,000 LPs, Sam Goody made his record store into a sensation, hosting 4,000 customers a day. By 1955, Goody's store accounted for 7 percent of all U.S. LP sales, grossing close to four million dollars that year.

Around this same time, the record companies saw a new source of revenue. Why rely on the Sam Goodys of the world when you could take your wares directly to the customer? Columbia started the Columbia Record Club in summer 1955, offering retailers 20 percent of the revenue from every member it signed up (a deal it still makes with the magazines that run its ads and the college students that post its application cards around campus). In a survey by *The Billboard* (as it was known at the time), a majority of retailers naturally opposed this idea. Most reported that it hadn't affected their sales, though over 30 percent said that it had cut into their bottom lines.

One of the methods the clubs used to recruit suckers—I mean, members—was to give away records as a premium, another practice that continues unabated. Thus, new artists and even more venerable artists without star-powered negotiating leverage (or a competent lawyer) found language similar to this in their contracts:

> No royalty shall be payable with respect to records given to members of record clubs as bonus or free records as a result of joining clubs and/or purchasing a required number of records.

The record business knew the clubs wouldn't replace the record stores, though. On the cover of the same issue of *The*

Billboard as the record-club story, the magazine predicted another record-breaking year of record sales. It partially attributed this rise to more advertising, especially display advertising. Another thing that might have accounted for the rise was the perception of value. As *New York Times* music specialist Robert Shelton pointed out, in the change from the 78 rpm glass-and-lacquer disk to microgroove vinylite, "A minute of music on a record today [1958] costs less than one-third of what it did before 1948, certainly a key factor in giving record and phonograph sales their great impetus in a period when prices for nearly every other product in the economy rose."

Indeed, record sales did rise to new highs, from $182.7 million in 1954 to $235.2 in 1955, and in two more years they had risen to $360 million. Shelton predicted:

> The happy tunes that have been playing on the nation's cash registers during the age of vinylite are by no means ended. The industry is at the brink of a new era, the age of stereophonic sound, and observers feel that the addition of a new dimension in music reproduction on disks and tape will add another dimension to the cash sales of a flourishing industry.

This kind of prediction might have led to some irrational exuberance. By 1959, Goody had expanded aggressively, so aggressively that that he was forced into Chapter 11 bankruptcy. Partially, it was a disaster of his own design. Discount retailing had caught on across the board, so Goody was no longer the only game in town for marked-down music. The retail record business had rapidly turned into what then–RIAA head Henry Brief described as "a low margin, high turnover business. . . . Where once a typical consumer was able to buy, say, one album for $4 or $5, now he can often afford two albums with a total outlay of $5 or $6. . . . Such discount price records make natural traffic builders or loss leaders for stores."

So they didn't necessarily have to go to Goody.

A study commissioned by John Wiley of Columbia Records said that the business had grown 250 percent in the decade between 1955 and 1965. It predicted the record business would double in size again within the next decade. "The end of the upward trend is not yet in sight," added Wiley. "Our future has never held more promise."

Even at that rate, it took seven years for Sam Goody to clean up his debts, but two years after he pulled his company out of bankruptcy, he floated stock over the counter. By 1969, at the age of 62, he was rebuilding an empire. He had eight stores and a new, computerized warehouse in Queens to get product to them. The company turned over a third of a million dollars in profit based on sales of $14.3 million, and things continued to look up. He had expanded into cassettes, both blank and prerecorded, an item he saw as having high sales-per-square-foot potential—a concept that would become increasingly important. He also franchised his name. He even looked into videotape rental, though the VCR would not arrive home for another five years.

By 1977, the Sam Goody chain had 28 stores and grossed about $60 million a year. In his 70s, Goody decided it had been a good run, but it was time to go. Unfortunately, he couldn't leave the company to his children. "They loved each other," he said, "and they still do, but they competed with each other on everything and soon even the help was taking sides. I could only see them breaking it all apart, so I sold the company."

The buyer was, unlikely as it sounds, the American Can Company, which had bought record distributor and retailer Pickwick International a year or so earlier. American Can merged the two music companies. "I agreed to this transaction," Goody said at the time, "so that the company would perpetuate itself and grow. I have my two sons with me, Howard, 35, and Barry, 33, and a lot of young eager beavers who have put a lot of effort into building this business with me." At the time of the sale, over 1,000 people worked for the chain.

In the nearly 40 years he ruled the roost in retail records, Sam Goody had revolutionized the way America bought sound recordings. Now he would see what that revolution had wrought.

Like Sam Goody, Jack Eugster once sold tchotchkes, albeit as the head of a department store chain. Also like Goody, Russ Solomon started selling records as an ancillary to another business, in this case his father's drugstore at the base of Sacramento's venerable Tower Theater. Both, in their own ways, were Goody's heirs.

Solomon took his success in the "record department" of his dad's store and moved it to its own space in 1960. By 1968, he was opening the sort of store contemporary record buyers have come to associate with Tower Records: a freestanding (as opposed to mall) store. Located in San Francisco, it capitalized on the music of the Summer of Love, and became a favorite place for the denizens of the Haight to hang out. The store became a huge success, and Solomon started to expand. At the height of Tower Records' success as a chain, Solomon owned (the company remained private until very recently, and even now does not offer stock) and oversaw almost 180 stores on four continents, with over $1 billion dollars in gross annual sales.

Part of this success had to do with staying ahead of the curve of what customers want—but only slightly. Said Solomon:

> Our company policy is to support new technologies, or, for that matter, to support anything the record companies come out with. It's a natural thing for us to go along with the program, whatever it is. We don't have an awful lot of risk, either, if you analyze it. If it doesn't sell, we send it back.

As for Jack Eugster, when he took over the Musicland record chain in 1980, it was part of the American Can (Primerica by that time) retail music division that included Sam Goody. He led a leveraged buyout of the chain eight years later and by 1993 controlled 8 percent of U.S. music business sales, harking back to Goody's similar achievement some 38 years earlier. However,

Eugster played a considerably higher-stakes game. In 1955, Goody accounted for 7 percent of the market with about four million dollars in sales. In 1992, Eugster accounted for 8 percent with sales of about one billion dollars.

Fast forward a decade, and both Musicland and Tower are in deep trouble, along with almost all record retail. Not only have sales plummeted, but so have margins and foot traffic. The RIAA reported that between 1989 and 2004, the people who actually bought records did it . . . differently. Record-store sales had accounted for 71.7 percent of total record sales; that number fell to 32.5 percent. Those that went to "other stores" rose from 15.6 percent to 53.8 percent. (This was even before online stores like CDNow and Amazon dug out a significant niche; online sales as of 2004 still only accounted for 5.9 percent of total business.) The only thing that had not gone down at specialty retail record stores was the overhead.

Anyone who has been in a modern record store will tell you it takes up a lot of prime retail space. A freestanding store—the kind Solomon specialized in—might use 10,000–20,000 square feet or more. Even mall stores have had to grow to carry enough music to compete, especially if the mall has a discount department store that might use music as a loss leader.

At a time when this retail space can average $40 per square foot in a mall, can cost upward of $200 per square foot along a main shopping drag in New York to as low as $35 per square foot in the city's Garment District (not the fanciest neighborhood); and range between $180 per square foot on the Strip in Las Vegas to an average of about $20 off the Strip; some thought has to be given to the profit margin of a CD, especially in the context of a store that sells little else.

Not that the contemporary record store concentrates solely on CDs. You might find DVDs, cases, blank CDs, players, books, magazines, and even memorabilia in many of these stores. They carry what the traffic demands. And it all takes up space they pay for by the square foot.

Now, let's do a little math. At even the lower end of the rental spectrum, say $50 a square foot in New York, a 10,000-square-foot store costs half a million dollars a month in rental overhead alone.

Which brings us to margin. In 2003 Universal Music Group's Jump Start program started a trend toward a lower CD wholesale price, but even so, a CD generally costs a retailer somewhere between $11 and $13 for a new-hit, major-artist release, and around $10 for "midline" CDs. The Jump Start program's efforts proved to be too little, too late. When CDs first came out, they cost about 50 percent more than the vinyl albums they would ultimately replace. The record companies assured consumers that as the manufacturing prices came down, so would the prices of CDs. Only they never did. For years, the cognoscenti knew that it only cost about a buck to manufacture and package a CD, but the price of CDs continued to rise.

Since the retail competition is fierce, most stores cannot charge more than $15.98 for a new hit, or $12.98 for a midline CD. This gives the store a $2–$3 margin per CD, much less a percentage than Goody made when he devised the method of marketing music at retail. Divide an average margin of $2.50 into the $500,000 rent and the merchant has to sell 200,000 CDs a month just to pay the rent. This doesn't include salaries, interest, or inventory, or even keeping the lights on. Clearly, this business model becomes more difficult to sustain every year.

Mike Dreese, CEO of New England specialty record chain Newbury Comics, offered more specific details:

On Fiona Apple, we are getting an 11 percent profit margin. On Nickelback, 10 points; Sevendust, 3.9 percent margin; Kanye West, 8 percent margin; and on Green Day, 9 percent margin. On the new Depeche Mode, we are sowing costs of $11.51 with a 6 percent margin. . . . The majors' titles are coming out at crazy costs. You almost wonder what planet these guys are on.

Rather than making things easier, Universal's Jump Start program made things even more difficult. To get a discount on CD prices, retailers not only had to dedicate 25 percent of their shelf space to UMG product (not a hardship, as UMG accounted for close to 30 percent of sales), but also had to provide a third of the stores' prime marketing space to UMG for free. This space included the endcaps, hit walls, and listening stations, all things that record retail used to beef up its bottom line; a month worth of space on an endcap could cost a record distributor thousands of dollars, which added to a store's net and helped keep the lights on. And even if a retailer did not join the Jump Start program and get the discount, Universal wouldn't buy that space again. Further, UMG would no longer provide co-op advertising dollars. Just like in radio, these "split" ads helped the retailer get traffic into the store. The record company paid for space on the store's or chain's advertising, each company promoting its hot program records for the month or week.

With the largest record company in the world stopping the practice, retail was well and truly screwed. So while the Jump Start program looked good for retailers on paper at first blush, it mostly benefited Universal. It no longer paid for space that used to cost it. If retailers chose to get the discount, Universal got the space for providing the discount. If they didn't give Universal the space, they didn't get the fee anyway. It might have left them with more space for the other three companies, assuming the other three majors saw fit to pick up the slack. It was a lot of slack, however, in a time of diminished returns.

The proof of the problem's seriousness lies in the obvious financial trouble that retail is facing. The phrase *Fortune Magazine* correspondent Andy Serwer used to describe the situation at Tower is "hemorrhaging money. . . . Solomon and his family are surrendering 85 percent of the company's equity to the bondholders. And the company is for sale. And it sure beats the heck out of me how this company will make a go of it long term."

Add to this the devastating effect of the terrorist attacks on New York and Washington, D.C., on September 11, 2001. Sales growth had already started to slip, falling from a 9.3 percent increase the previous year to a 3.3 percent decrease. The attacks shut down virtually everything in America for a week. The emotional vulnerability, shock, and sadness the nation felt was coupled with the physical problems of all air traffic being grounded so checks could not be transported, the stock markets closing (and the commodities exchange effectively getting wiped out in the collapse of the World Trade Center), and certain financial records being lost. The record business had ceased to continue sales gains the previous year, slipping from a 1999 peak of $14.6 billion to $14.3 billion. In 2001, the slide continued to $13.7 billion.

Thus, when Best Buy purchased Musicland in 2001 for $685 million, it thought it had bought at the bottom of the trough. It was wrong. In 2003, it basically gave the chain to a Florida investment firm in exchange for assuming the company's debt. Another chain, Wherehouse Entertainment, filed for bankruptcy twice over the course of nine years. Still other chains fight the good fight, closing stores to try and shore up their profits. By 2003, total recorded music sales slid to $11.9 billion, lower than 10 years earlier.

This slump doesn't only affect the chains. The independent record store has nearly fallen by the wayside. Many of the owners of the stores that remain open think about shutting down on a daily basis. "This industry is in trouble," said the owner of a 14-year-old Illinois shop. "I'm scared. I love what I do."

Some stores and chains have survived, through the writing of this book at least, by filling a niche market. A small California chain, Amoeba Records, beat the larger chains at their own game by actually paying a staff for their musical knowledge. Chicago's Dusty Groove put much of its inventory online, leading some to describe it as "one of the most exciting record stores in the country." Gary's Record Paradise in Escondido, California, caters to an audience that wants rarities, oddities, and specialties. "Wherehouse and Sam Goody have a fast-food mentality," Gary's owner Eustaquio Kirby said. "They are not really record stores."

Science of Shopping author Paco Underhill agreed. "The industry views music as a consumable product: You consume music in the same way that you'd drink a Pepsi. Amoeba thinks of music as a tradable commodity, a durable good that has long-term value."

What this means is that these stores carry used records and CDs. With a 70 percent margin on a used CD, they can moderate the margin needed on their new albums.

But even these stores may feel the pinch as the rental rates for retail (and all other) properties spike. By fall 2005 in New York, the rents drove even revered specialty stores out of business, noted the ARChive of Contemporary Music's Bob George:

> CBGB's was not the only East Village institution to disappear at the end of August, as venerable soundtrack and theatrical shop Footlight Records closed down the bricks part of their operation. While the store is now dark, this vast historic collection documenting the lively arts will be largely kept intact through a generous donation of over 25,000 recordings to New York's ARChive of Contemporary Music. For nearly 30 years Footlight has been one of America's most important sources of out-of-print and hard-to-find LPs and CDs. As the name implies, theater and film materials were their primary focus, but the store also stocked one of the largest inventories of recordings by cabaret singers, big bands, crooners, and pop vocalists from the '20s to the present time. Fans, collectors, and the music industry itself often combed the bins for just the right satisfying sound. Ron Saja, Footlight's owner since 1993, tells of the time film director Nora Ephron came by to search for music to enliven the soundtrack to *Sleepless in Seattle*. However, as early as 1991 sales were inching toward 50 percent online at Footlight, heralding the eventual demise of their high-rent physical space.

The same issues caused huge international record seller HMV to pull out of the U.S. market after five years. "In our case it was about the fact we had very poor real estate deals," said the chain's CEO Alan Giles, "where the majority of the stores we had were either poorly located or over-rented and that always gave us a mountain to climb."

Had the music business thought ahead far enough, it might have found in MP3s (or some other digital compression format) the answer to many of its most expensive problems—but, then, it has those infamous control issues. "Prerecorded media will disappear," Todd Rundgren postulated early in the 1990s, not accounting for the record industry's stubborn, backward reaction to the digital retail space.

> You will never go out to buy a prerecorded CD. All you will do is buy blank media and say, "Okay, I want this particular record, or I want these songs off of this record, or I want to buy six pounds of Michael Jackson." They'll just download it to you and it will appear on something like a MiniDisc, and you can listen to it at home, or you can pop it into your portable player or listen to it in your car. It's just the delivery medium will be different. It will be much more efficient, I think. They won't have to send the record to the pressing plant and press and send it to the record store. All the packaging that you just throw away anyway will just disappear.

With the digital transfer of music files, the medium becomes whatever bottle the end user chooses to keep the lightning in. "The Web eliminates two-thirds of the cost factors," the Smithsonian Institute's Richard Kurin pointed out. "You don't have to produce a hard product and you don't have to pay a middleman. The prospect is for greater dissemination."

Of course, the digital space still accounts for less than 10 percent of the record industry's sinking sales. We'll see, however, as stores close down, people have fewer and fewer choices about where they can actually buy records, and those stores offer fewer and fewer choices as to the kinds of records customers can buy. It turns into a vicious cycle—the fewer places to buy records, the fewer potential sales.

Then there are the space considerations. Retail density ranges from 5.5 CDs per square foot of floor space at a Tower location to 20 per square foot at a smaller independent store. That means the 10,000-square-foot store (with the half-a-million-dollar rent) we looked at earlier would carry between 55,000 and 200,000 titles if it stocked nothing but CDs. Of course, most record stores carry far more than just CDs, if only for the margin. And as Doug Mashkas, owner of a store at the high end of the density spectrum (carrying 30,000 CDs and 10,000 DVDs in a 1,500-square-foot space) admitted, the effect is "not very pretty."

Figure most stores stock less than 10 CDs per square foot, and carry an inventory of between 10,000 and 100,000 CDs, depending on floor space and inclination. Even if they carried only one copy of each title (not a likely scenario) and crammed the racks at the high end of this inventory, they could still only fit one-third of all available titles.

Certainly the department stores sell only the hits. And as the dedicated record stores give up more space to higher-margin items, they can devote less space to marginal music and catalog items. The fewer stores selling deep catalog, the less deep catalog gets sold. And if you wondered why 0.45 percent of the records sold accounted for over 50 percent of the sales, just try and find some of the other 99.55 percent of the available titles with any regularity at most record stores.

19

Censorship
Wal-Mart Tippers the Scales

SPECIALTY RECORD STORES—even the huge chains such as Tower, Trans World, or Musicland—pale in penetration when compared to Wal-Mart. With more than 2,300 locations around the country, the huge discount department store often represents the only choice people have to buy records within an hour of where they live, particularly in rural areas. Since the mid-1990s, Wal-Mart has sold more pop music than any other retailer in America, accounting for around 52 million of the 615 million compact discs sold per year on average. Not bad for a store that stocks records as a part of a mix that runs from pillowcases to shotguns.

Not only does Wal-Mart sell the most records of any retailer in America, but often it sells them cheapest, too, which makes sense: get a customer into the record department (usually in the back of the store) and maybe he or she will buy a toaster, a tractor, a television, or some towels as well. For a department store, margin cuts both ways—it's willing to gamble on a slight loss on a product to lure customers in to buy higher-margin items. Records are the classic loss leader.

But Brian K. Smith of Value Music Concepts explained the downside:

> For the sake of a possible big first-week ranking, some front-page flier exposure, and power-aisle placement (next to the greeting cards or candle rack), the labels have sold their souls to a sector that has not developed an act, will not develop an act, and has no desire to develop an act. All the [high-volume depart-

ment stores] care about is loss-leading and add-on transactions, and they do not care where the add-ons come from. In the process, the labels have allowed their product to be devalued in the eyes of the consumer thereby creating a situation where the traditional players look like thieves for expecting the same margin on sales as the [department stores] get—only we have to do it without the benefit of a lawn-and-garden department.

In addition to marketing its store brand as a place for bargains, Wal-Mart takes great pains to promote and maintain an image as a "family" store. In certain areas, the local Wal-Mart serves as a social center. Even where I live, in an exurb-cum-suburb of New York City, one of the larger religious communities in the area uses the local Wal-Mart as a place to get together, schmooze, and, of course, shop. It even has elements of a pick-up bar—I've seen dates made by people who meet there.

"Our customers understand our music and video merchandising decisions are based on a common-sense attempt to provide the type of merchandise they might want to purchase," a Wal-Mart spokesperson explained.

And what type of merchandise might they want to purchase? The answer is actually more what they *don't* want to purchase, or perhaps what Wal-Mart doesn't want to sell—entertainment with curse words, nudity, or violence—in short, no CD conveniently decorated with a "Parental Advisory Warning" sticker, otherwise known as "Tippa Stickas."

Which brings us to a point where we need to back up. The sticker itself is a bit of "self-policing" by the record business; it resulted from an accident that started an avalanche. The controversy over the lyrics in popular music and what's appropriate family entertainment made for some of the most entertaining moments in congressional history, but bloomed into one of the record business's worst cases of agita and angst.

The simple beginnings involved an Ohio family named the Alleys, who liked the song "1999" from the Prince album of the same name. So one day in 1984 (how appropriately Orwellian),

Mrs. Alley went to the store and bought a copy. So far, the record business approves and everybody's happy.

While playing the album that evening, however, Mr. and Mrs. Alley stumbled on "Let's Pretend We're Married." They found the lyrics so explicit that they turned down the volume lest their just-prepubescent daughter or seven-year-old son catch them.

It would have stopped right there, with Prince getting relegated to the hours after the kids went to bed, except that the Alleys were members of the Delshire Elementary School PTA. They proposed that some sort of warning be put on records to make parents aware of profanity, sex, violence, or vulgarity. In June of that year the PTA's National Convention passed a resolution to that effect.

The mayor of San Antonio, Texas, saw this as an opportunity and made a lot of noise about a similar ratings system for concerts. All this was disturbingly reminiscent of the sort of film footage you can see from the 1950s, wherein Klansmen and White Citizen's Council members talk about the evil influence of rock, and claim it as a conspiracy of communists, African Americans (not exactly in those words), and Jews. But the PTA's resolution was relatively toothless—it really had no enforcement power and stopped short of calling for a boycott of all recordings.

However, before all controversy over Prince's alleged "profanity, sex, violence, or vulgarity" (pick one or two) had a chance to blow over, Mary Elizabeth "Tipper" Gore, wife of then-freshman Tennessee senator Al Gore, overheard her daughter listening, once again, to Prince. This time the sonic culprit was his somewhat less innocuous song "Darling Nikki" (whom the singer finds "masturbating with a magazine"). Mrs. Gore compared notes with Susan Baker, the wife of Treasury Secretary James Baker, and the two of them formed the Parents Music Resource Center. Bolstered by the PTA mandate, this group used their clout in Washington, and convinced the U.S. Senate to convene a hearing on the issue of monitoring the music industry with a ratings system similar to the one used by the film industry.

On one side of the room were the members of the PMRC, several senators, and foes of "porn rock," as the subject of the hearing came to be referred to. On the other side sat one of the most unlikely troikas of performers from the world of popular music: Dee Snider of the theatrical heavy metal band Twisted Sister; mellow, middle-of-the-road pop star John Denver; and virtuoso iconoclast Frank Zappa.

The festivities kicked off with Senator Paula Hawkins playing the videos for Van Halen's "Hot for Teacher" and Twisted Sister's "We're Not Gonna Take It," before giving a symposium on album covers she claimed glorified sex and other "unacceptable behavior" for young people.

Snider countered this by describing himself as a practicing Christian who didn't drink, smoke, or use drugs, and saying that everything he did professionally as the leader of Twisted Sister was consistent with his beliefs. He remarked that the violence in the video of "We're Not Going to Take It," which shows a teenage boy throwing his father against a brick wall, down the stairs, and out a window, "was simply meant to be a cartoon. It was based on my extensive personal collection of Road Runner and Wile E. Coyote cartoons."

The Reverend Jeff Ling, a PMRC advisor, recited lyrics to songs he found objectionable by such "popular" bands as the Mentors (which has not sold more than 5,000 copies of any record it's released to date, even after all the publicity from the hearings), quoting lyrics like "Smell my anal vapors/Your face my toilet paper." This inspired committee member John Danforth to inform Ling that his time was up.

Denver countered by pointing out that the amount, availability, and indeed the market for some of the songs Ling had quoted was a very small part of the pop music universe, small enough that "it's not going to affect our children to a degree that we need to be fearful of."

The star of the day, however, was Frank Zappa, whose life mission always seemed to be hoisting jerks on their own petard anyway. After refreshing the committee's memory with a reading of the First Amendment to the U.S. Constitution (ostensibly for the members of the foreign press), he began:

> The PMRC proposal is an ill-conceived piece of nonsense which fails to deliver any real benefits to children, infringes the civil liberties of people who are not children, and promises to keep the courts busy for years, dealing with interpretational and enforcement problems inherent in the proposal's design. . . . No one has forced Mrs. Baker or Mrs. Gore to bring Prince or Sheena Easton into their homes. . . . A teenager might go into a record store unescorted with $8.98 in his pocket, but very young children do not. If they go into a record store, the $8.98 is in mom or dad's pocket, and they can always say, 'Johnny, buy a book.' . . . The parent can ask or guide the child . . . away from Sheena Easton, Prince, or whoever else you have been complaining about.

Zappa really got to the heart of matters, noting the smoke and mirrors surrounding the Reagan tax reform package that was working its way through Congress, designed to raise the national debt while lining the already well-laden pockets of America's wealthiest. Zappa pointed out that while the PMRC circus was going on, "people in high places work on a tax bill that is so ridiculous, the only way to sneak it through is to keep the public's mind on something else: 'Porn Rock.'"

Indeed, the hearings and his high-profile wife brought Al Gore into the limelight, as well as 1984 presidential aspirant Ernest Hollings. But beyond that, they caused the RIAA to fold like a bad poker hand. The record companies capitulated and adapted the Parental Advisory Sticker.

This brings us back to the aisles of Wal-Mart, where albums dressed in Parental Advisory Stickers are taboo. Since Wal-Mart represents such a large percentage of the records sold, record companies and bands redesigned (or created alternative) covers for albums, released versions of CDs with masked lyrics, changed lyrics, or removed songs altogether.

Artists who will not give in to this sort of self-censorship will not get into the racks at Wal-Mart. Not getting into the racks could cost artists 10 percent of their sales, estimated Al Cafaro, former head of A&M Records.

Beyond the sales, however, this has had a chilling effect on the artists. When Perry Farrell created a papier-mâché sculpture for the cover of Jane's Addiction's *Ritual de lo Habitual* album, he hadn't given Wal-Mart a second thought. Until he had a pre-release meeting with his record company. "They said they thought I should consider a second cover, because we'd probably only sell a thousand copies." The *Ritual de lo Habitual* albums in Wal-Mart had a white cover with the band's name on it, along with the First Amendment.

"If you're an artist," noted retailer Don Rosenberg, "and want to write something about race, religion, politics, or sex, and you know it's not going to be carried by a large percentage of retailers, you're in the position of either singing what's on your mind or selling records."

"You may need to show ID," wrote *Rock and Rap Confidential* editor Dave Marsh, "to buy records that make any meaningful commentary on the world."

Or you might not be able to buy them at all if the only place near your home that sells CDs is Wal-Mart. But then, there's an awful lot of music that you cannot buy at Wal-Mart. Wal-Mart stocks its stores like the retail reflection of radio. Even online, the chain stocks only 80,000 titles, not quite a quarter of the number available. Many artists needed to expurgate a goodly chunk of those albums to get them on the shelves. Some artists don't need to bother, as their company couldn't get the records into Wal-Mart regardless—they're too small, too low-profile, too anything, really. As with most of its merchandise, the music at Wal-Mart tends toward inoffensive, middle-of-the-road blandness. The quirky or controversial need not apply.

20

A Voyage Down the Amazon.com

FORTUNATELY, THERE are alternatives for those who cannot get to a record store besides Wal-Mart but don't want the expurgated version of their music. The age of McLuhan has arrived, we live in a global village, and anywhere in the world you can find an Internet connection, you can access one of the dozens of online record retailers and booksellers.

Indeed, CDNow cofounder Jason Olim saw this need for an alternative as the main reason people would come to his online store. "Breadth of selection," he said of his store that sold a quarter of a million different items, "is the most important thing."

This wasn't always an option. E-mail and usegroups and other Internet (as opposed to Web) functions had been available generally since 1969, when Compu-Serv (as it was called then) went into business; however not many people were even aware of it. Modems certainly were not standard equipment for the few people who had a home computer before the 1980s, and most people who had modems had them crawling along at about 300 baud (in contrast, a modern home DSL line exchanges information at about a thousand times that rate).

The trend toward personal computers becoming truly personal had only slightly improved by 1998, when home computer penetration in the United States was a mere 42.1 percent, and of those a scant 26.2 percent had Internet access. It took until 1993 and the advent of Mosaic (a forerunner of Netscape) to move the Web out of the hands of solely the geekerati and into the realm of technological early adapters. Where previously navigating the Web involved "knowing the code" of Universal Resource Locators (or URLs), with the hypertext features Mosaic's graphical interface added, new information was just a mouse click away.

Within a year, the number of Web servers had risen from 500 to 10,000, and the number of netizens was doubling every few months. It didn't take long for businesses to smell money and start swarming around the Web like sharks at a chumfest. By the end of 1994, you could tour Graceland, book airline tickets, and see clips from Fox television shows online.

And, of course, buy CDs. In August 1994, 26-year-old twins Jason and Matthew Olim opened CDNow for business on the Internet. "CDNow was founded because of a disastrous search for some jazz albums after I first listened to Miles Davis," said Jason Olim. "Unable to get good advice on how to introduce myself to the genre, I decided to build a music store that provided customers not only with discs, but also reviews, related band information, personalized e-mail recommendations, and Real Audio samples. I built CDNow to help people discover music."

By December 1994, companies such as Geffen Records were linking their Web sites to CDNow. In addition to finding information about a record on a company's Web site, visitors could now click a button that said, "I want to buy this now," and open up a window to that record's page on CDNow. By November 1995, 210,000 people were checking out the Olims' site every month, bringing them monthly sales of about 8,000 CDs, monthly revenues of $325,000, and monthly profits of between $20,000 and $40,000.

Seeing that, New England retailer Newbury Comics set up its own "virtual storefront." In another sector of the music business, former GRP Records owner Larry Rosen opened a virtual storefront called Music Boulevard. All this action had people predicting that the Web would become a nexus of commerce, and soon the larger retailers would have to get online just to compete with the upstarts. Music became the most popular item to purchase via the Web. By 1998, CDNow stocked more than half a million different CD titles.

Part of the reason for the popularity of buying music online was that you could actually hear the music on most of the sites. While "fair use" proscriptions required that the clips be no longer than 30 seconds, a Web surfer could listen to pretty much any song on any record CDNow and Music Boulevard sold. Beyond that, both sites (and all the others that followed) offered a vast amount of editorial content, including short artist profiles and reviews. Even at low bandwidth (at the time, most people surfing at home used a 28.8K baud dial-up modem) music streamed with acceptable enough fidelity that a listener knew the song to which he or she was listening. Music didn't take up much bandwidth.

This led Music Boulevard to start an experiment in 1997. It was aware of the collegiates using MP3 to exchange music files. Why not, the company asked, try to actually *sell* music online? It hooked up with a proprietary music compression technology called Liquid Audio and started to sell tracks on its Web site for 99¢. Most of them were either advances of more conventional CDs, or non-CD tracks. It was not an idea whose time had quite come yet, and even Music Boulevard realized it. For one thing, it was still very inconvenient to download a song at that speed. "A three-minute song," Liquid Audio's Scott Burnett said, "with a 28.8 modem, you're looking at somewhere around 12 minutes."

However, with the introduction of secure Web connections that made financial transactions possible without endangering your credit rating, the online marketplace boomed. Amazon.com, already one of the biggest sellers of books on the planet, expanded into music during summer 1998. Its site, like CDNow, was information rich. Said Amazon's David Risher:

> If you don't know the difference between, say, acid jazz, traditional jazz, free jazz, or ambient jazz, we describe each of these, plus we list the essential CDs for each genre, with reviews. It's a way of learning about a genre so you don't wind up with a

couple of ridiculous easy-listening jazz discs that'll embarrass you in front of serious jazz listeners.

The ability to preview records, a hallmark of the days of glass and lacquer, when most record shops had listening booths, became such a popular aspect of the online buying experience that brick-and-mortar retailers started to install listening kiosks in their stores. Some discovered that record companies were willing to pay for them to put certain artists in their listening stations. Others had their entire selection of recordings available for listening by putting on a pair of headphones and waving a CD's barcode under a scanner.

The competition became intense as the online CD stores had at it on the battlefield of commerce. Columbia House bought out CDNow in 1999, making it the online arm of its mail-order operation. Similarly, Bertelsmann wound up buying out Music Boulevard, putting it under the aegis of the RCA record club by the early years of the new millennium.

Despite the fact that a consumer can buy pretty nearly every CD in print and quite a few out-of-print CDs online, not many people seem so inclined. While online sales of physical CDs continued to climb over the course of the last five years, they still account for less than 6 percent of total physical CDs sold. Why? Perhaps simply because of the culture of instant gratification—we want what we want and we want it NOW! Some people do not trust online commerce, feeling a little suspicious about putting credit card information into cyberspace. And perhaps people just don't have enough information to take advantage of all the choices the Internet provides, an ironic situation for the information superhighway.

Beyond this, technology has taken hold in a different way as more and more people gained access to more and more speed on the Internet. At 28.8K or even 56.6K baud, downloading music was a painful process, but as broadband started to penetrate deeper and deeper into U.S. households via DSL lines and cable television company online services, suddenly you could download a song in less time than it would take to listen to it. Many people began to explore the possibility of eliminating (or reducing their intake of) physical product, choosing a new digital container for their digital music.

"Five years out," Scott Burnett predicted of downloading music in 1997, "you may look at this as becoming a mainstream distribution alternative." He didn't know how prescient he was.

Part IV | **Technology**

21

We Recorded This in Only Three Months!

From One Mic to 128 Tracks

I MET FRANK FILIPETTI while he was working as an engineer on Foreigner's *Agent Provocateur* at Electric Lady Studios in Greenwich Village in New York. We got to know each other, not because I had been an engineer, but because I was managing a music and video store about a block from the studio on Sixth Avenue. He would rent four or five videos at a time for his wife, who was ailing, while he tracked the album. He became a regular, and once when I asked him for a progress report (on Foreigner, not his wife), he told me that he wasn't sure. They had been working for nearly a year, twelve hours a day, and he really didn't feel any closer to finishing than he had six months earlier. The process eventually took about a year and a half.

I mentioned this to Todd Rundgren some time later on. "Some people think that unless it takes a certain amount of time, it isn't good," he said.

> That's not necessarily true. I don't know how many times people have done their best take on the first take, if you can ignore the glaring errors. Then, what happens is people try to get rid of the errors; they concentrate more on precision and less and less on performance. It may be more perfectly played, but the feel of it will be less pleasant, less human.
>
> You have to realize that by the time the second month rolls around, you're not looking forward to it any more. You're sup-

posed to be creating pleasurable and meaningful stuff, and what happens is it's the last thing in the world you want to do, to go into the studio and go through that grind again. I don't comprehend it myself, but I guess the ends can justify the means. If anybody does it and they manage to get the sales, that's fine.

"A lot of guys couldn't possibly think that way," Les Paul, inventor of the multi-track technology, noted about the trend to cold, faultless recording. "They let it go until they get it perfect with no feeling."

In the early days, this was not possible. The entire nature of recording was different. Of course the record company wanted the best-sounding, best-recorded music. But up until the very late 1940s, everything had to be recorded direct to disk (remember, the tape recorder really didn't even come to these shores before 1946). If someone made a mistake, the engineer in the control room had to scrap the transcription disk and start over. It behooved the musicians not to make mistakes, to get it right the first time. To achieve that, the producers relied on great musicians, some rehearsal, and good charts. Sessions only lasted three hours back then, with the objective of leaving the studio with three or four serviceable sides.

"The whole point," said Mitch Miller, who spent a lot of time making these recordings as an artist, A&R man, and ultimately president of Columbia Records, "was to be ready when you did the take. Otherwise, it became an exercise in exhaustion. Nobody wanted to be the one who screwed up the record."

Initially, in the days of the wax cylinder, recordings weren't even made electronically; captured acoustic energy dug the grooves into the wax. One of the hardest aspects of recording then was arranging the musicians to achieve the balance that would present the music at its optimum. When electronic recording and transcription were initially introduced, there was still only one microphone, so the musicians all had to arrange themselves toward that one locus. Even the initial tape recorders were monaural and so were the records that were made on them—though tape certainly offered a less expensive, simpler means of recording than cutting a disc on a lathe, especially when it came to multiple takes.

The tape recorder led to a major economic shift in the record business. No longer did each track involve cutting a master. Now, recording merely required some relatively inexpensive tape, and bad takes could either be fast-forwarded over or erased entirely. With the advent of the LP, as Robert Shelton pointed out earlier, suddenly the perceived value of recorded music shot up even as the cost of producing it came down. This spurred some 133 new independent record companies to open for business by 1952.

But as in Miller's day, it was important that the artists came in prepared. Sessions for a recording were still a matter of hours rather than a matter of days or weeks. As legendary English producer and manager Mickie Most recalled of his first recording with the Animals, circa 1964:

> I paid for the production of the records. Of course in those days they weren't that expensive. . . . The Animals' first record was "House of the Rising Sun." They had been playing it onstage. You'd have to be deaf not to hear that as a hit record. It was magic and we made the record. They had been on tour with Chuck Berry, and they took an all-night train. We picked them up at seven fifteen in the morning. Took their equipment and them in a truck around to the recording studio. We started recording at around eight o'clock in the morning and by eight fifteen, "The House of the Rising Sun" was finished. The studio cost eight pounds an hour, which was about twenty dollars in those days. And we recorded the song in fifteen minutes, so you're talking about five dollars. And because they were scheduled to catch a twelve thirty train to Southampton to continue with the tour, I said, "Let's do an album." We finished the album by eleven, and they made their twelve thirty train.

For Les Paul, however, this would not do. Paul's career spans almost the entire history of sound recording, from "gouging a record out like a farmer with an ox" with transcription turntables to building and recording in modern digital studios. Early on, he came up with the idea of "sound on sound," playing one track onto one transcription turntable then plugging his electric guitar (another of his innovations) *and* the first turntable into a second turntable and playing along with the first transcription to add a track. In the process, he broke another bit of prevailing conventional audio engineering wisdom: since he was the only one recording, he decided it was silly to stand three feet from the microphone. He moved it to six inches away and found that the sound he got was a lot cleaner—the technique is now called "close micing." He found that it worked even when he was recording several people. And he discovered that if he put several microphones into a preamplifier, each with its own volume control, he could close mic a bunch of people at the same time. In such ways, he improved the sound of records.

However, some of his biggest innovations came with the advent of tape. Already legendary for his technical prowess, Paul procured one of the first tape recorders to come to the United States. Immediately, he started tinkering with it, putting in an extra record head so he could do sound on sound with just one machine. However, that method was risky. If he made a serious mistake at any time, he had to start the whole thing over. This is illustrated by a scene in the film *The Buddy Holly Story* in which Holly, after crediting Les Paul for the idea, blows a sound-on-sound dub, causing the band to have to go back and do the initial track again.

In answer to this problem of his own making, Paul came up with another idea. Instead of recording with the head onto what had already been recorded, how about stacking several tape heads together and then recording onto different areas of a larger tape? He took this idea to Ampex. What it came up with Paul affectionately nicknamed "the Octopus and the Monster." an eight-track mixer with a set of eight cables (the "octopus") leading to a six-foot-tall set of pre-amplifiers that attached to a reel-to-reel tape machine with a two-inch-tall tape head where the quarter-inch head used to be, that transported an oversized reel of two-inch-thick (as opposed to quarter-inch-thick) tape.

For many years, however, if you wanted to use an eight-track recorder, you had to venture to Paul's home and studio in Mahwah, New Jersey. The Beatles' first studio recordings, nearly a decade after Paul's studio was up and running (albeit not quite debugged), were still done on a three-track recorder at Abbey Road. They would play live in the studio, using Paul's multiple close micing, onto two tracks, and the third track could be used to fill in anything else or to "bounce" the first two tracks—taking the material on those tracks and mixing them to the open track—giving the group two additional tracks on which to record. As a famous engineer and producer once said, "Who needs more than three tracks?"

Four-track recording became de rigueur around 1964. With each subsequent bump in technology, the process of making a record became both potentially more complex and, consequently, more time consuming and costly. In 1971, Beatles producer George Martin said:

> I cannot see the need for any more than sixteen tracks for recording. In building our new studios in the center of London, I had to decide how sophisticated our facilities should be, and while 24 and 32 tracks are possible, I think it makes the whole business of recording far too expensive. Multi-track recording does not give you a better sound; it only postpones the moment of truth and then you have to decide what your mix is going to be. I use 16-track quite a lot because I have all these facilities at [my own] AIR Studios, but I would be quite happy with less. Sorry to repeat myself on [the Beatles' Sgt.] Pepper, but I think it is worthwhile mentioning that this was done on four track. I think the main point about recording studios today is that they should provide modern facilities instantly and with great comfort so that the artist is made to feel at home. After that, it is up to the artist and the producer.

If you have never seen a 16-track recording console, it looks something like the controls for a spaceship, and while each track has essentially the same controls, depending on the board these controls can look intimidating and off-putting. The recording engineer's job is making sense of this world of gear and getting a sound from one place to another place as transparently (to everyone else) as possible.

However, progress didn't stop at 16 tracks. By the early 1990s in the Power Station recording studio, a room geared for sound for the film industry had in excess of 100 tracks on a recording console that was over 16 feet wide. "I started when four track was in," noted the Power Station's owner, Tony Bongiovi, "Through 8-track, 16, 24, and 32. In my generation, I spent a lot of time in the studio. I watched the technical side of our industry evolve." Pictured below is a 48-track console.

The problem for each particular studio is striking the correct balance. How much equipment does the studio need to own? How much can it rent at the client's behest and expense without losing the client? Can a facility be state of the art and charge top-line prices, or can it book enough hours with equipment merely adequate to the client's needs and still turn a profit? How does a studio bring in the clients in the first place? How much needs to be spent on advertising and promotion to keep the room or rooms filled?

When I cut my teeth as an engineer at a small eight-track studio in Manhattan, we faced these challenges on a daily basis. The studio had a good-to-great location in a relatively shabby building on 49th Street, by Eighth Avenue, with a rehearsal studio two floors above us. Sadly, the owner proved not much of a business man (he initially opened the studio in the hope of promoting his own musical career through the record company attached to the studio), and after expanding to 16 tracks, then renting out the space for video production, eventually the sheriff came around, chained the door, and auctioned off the contents for nonpayment to any number of creditors.

In the recording studio business, this is a pretty familiar scenario. "We invested millions of dollars into the business," noted another studio owner as he shut his doors and sold off his assets, "only to turn around and charge peanuts. We did 85 percent booking at full rate, which must be a record, so we really couldn't make it better. We reached the top for us, and the top wasn't good enough."

The trouble at this studio began when the console it installed, one of the first of that particular kind in its city, became commonplace. Then the console company started to lower the price of the console—the cost of being an early adapter. Said the studio owner of people in his position, "You never win. You put in [a console] and you sell your room for $2,000. Then the next guy puts one in and charges $1,800. Then the next guy charges $1,600."

Producer, artist, and studio owner Larry Fast noted:

> During the heyday of big-format studios like the Record Plant, Power Station, Hit Factory, Media Sound, etc.—all now gone out of business—the big console and tape machine manufacturers extended easy credit at the prevailing interest rates (9–13 percent) to buy (actually infinitely lease) their products. They flooded the market with product, but their money was made on the lease-to-buy arrangements where a $750,000 console could easily cost $2 million over the life of the lease. And they'd sell to anyone, forcing rate wars among the studios which the labels leveraged to drive their own recording budgets downward.
>
> An illustrative example from House of Music: In 1976 we had an MCI console on lease purchase, which cost $60,000. We could get a book rate of $200 an hour for studio A. As you can imagine other costs for staff health coverage, property taxes, energy, etc. were pretty low by comparison back then. By 1994, we had a $600,000 Neve "V" series console in that studio and were lucky to get the labels to cough up $80 an hour. Other costs had gone through the roof. The biggest monthly hit was to Neve's parent organization, Siemen's Financial Services, which held the lease purchase paper.

As I write this, a good console could cost a million dollars or more. With the cost of the audio accessories not included on the board, designing and building a room, buying the actual tape and/or digital recording system, and lease or mortgage payments, a good studio in a good location could set the owner back two million dollars before it ever books an hour. And then it has to start booking those hours, no mean trick in itself. "The folks that . . . use A-list studios are among the most conservative in the world," said producer Vic Steffens, a studio owner in his own right. "They generally do not take chances unless they absolutely cannot get another place."

Beyond building a clientele for a studio, you need to maintain your customers. As with any business, the prevailing wisdom says that retaining a customer is about 90 percent easier (and more cost effective) than getting a new one. For many studios, retaining customers meant keeping their prices low so that a similarly equipped space could not woo away hours with severely undercut rates. However, in keeping up with the competition, rising rents in the most desirable areas, rising salary requirements for staff, and all the other costs of doing business, this could squeeze a studio's margin like an old whalebone corset.

Billboard columnist Paul Verna elaborated:

> One studio owner recently told me that he was looking at early-1970s receipts of one of New York's top facilities and was astounded to learn that the top rates were exactly the same then as they are now, a quarter-century later. However, the average investment necessary to construct and equip a top-notch room has increased more than tenfold in that time, according to sources, from approximately $150,000 to at least $1.5 million. . . . A big reason for the increasing costs, besides inflation, has been the need for an ever-growing number of tracks in recording/mixing situations. Whereas recording projects in the '70s and '80s seldom exceeded 24 tracks, today it is not unusual for a major mix to require up to 96 tracks. Accordingly, consoles and tape recorders—which account for the bulk of a studio's investment—are bigger and therefore expensive.

"In some cases," Steffens concurred, "having an SSL or a Neve might make the difference between being booked or not."

Kit Rebhun, studio manager at Glenwood Place Studios in L.A., also agreed on the importance of having a board people know: "Right now, the market wants tried-and-true. People aren't comfortable with new consoles, even if they're absolutely incredible. They don't want to sit down with a learning curve; there just isn't time for it."

However, all those tracks lead to several issues for the musician, the record company, and the music. Where the Animals could get off the train at eight in the morning, load their equipment off the train and onto a lorry, get to the studio, load their equipment off the lorry and into the studio, set up, *record an entire album*, tear down their equipment, load it back onto the lorry, and get on a train again all in about five hours, these days it might take that much time just to mic the drums properly. The recording process has become long and drawn out, and lacks the spontaneity and energy that powered an adrenaline-fueled, well-rehearsed three-hour session. While recordings have become far more *precise*, precision was never really a hallmark of popular music until very recently. As Paul and Rundgren pointed out, the human element gets lost. Then there's the cost. Most's session for the Animal's first album, by his own estimates, including studio time, tape, and hauling equipment, probably cost around $100. At that rate, releasing an album had very, very little in the way of up-front costs, compared to even a couple of weeks at a modern recording studio, which could cost tens of thousands of dollars, even at the discounted rates fueled by the intense competition in the business.

The rise of home studios and inexpensive digital equipment wrought yet another major change in the recording business. At my right elbow on my desk is a digital four-track recording studio on which a competent musician can make a serviceable demo. It cost just under $200. Most new Macintosh computers—even the under-$500 Mac minis—come with Mac's Garage Band, a functional digital recording program. For about 10 times that, an artist can assemble state-of-the-art equipment for a digital audio workstation.

The big dog in digital audio workstations is Pro Tools, a program that works on both Mac and PC. An artist or entrepreneur can purchase Pro Tools at several levels, from a free sample program that the parent company, Digidesign, offers on its Web site, to a program that comes with a recording and mixing console and software emulators for just about any kind of effects equipment any studio could want, all for less than $5,000. A few days in an A-list studio could cost that easily.

"When computer and hard-disk recording really got cheap and better at the same time," lamented Wolf Stephenson, owner of legendary Muscle Shoals studios, "it just knocked the socks off a lot of studios, [Muscle Shoals] included."

To exacerbate the current financial bind the recording studios find themselves in, recording advances have gone way down. Many artists opt to do at least the initial recording for their albums using digital workstation equipment, even if it means hiring an engineer to run it—or even better, hiring an engineer who owns the equipment to do the tracking. "You can buy a 24-track digital machine now for four grand," railed Green Street Recording studio manager David Harrington. "It's insane!"

"Many producers and artists feel that if you get a $30,000 to $50,000 budget to make a record, a home studio is a better investment," noted one of the owners of the now-defunct Unique Studios in New York as they shut their doors. "If the record flops, at least you still have a home studio."

The recording industry economy forced Unique to close up shop after 26 years in business. Still, the studio's owners didn't leave the business entirely. They invented several software tools for the digital audio workstations.

In 2004 and 2005, the fallout began in earnest, as some of the biggest-name recording studios shut their doors. Unique, Power Station, Muscle Shoals Sound Studios, Cello Studios, the Enterprise Studios, and the venerable, renowned Hit Factory all closed down. Beyond the home studios and the equipment wars, the recording studios had a similar fight at the beginning of the process of making a record as the retail stores had at the end of the process of bringing music to market. "In a rising market," said George Petersen, editorial director of the recording industry trade magazine *Mix*, "a studio space's land value can far exceed its business value."

Other, surviving studios added Pro Tools rooms, figuring that even if artists record entire albums at home, if the record company is providing a budget, they might want to get it mixed professionally.

But this still can lead to a loss of the spark that leads to great music. Even more so than at a recording studio, where you know every minute spent eats away a bit of your budget, when you as an artist own the means of production, you can spend as long as you can stand it to get the sound *just right*, even if all real feeling gets lost in the process. Digital effects can even tweak the sound to make it more precise.

Still, if this is how the artist hears the music, and more importantly *feels* the music, then that's the way the music *should* be recorded. For some artists, particularly in electronic, synthesizer-driven music, precision is the hallmark of their sound. It may not work for everyone, but it works for them. As Bongiovi said (albeit, before he sold The Power Station):

> It is the musicians and singers who make the music. Not the engineers. I'm a producer and mixer myself. I've produced a lot of hit records, and I'm smart enough to know that the musicians I get around me are the people who make the records, not how much bass or treble I put on the record or what kind of microphone I use. It's the song you're selling and the musicians who are playing it. That's what this business is all about.

22

The Internet
Friend, Foe, or Just a Tool?

WE'VE ALREADY established that the record industry likes to blame
new technology for its woes. In the 1930s, the culprit that nearly
drove the record business out of business was radio. In the 1970s,
it was the compact cassette. And from the late 1990s through to
the writing of this book, it's been the Internet. It brings to mind
two great quotes from two members of the Who.

One is attributed to the late Who bass player John Entwistle.
During the slump of 1979, he was asked whether he thought that
the reason for record sales falling nearly 30 percent had anything
to do with home taping. He thought about it for a moment and
replied, "No. I think it's because the record business has put out
30 percent less good music."

The other quote is from the bard of rock, Pete Townshend,
the Who's guitarist and primary songwriter. It came from a series
of interviews related to a webcast of his Lifehouse concert from
Sadler's Wells. Townshend is often credited with being one of the
predictors of the Internet (the concept of Lifehouse is a concert
that everyone can experience live through a communications web,
an idea Townshend proposed in 1971), so in 1999 we wondered
if he still thought the Internet was a good idea. He replied:

> The Internet is definitely a friend to the music industry in so
> many ways. The growing new Internet companies need estab-
> lished artists like me to focus their activities on. For new artists,
> it's a direct line to the general mass of the population so they can
> get some early response to their finished work.

"The Web is a fabulous marketing channel with a built in feedback loop that never existed before," recording artist–turned–web entrepreneur Thomas "Dolby" Robertson agreed. "Both world-class acts and wannabes alike can reap the benefits."

Case in point: the meteoric rise of the English band Arctic Monkeys. From Sheffield, England, the band made its London debut not long after New Year's 2005. By fall 2005, it had the #1 single on the English charts. When the record hit the United States, it debuted at #24, based on nothing but the residual British buzz.

What caused that buzz? The band made over a dozen of its songs available for free on the Internet, and the music spread virally. (It helped that the Monkeys make intriguing music, of course.) Using the Internet, it built its following on a grassroots level, reaching directly to fans and potential fans. When it finally released its first physical product, via U.K. independent company Domino Records, it sold 360,000 copies in Britain in the first week, the best first week by any album ever sold there.

Faced with the scenario of losing not only their audience to downloading but their artists as well, some record companies, particularly independent ones, discovered that peer-to-peer downloading actually helped them promote their artists, especially as the radio noose tightened. Richard Egan, a principal at Vagrant Records, figured that his label would have gone out of business without peer-to-peer downloading. Peer to peer, after all, is like that most convincing form of marketing, word of mouth. Taking enough ownership of a band or a song to introduce a friend to it is a big risk and responsibility. That's powerfully persuasive.

"In artist development," said Chris Blackwell, former head of Island Records and owner of Palm Pictures, "file sharing—it's not really hurting you. You want people to discover your artists. You're building for the future."

Todd Rundgren is another very technical fellow, an early adapter of most things technological. In the early 1990s, he presaged the way the music business would shake out a decade later:

There will be a lot of hidden channels for people who aren't traditionally musicians, or haven't signed a record deal with somebody—in other words, they don't have a company bankrolling the record. The cost of equipment is coming down further and further. You get yourself an ADAT and a couple of synthesizers and make your own records and completely do an end run around the record companies. You could go to some kind of equivalent of public access on the data lines.

This revelation came about as Rundgren began to seriously reevaluate his career. In 1992, after 19 years with Warner Bros. (through Bearsville Records), a half dozen or so moderate hits, a gold record early on, and a reputation as both an innovator and a pain in the ass to deal with professionally, the label and Rundgren came to a parting of the ways. Ever the fan of technology, he had been actively involved in the Internet as early as 1985. He saw it as a way to disseminate his information, and anticipated the concept of a FAQ site: "I'd rather have someone dial up my computer terminal, punch in the questions, and the answers would all be online."

His adventures in technology took him to an experiment with interactive music on the abortive CD-I format and pioneering work in desktop video, and finally led him back to the Internet. During spring 1997, he opened up a Web site that, for an annual subscription, made his music available as he made it, and offered access to online chats and e-mail messages. He found a lot of things attractive about the idea. "I can write music all the time, because I have the assurance that it will get distributed and heard," he said. "I also show up in the chat room just to see how everyone's experience of the site is going and what it is they'd like to have happen."

Rundgren's idea became a recurring theme in the late 1990s and the early years of the 21st century, at the height of Internet giddiness, when investors would throw money at anything that required a modem and had dot com in the name, and Web music companies had public capital to burn. "I'm leaving the major label system and there are hundreds of artists who are going to follow me," said Courtney Love.

> There's an unbelievable opportunity for new companies that dare to get it right. . . . Since I've basically been giving my music away for free under the old system, I'm not afraid of wireless, MP3 files, or any other threats to my copyrights. Anything that makes my music more available to more people is great.

Prince changed his name to a glyph and the Artist Formerly Known as Prince set up a Web site, the NPG Music Club. There, members could download unreleased songs and videos. He also sold his album *Crystal Ball* to a quarter of a million fans, more than half of them directly to the public through his Web site. "People are under the collective hallucination that you have to sell X amounts of records to be a success," he said, noting that he made more money selling 25 percent of the volume of a major label and keeping all of the profits than he had under the record company's system.

"The exciting part of music on the Internet is the impact it could have on delivery systems," added David Bowie, another early Web adapter via BowieNet and several other multifaceted and multifarious Web presences. "Record companies may resist the Web until the last minute before being forced into action. My record company isn't exactly jumping on board, but I'm indifferent to it. You don't have to stay with a record company forever."

Younger bands started discovering this in a big way. "Clap Your Hands Say Yeah, the Arcade Fire, and Sufjan Stevens—not to mention Arctic Monkeys in the United Kingdom—all can thank this grassroots community for the fact that they are selling hundreds of thousands of albums," noted Nettwork Records president Terry McBride.

Nor is viral marketing on the Internet the sole domain of rock and pop bands. Country artist Michael Lee Austin created an Internet-based fan club, giving away memberships and music. Armand Morin, from Austin's record company, Alive, explained:

> With the creation of the Internet, it is more about relationships now than ever before. A high-tech marketing strategy needs to be supplemented with a high-touch system to stay in constant contact with your customers and fan base and build that relationship.

In marketing, there's a buzzword for this sort of relationship: branding. It allows the customers to take ownership of an artist as "their band" and develop an emotional attachment. What judicious use of the Internet has changed is that now artists don't necessarily need radio or even vast resources to create this relationship. One of the leading tools costs nothing for the user or the artist: the Web-based community, epitomized as of this writing by MySpace.com. The site allows artists to post tour dates, bios, information, and most importantly, music. They can communicate back and forth with existing, new, or potential fans. As Hawthorne Heights lead singer JT Woodruff recalled, "When we were trying to get going, all of us would spend at least four hours every day just adding MySpace friends."

As with any discourse, especially in the record business, even veteran artists with similar points of view disagree. David Bowie feels that "the lack of control which people criticize the Internet for is what I've found most attractive about it. . . . The idea of formalizing the Net is awful—and it won't happen."

Pete Townshend, on the other hand, noted, "What bothers me about the Internet is that rapidity of change. That speed of change means that there's no academy, there's no process. Nobody can teach anybody anything. In 1985, just before the Internet became established, I did a lecture at the Royal College of Arts. It's the only one I've ever done. . . . At this particular lecture, I said that music would be sold down telephone lines. The audience got up and walked out. The couple that remained, remained only to heckle, to say why would anyone want to do that?"

However, as the 1990s matured, music down phone lines and through personal computers became the hot topic around the record business. Especially as most of the music going down those phone lines had only been paid for once and shared dozens, hundreds, or even thousands of times. The Internet music genie was out of the bottle and devising new ways of creating mischief.

Not that everyone in the record business thought file sharing was necessarily a bad thing. "We should thank the heavens if we come up with a record kids want badly enough that they're willing to waste their precious, hormonally infused minutes downloading them on their Internet," chided one independent record company president. "Internet music sites don't threaten the record industry nearly as much as greed and stupidity."

Some companies tried to develop an online business model, like the Liquid Audio partnership with Larry Rosen and Phil Ramone's Music Boulevard. They made live tracks from various artists on their N2K label available on the Internet only, things like Richard Barone doing the closest thing his old band the Bongos ever had to a hit, "Barbarella," live. They had the right idea but they were too far ahead of the curve.

In the meantime, the fearless prognosticators began to fearlessly prognosticate, saying that four years down the road, direct digital delivery of music would account for between 7 and 13.5 percent of the music business. Lighting up at these suggestions, dozens of legitimate companies tried their hand at the online music business. As it happened, from 1999 through 2000 I worked for one of these "legitimate" online music sites, MCY.com. As with Liquid Audio, the key was encryption, along with high sampling rates and compression. The company had its own proprietary software player, and the purchaser could also load the music into an early MP3 player, the Rio. Before we changed our business model to proprietary webcasts, and made the online music sales a secondary part of the business, we had sold dozens of downloads. Consumer thinking, by that point, was why buy when you could swap?

As Warner's chief information officer Tsvi Gal said:

Now there is a generation of people who are not used to paying for intellectual property, not because they are bad people, but because we never insisted on teaching them that it has to be paid for. So the industry is now trying to reconcile *its mistakes.*

Some wonder if the record business can come back from these mistakes. Many fear that a decade of free downloads, coupled with the sense of entitlement that brings, may have killed any intrinsic market value of recorded music.

One of the major problems for the record business that led to this situation was that even at the turn of the millennium, over a decade into the Internet age, it was still far easier and certainly cheaper (as in free) to get digital music from the "pirate to pirate" sites than it was to deal with anything legal the music business had set up. A Red Herring Research study on the topic concluded:

The only successful companies will be those that can license a database of digital music, that can successfully syndicate online music technology or that can develop a subscribership whose monthly remittances to the online music firm are great enough to cover both the demand for profits from the recording industry and music artists, and the costs of operations. . . . They must get users to pay for content, and as we know, there are very few Internet entities that have been able to make that successful.

In the meantime nearly all the major record companies, and some independent firms, tried to get the pay service right. Ultimately, it took Apple Computer founder Steve Jobs to do the job. First Apple introduced the hardware, a player called the iPod that could hold upward of 10,000 songs. The device took off, the hot electronic gadget of 2001. Then Apple introduced a place to buy songs for the iPod, one at a time, for 99¢ each—iTunes. Jobs had managed to convince the major record companies, many independent labels, and even some unaffiliated artists to put their music onto Apple's iTunes music service. Unleashed on the public in April 2003, by the end of its first week iTunes had sold a million downloads at 99¢ each. And that was only to the 5–10 percent of the computing public that used Apple computers. The chief downside to iTunes initially was that PC users couldn't use it.

By October, Apple programmers, no doubt holding their noses the whole time, had come up with a Windows version of the program so the 90+ percent of humanity subservient to Microsoft's software whims and wiles could use the iPod and iTunes. They came into a market that suddenly had a bunch of competitors: Real Network's Rhapsody, MusicNet, BuyMusic, a relaunched Napster (in name only—you couldn't share files this time, only buy them), the dreaded Microsoft itself, and even Wal-Mart (which, in typical fashion, undercut everyone by selling its downloads for 88¢). Apple partnered with AOL, did promotions with Pepsi, and soon iTunes became the most popular online music store in the United States.

Another answer came from sites that allowed users to subscribe and stream music to computers and devices (albeit not the iPod)—more like the model Red Herring suggested. For $5–$10 a month, these sites offered access to millions of songs, with the record companies' and music publishers' blessings, provided the sites paid royalties. The customer could stream nearly any song he or she could name, and recent initiatives made even long-out-of-print music accessible to the music fan.

By February 2006, iTunes had sold a billion songs—the billionth being Coldplay's "Speed of Sound."

Now, as early as 1997, people had predicted that the death of the CD to the digital domain was inevitable. A generation that grew up downloading MP3 files might feel about going to a store to buy music the same way people in their 20s feel about vinyl—it's a pleasant little anachronism that older people enjoy. However, this same generation that gave up the object fetish item of the musical hard good like CDs also grew up in a "mall culture." They meet and mingle in malls and bring a significant social standing to shopping, especially shopping for entertainment software. So even if accessing music via the Internet ultimately becomes easier than going to the store, it might not be as much fun.

"It's like saying home shopping networks will keep you out of the stores," said Phil Ramone. "It's the old story about dancing. People will never stay home and dance. They go out to dance, so you have to have a club with personality. I think that's what makes the musical world tick."

"Human nature requires interaction with other people," concurred Sony CEO Michael Schulhof, "the kind of interaction which specifically occurs in record stores. I believe people will still want to experience firsthand the emotional aspect of stores, malls, etc. It's a destination as well as a social experience."

However, after years of threats and lobbying, the retail community finally joined the digital fray. In a way, you could hear the sighs of relief all up and down the record industry grotto on Sixth Avenue. Now the manufacturers didn't have to worry about any aspect of distribution of digital files except getting paid—business as usual.

Of course, just because legal downloads were now available, it didn't stop people from downloading from P2P sites. Estimates put the ratio of legal to P2P downloads between 1:14 and 1:150 in 2004. The biggest downloaders, naturally, are younger people, who have a larger time-to-budget ratio and are generally more Internet savvy than their elders. A survey of Canadians showed that while 12- to 24-year-olds composed about 21 percent of the Canadian population, they accounted for 78 percent of P2P downloading, and that Canada had the largest per capita percentage of file sharers in the world. However, another study revealed that among that same demographic, the heaviest downloaders are also the most apt to buy.

Despite (or perhaps because of) all this, record sales rose 2.3 percent in 2004. So the downturn that the industry placed squarely on the shoulders of P2P may well have had to do with the general global economy, as a report from Pricewaterhouse-Coopers observed:

> In mid-2004, the entertainment and media industry is in an upswing following three years of sluggish growth in reaction to economic weakness and terrorism. While terrorism remains a grave threat, economic conditions in most countries have improved, and the entertainment and media industry is expanding.

Or maybe not. Early indications are that sales dropped precipitously in 2005, falling close to 8 percent. By the middle of 2006, CD sales had fallen over 5 percent comparable to the same period in 2005, and even digital sales were reportedly slowing down.

One of the positive signs in all of this is that after over a decade of first sticking their heads in the sand, and then becoming the ninja ostrich and going on the attack, the record companies finally seem willing to explore, if not embrace, the possibilities of the Internet, and show signs of beginning to accept that a goodly hunk of their future involves the electronic transmission of their "product."

Evidence of this could be seen in the industry's reaction to the shutdown of Grokster in 2005, as compared to the victory dance surrounding Napster only four years earlier. "However valid the industry's desire to protect its products," reported the *New York Times*, "trying to stop file sharing has become a Sisyphean exercise."

Even Hilary Rosen, who in her former role as head of the RIAA had been the single most vocal anti-downloading champion on the planet, noted with a certain air of resignation that while the Grokster ruling might have been "important psychologically, it really won't matter in the marketplace. . . . [Knowing] we were right legally still isn't the same thing as being right in the real world."

The Internet, via sites like MySpace, which offers exposure to half a million aspiring artists, has become a key tool in finding new talent for both record companies and managers. That assumes, of course, that the bands want to get involved in the musical industrial process at all. Artists can sell downloads, ringtones (more on this also in the next chapter), and CDs, and build a following worldwide via Web sites and Internet affiliations. "Fifteen years ago bands would have had to build up that audience with constant touring," said Paul Smernicki of Fiction Records. "Now you'll see groups without a record out and 300 people will turn up for a gig."

"Sales of 20,000 on a major label would have you kicked off because of the enormous overheads," said David Cool of Stand Alone Records. "But as indie musicians, that's a good living. . . . More and more artists are realizing they can do it themselves, build up a fan base and keep control over their art as well."

Aiding in this endeavor are sites like CD Baby, an online record store for independent artists that sells both hard product and downloads, keeping $4 on the sale of each CD and 9 percent on the sale of each download. The site offers a free Web page for each artist, along with practical advice and a weekly check (provided, of course, the CD sells). It claims to get 150,000 hits a day.

In his use of and attitude toward the Internet, as in so many things, Rundgren proved about 10 years ahead of his time. In 1997, when he opened up his subscription Web site, he recommended it to record companies as a means of subsidized artist development:

> A record company can underwrite a band, promote them through the Internet, and build a core audience of even as few as one or two thousand people. Let's say they get 5,000 people to commit at a level of $20 [a year]. That's $100,000 in cost defrayment right up front, $100,000 that would essentially be loaned to the artist to do production or whatever. All they have to do is build that small, core audience who are willing to pay around the cost of a CD.
>
> If I'm distributing electronically, I can make music that I might not normally put on a CD. It wouldn't fit the concept, it's only a minute long, or it's 20 minutes long. All kinds of restric-

tions to giving up real estate on the CD don't exist when you're distributing electronically.

This sounded surprisingly similar to an announcement his former record company, Warner Bros., made nearly a decade later, in summer 2005, about the coming of its e-label subsidiary. "An artist is not required to have enough material for an album," noted Warner Music Group chairman Edgar Bronfman when he made the announcement, "only just enough to excite our ears. Rather than releasing an album every couple of years, every few months the label will release clusters—three or more songs—by the artist."

Additionally, the artists signed to the e-label retain ownership of their masters and copyrights. The parent company saw this as a way to exploit the Web as a means of talent development, slashing the cost of marketing a new artist from millions to minimal.

By November 2005, that label had taken shape and hit the Web as Cordless Records, headed by Jac Holzman, who had founded Elektra Records 40 years earlier. "Physical product has its place in the world," Holzman said, before pointing out that using the Web let him find and test artists with greater speed and far less cost. With the same money that it would take to make, market, and distribute a single CD, Cordless could release songs by between 7 and 10 artists.

Even during the darkest days of the Internet's relationship with the record business, there have been cheerleaders for the digital music business. EMI's former senior vice president of digital development Ted Cohen took his record company position rather than a similar one offered by the emergent Napster in 1999. In that position he cajoled and needled the business to the point where it now teeters on the brink of dealing with online music as businesspeople rather than combatants—and he has started his own consultancy to further and broaden that effort. "The future has never been more exciting," he said. "We're going to figure out how to make this work!"

23

Hardware and Software
On Demand and on Your Hip

SAY WHAT YOU will about his music or his politics, Ice-T is smart. When he addressed the MP3.com convention in San Diego in 2000, he offered a funny, biting, and ultimately very true reading of the state of digital music. Among his comments on the subject, he succinctly got to the heart of why people weren't getting wealthy from downloadable digital music files yet:

> Right now, you can't get MP3 two feet off your computer. How many people got their computers hooked up to their stereo system? It's not really happening.
>
> The Internet, music, MP3 is not going to move until the hardware catches up. The Christmas of the MP3 car stereo, the Christmas of the MP3 home system, the Christmas when the Rio player is playing six and eight hours, when that shit happens, sites are going to be bombarded because people are going to need content.

Christmas that year was supposed to be when hardwired digital music players would be introduced to people's homes, the year downloadable files would start to migrate off the computer and onto entertainment systems. However, with the exception of the already available digital music players like the Brujo, which had allowed early adapters to burn CDs of MP3s and play them back as MP3s (as opposed to reconstituted CD audio files), and, of course, the Rio, a prospective marketplace full of brio and brouhaha fueled by hyperbolic press releases in May had turned suspiciously quiet by September.

This didn't bode well for the kind of quick penetration into the marketplace that people promoting digital music anticipated. And, as T pointed out, it had more to do with the hardware than the software. Files using MP3, A2B, NetTrax, and a bunch of other proprietary compression systems could have gotten onto stereos around the world but for the lack of actual players.

People wanted the convenience of digital music on demand; they wanted the ability to put 11 hours of music on a CD-R or load thousands of songs onto a player and not have to worry about changing the record. "I had my record out on MP3 download," Ice-T told the convention audience, "but it's stuck on my fucking computer. I'm not burning no fucking CD. I'll go out and buy the goddamn thing." Some people, however, would sooner burn than buy, even—perhaps especially—now.

At the time, several pieces of audio equipment allowed compressed music files to migrate away from the computer and into the realm of home audio as components of a home audio system. The aforementioned Brujo MP3/CD player came out during summer 1999 and sold for around $300—not a bad price point for early-adapter technology. The first player of its kind, it played traditional compact discs, but also CD-ROMs, CD-Rs, CD-RWs, and ISO-9660s, as well as MP3s. This allowed a listener to put 11 hours' worth of music on one CD with the CD burner on their computer and play it on a home sound system. Several similar players came along and upped the ante, allowing people with DVD burners to play DVDs and SVCDs, as well as all CD formats and MP3s.

For people who preferred to take that 11-hour CD on the road, there were the portable CD players, starting with a player called the Genica, which had all of the functions of most popular portables with the additional advantage of playing MP3 discs. More traditionally, if anything about MP3 players could be considered "traditional," the chip-based Rio, introduced in the latter part of the 1990s, continued to allow for MP3 play and music reproduction without moving parts. However, as T pointed out in his speech, it only held about two hours of music, and that at a lower-fidelity setting.

Around this same time, hard-drive-based iPod progenitors began to show up as well. The portable Personal JukeBox and the home-stereo-compatible SongBank were both based on hard-drive technology. The JukeBox used a very small-sized six-gig hard drive that held 1,500 songs. The unit was about six inches long by three inches wide and an inch thick, weighing in at a little over half a pound, about the size of a paperback book, and sold for about $750.

Unfortunately, while downloadable digital music had broken through the underground like spring crocuses, via the peer-to-peer services on the one hand and Liquid Audio and MCY and their ilk on the other, the hardware that would take digitally down-loaded music off the computer and onto the living room (and the car) stereo remained buried. Very few mainstream audio mer-chants carried the Brujo, and you could only use it for digital files if you had a CD burner on your computer—still a fairly expen-sive option in 2000, rather than the standard equipment it has become. All of the products for playing digital files available in America required a computer at some point in the process. In other words, they might allow the music to be *taken* away from the computer, but they didn't necessarily get music away from the computer yet.

While the word "music" doesn't even appear in the index to his book *The Innovator's Dilemma*, Clayton M. Christensen might as well have been writing the book for the emerging digital music business; digital music files and players exemplify what he calls a "disruptive technology." The example he cites is the hard-drive industry and the developments that allowed the drives to get smaller yet have more available disk space. Each time this kind of change occurred, the company that brought on the change challenged the market leaders and ultimately toppled them.

"Disruptive technology should be framed *as a marketing challenge,*" Christensen wrote (though the italics are mine), "not a technological one." Unless you can:

➤ identify potential customers
➤ convince those potential customers that they need the technology
➤ find a price point that works

then the gear is destined for the great technological scrap heap.

On a consumer level, entertainment technology develops in a pretty standard curve, particularly hardware. When a new component or format comes out, initially only well-to-do gadgeteers can even touch it. Eventually, depending on marketing and how well the product does among the first-wave, early-adapter gadget buyers, the price starts to come down and the item becomes mainstream; think of DVD in the mid-1990s. Or else it doesn't sell and vanishes; think DAT or digital compact cassettes before that.

"You'll always have a certain amount of—I don't want to call them elitists, but people who are on the cutting edge of new technology," Russ Solomon, head of Tower Records, mused. "A lot of brand-new electronic machinery gets bought for that reason. It's just new. People buy it. That's their hobby. But that doesn't create a mass market. They actually sold an awful lot of DAT machines. I've got one. I never use it, but I've got it."

Of course, for this curve to even have a chance to develop, the product has to come to market. Take the aforementioned SongBank. In June 2000, its creators announced their revolutionary system that would allow you to make compressed digital copies of your own CDs. The unit also would come with a modem and network connection to allow you to eliminate the computer from the process, downloading music directly from the Web to your stereo. In all, you could create a possible database of 7,000 songs on a SongBank, almost 500 CDs' worth of music, which would blow the capacity of CD carousels—up to that point the only way of getting even close to that much music onto your stereo—out of the water, especially when you consider that you wouldn't have to put an entire CD on the system, only those songs you wanted.

By August 2000, however, the company had begun to have second thoughts. Dwight Griesman, the head of marketing for Lydstrom, the parent company of the SongBank, explained:

> Rather than rush to market with a product that was good but perhaps not outstanding for the consumer state, we decided to finish, if you will, and integrate other improvements and technology. While we're doing that, we're also working with consumer electronic manufacturers in hopes that we can compress some of this traditional product lifecycle, so that perhaps it won't be two to three years before some of these products come to market at reasonable price points.

Another piece of musical techno-geek wet-dream hardware announced in May that became vaporware by September was the Indrema. While on paper it would have had most of the music capacity of the SongBank, the Indrema would have added digital video—not unlike Panasonic's then-new set-top digital video unit or TiVo—as well as video game capabilities, making it a virtual digital home entertainment center in a box.

"Personal TV is just beginning to take off," Indrema marketing manager Yana Kushner said. "And you know MP3 is an enormous potential market. We are offering an entertainment system that does it all, and it does it very well. The graphics subsystem is mind-blowing."

Instead of tallying up holiday sales, by the spring of 2001 the company closed up shop, the victim, like so many technology companies at that time, of more burn than capital. As for the SongBank, a product with that name finally came out in 2005, but it hardly resembled what Griesman described. In the intervening half a decade, the digital music hardware marketplace had grown a little more conservative, but it still had all the stability of plutonium.

"The reality of the marketplace is, it moves awfully damn quick," Griesman almost prognosticated.

> We are arranging or trying to arrange a variety of different partnerships that will give us the flexibility to adapt to how the market unfolds. So, for example, should the market turn out to be subscription based, we'll be able to support some sort of subscription service. Should it turn out to be a more traditional download basis—purchase albums, purchase tracks, whatever—we can do that. We're working on streaming capabilities, as well. . . . Everything we've done comes from the consumer music lover's perspective.

The automotive frontier presented the largest array of options for early adapters. Using a direct wire or an adapter, any of the portable devices could be used for car audio. In addition, by 2000 there were several hard-drive-based MP3 players for the car, each costing around $1,000 and holding between 2,000 and 7,000 songs. These systems were basically removable hard drives installed in the trunk of a car that you could plug into your computer and transfer files. One of the early adapters in this market was Ted Cohen, who marveled at the ability to have 20 gigabytes of music—larger than many people's record collections—at his fingertips as he drove through L.A.

Automaker Ford and digital wireless phone technologist Qualcomm began working on a product called Wingcast, a way to allow the consumer to, among other things, access Internet music in his or her car, as well as integrate with the car's onboard computer system. They expected it to be available in 2002 models and projected that it would become as common as the proverbial AM/FM/cassette package by 2004. Instead, by 2002, they had dissolved the partnership, and by 2005, GM was still the only auto manufacturer using telematics—as the system was called—albeit without the Internet component, via its OnStar system.

In a move similar to the Qualcomm venture, though geared to pedestrians rather than automobiles, Korean LG Information and Communications, best known in the States for monitors, had put out an integrated cell phone and digital MP3 player. The Cyon MP3 allowed the consumer to download music right to flash memory on his or her phone, without having to access a computer. A similar phone finally came out in America late in 2005.

The bastard-stepchild status of the digital music files themselves slowed the hardware process to a crawl. Legal downloading of files remained in a state of hit-or-miss chaotic flux. The record companies were upset unto legal action with P2P users, and were none too happy about people using readily available consumer software to "rip" songs from CDs on to their hard drive as MP3 files (they regarded this as a prelude to P2P—more often than not, correctly).

This software element, the MP3 file, was a true disruptive technology—everyone had MP3s and for the most part they were at everyone's favorite price point: free. The brouhaha surrounding the very act of downloading had spread the word in a way that should be the envy of any marketing professional. Yet the hardware failed to be the disruptive technology it could have become, mostly because investors became risk averse during and after the dot-bomb. Until the music's owners found some legal way of distributing their product over the Internet, very few pieces of MP3-friendly hardware came to market, and those that did had a lot of difficulty finding retail space, especially at the "big box" stores that sold both audio equipment and CDs.

For the most part, the companies that made these products tended to be small. They also were generally run by technologists intent on inventing the better musical mousetrap without any clue how to get retailers excited about them and get the product into stores. In other cases, all the money went to R&D and manufacturing, leaving little for the necessary sales and marketing. Some also point to the musical-industrial complex—the big-box stores live and die by brands like Philips, Sony, and Panasonic, which all have convenient ties to the record business. These companies were not about to put out one product that would actively undermine another, nor would they happily and cooperatively do business with stores that did. So while sheer customer demand got the Rio into some stores—more computer-oriented retailers than audio dealers—the Brujo was generally available through the same means as most of the music played on it—the Internet.

It took the exceedingly deep pockets of Apple founder and CEO Steve Jobs to create the first truly disruptive technology in the digital music hardware world, ironically making use of one of Christensen's favorite examples of disruptive technology—the ever-shrinking size and ever-growing capacity of hard disk drives. Whereas his competitors had done very little consumer outreach in the market, Jobs had the wherewithal to create a masterful piece of marketing: the iPod

The iPod was a $500 toy, and its signature white headphones became a status symbol, a sign of the discretionary income, musical taste, and technological savvy the piece came to represent. Introduced toward the end of 2001, when the SongBank and so many other pieces of digital music hardware had turned to vapor, the device demonstrated that timing was not the problem. Indeed, several other players did come to market, but with limited success—Sony had a smaller player, but it only held a couple of dozen songs. The Creative Nomad was a large, unwieldy piece of equipment. By combining a pocket-sized footprint with a capacity for thousands of songs and ergonomic controls, most people regarded it as the most advanced digital music player on the market. The iPod became the generic name in MP3 players very quickly, perhaps this one object replacing the space-consuming fetish object represented by the record collection.

It helped that Jobs threw all of the company's marketing muscle behind the product. A series of television commercials combined with 22 million magazine inserts. The slogan for the accompanying iTunes software made digital music fans cheer while making record executives' blood run cold: "Rip. Mix. Burn." Where, before the introduction of the iPod, the other hard-drive-based players had sold 26,000 pieces, within three years, Apple had released four generations of iPod and sold over 10 million units.

It did everything Ice-T had wished for—it could play nearly two weeks' worth of music, go anywhere, and attach to a home or car stereo. The hardware had finally caught up with the revolution, and now the revolution was going mainstream.

As noted in the last chapter, it took until 2004 before the major labels allowed the consolidation of their copyrights onto one system, and that feat took Jobs to accomplish it. This kicked the legal genie out of the bottle, and before long, consumers could download music from the major record companies legally from over a dozen places. According to a 2005 survey by Forrester Research, 25 percent of 12- to 17-year-olds planned to buy an MP3 player during the course of that year. Forrester further found that 20 percent of the people in that same demographic actually buy their downloads, but pointed out that better than half also "share" music via CD exchanges, e-mails, blogs, and local networks. However, the "promoters" who do the most sharing, they found, also do the most buying.

Another disruptive technology was advancing by leaps and bounds alongside the digital music world. Cell phones had gone from expensive luxury item for the very wealthy to a mainstream item that achieved about a 66 percent market penetration in the United States and over 100 percent per capita penetration in Sweden, Italy, Austria, and the United Kingdom, with many people owning multiple phones. Many people use their cell phone as their primary (or even their only) phone.

As sales increased, the technology also followed Moore's Law, doubling in power every couple of years. One area where this became highly evident was the development of the ringtone. Ringtones initially just played a melody line, then they gained the capacity for entire computer-generated arrangements, and finally they were able to play actual digital recordings of favorite songs.

Record producers not only had to concentrate on where to edit hit singles, but also had to separate out 15-second snippets of songs for potential ringtones. "Once considered a passing craze," trumpeted one ringtone Web site, "ringtones now account for more than 10 percent of the global music market and are overtaking CD sales sooner than expected."

"That's something the artists are really into, especially producers," said Greg Clayman, MTV's VP of wireless strategy and operations. "They begin to think about all the different places where their music is heard—booming from cars, computers, stereos, iPods, and also from phones."

In slightly less than a year, for example, a company called Bling Tones sold over four million ringtones. "Artists are playing with a medium that isn't fully formed," said Bling Tones' VP of A&R Jonathan Dworkin. "Mobile content can be used for retail and promotion. . . . It's a powerful promotional tool they built into an actual product."

On an episode of the hit television show *CSI: New York* for example, one of the characters' cell phones rang with the song "Let's Talk" by the band Coldplay, and the public availability of the ringtone was announced in a commercial aired right after the scene.

Artists have also started exploring other digital means of delivery. Ted Cohen helped make the Rolling Stones' *A Bigger Bang* available not only on CD, but also on a memory card for phones and computers. Similarly, Canadian pop stars the Barenaked Ladies released a recording that was only available on a USB flash drive. Called *Barenaked on a Stick*, the device contained 29 songs, album art, photos, videos, and a variety of other goodies.

While it took half a decade, MP3 players in general have gone mainstream in the wake of the iPod. For one thing, the big box stores have finally seen the digital light. For under $40, a consumer can buy a CD player that will spin that 11-hour CD of MP3s, or a disc player compatible with DVDs, CDs, and burned MP3 discs that will hook up to a television and stereo.

For the record companies, the mainstreaming of digital music almost felt like capitulation, succumbing to the inevitable. Since hardware manufacturers owned so many of the software companies, they opted to play so carefully that the upstart technology nearly walked away with the business. Some predict that Apple will become the dominant player in the music business, from both the hardware and the software perspective, taking over a majority of retail market share and perhaps even acquiring its own content for distribution.

In an almost symbolic victory, the company retained the right to use its logo on its digital music products, though the Beatles' Apple Corps said that Apple Computer had violated a 15-year-old agreement that gave Apple Corps the exclusive use of its similar trademark in the music business. Perhaps the upstart Apple's conquest of the former upstart Beatles' corporate interest indicated the record business's inevitable course.

Back when we were in high school, my friend Mike had the good fortune and good grades to spend his summers working at Bell Labs. He would come home very excited about the stuff he'd seen. "Man," he would tell us, "they have things there that they're doing with computers that you aren't going to even see for another 25 years, until everyone catches up to the technology."

Unfortunately, it took the record business more than 35 years, and it has yet to get up to speed. In spring 2006, many record labels, including all of the majors, renewed their licensing agreements with iTunes. For months before that—in the fashion typical of a business that either kills all the geese that lay golden eggs, or exhausts them until they start laying lead—they lobbied to raise the price on "front line," new, hit recordings from the 99¢ the Web site charged to $1.49, leaving everything else at the 99¢ price point.

Jobs laid into them mightily, chiding them for being greedy (really, Steve?). He insisted that the 99¢ price point was essential to the continued success of iTunes, and that the service held the record business's only possible hope of success in the digital domain. It certainly marked the first time that anything even made a dent in the "free music" ethos, and did it by creating a simple, comprehensive, and legal way of getting content for digital players.

The revolution finally became portable, with absolutely no thanks to the record industry. Ice-T must be pleased.

Part V | **We, the Audience**

24

A Touch of Grey
Boomers Grow Up and Grow Old

PETE TOWNSHEND, at the tender age of 23, wrote an anthem for his age called "My Generation." One of the most controversial lines in the song had the Who's lead singer Roger Daltrey stuttering, "Hope I die before I get old." When I last saw the Who, with Pete and Roger both facing their 60s along with the other members of their g-g-g-g-g-generation, they still did the song. It says a lot about baby boomers.

"When the Who first sang the lyric, 'Hope I die before I get old' it was a generation gap anthem," asserted *Sun-Sentinel* book editor Chauncey Mabe, "meaning 'Hope I die rather than become a fat old hypocrite.' Now it seems to mean, 'Hope I stay young until I die of old age.'"

Would the music business be where it is without the boomers, the post–World War II generation born approximately between 1946 and 1964? Author and former Mercury Records president Danny Goldberg calls himself "a baby boomer and an aging hippie." This would describe many of the people who work in the record business, and indeed, the people who work for, and especially *lead*, most businesses. These are the people who have the skill, talent, and *experience*.

In addition to forming the foundation of the record business itself, the baby boomers are the original rock audience, and to a lesser extent rock's driving creative force (though not its innovators—that would fall to the generation before). If not for the baby boomers' embrace of rock, it might have been a small, localized phenomenon, and the record business might have never grown to its present proportions. As historian Donald J. Mabry asserted:

> Rock 'n' roll became the dominant musical genre in the United States in the 1950s because young people between the ages of 13 and 19 listened to the radio, bought rock 'n' roll records, and watched *American Bandstand* on national television in the afternoon and movies which featured rock 'n' roll music.

NYU professor Herb London claimed that "a revolution in sensibilities," the core of which was rock and roll, happened in America during the 1950s, to the benefit of the baby boom generation. According to London, the rock revolution rivals such political upheavals as the French Revolution (although it was less bloody). The revolution, he argued, followed all the classic sociological stages of a "proper" revolution—incipient change, reform, active revolt, equilibrium, reaction, and restoration. As one reviewer put it, Professor London characterized rock as the litmus paper of contemporary culture.

Clearly, the baby boom caused a major social upheaval. Suddenly, questioning authority, social mores, and the status quo went from verboten to an almost mandatory right of passage. Boomers could do this based on sheer numbers—between 1940 and 1960 the number of live births nearly doubled.

Of course, while this enormous percentage of people happen to be the same age, it didn't necessarily make us a consolidated, monolithic bloc. For example where the extremes of youth culture, like the liberalism of "the movement," did not represent the majority of young people by any stretch of the imagination, it did set in motion the counterculture of music, drugs, long hair, free love, and not respecting authority for authority's sake that played an important role in what our society turned into, creating an overt generation gap and giving the masses of youth a voice it had never known before.

Baby boomers continue to make up an enormous percentage of the population. By 1990, when America began to feel the full impact of the tail end of the baby boom, boomers born over the course of 18 years accounted for more than 30 percent of the population, but the age group's self-referential gestalt outweighs even their sheer numbers. As much as they are self-aware as individuals, boomers also enjoy the power of being boomers, of having the sheer strength of numbers behind them. Dartmouth economist Joyce Manchester wrote in 1988:

> The baby boom generation is now in the prime of its young adult years, ranging from 23 to 41 with the biggest cluster around 31. The behavior of this cohort as it swarms into the labor force, clamors for home ownership, and borrows to finance commodities as well as children has far reaching effects on the economic patterns in the United States.

Nearly 20 years later, the leading edge of this key demographic faces turning 60, and the bulk are in their 40s. The generation that created the notion of youth as a separate realm of experience and knowledge now had children and even grandchildren of their own, yet still equate themselves and their peers with youth—the "baby" part of the "baby boomers." Not only don't we want to grow old gracefully, we don't want to grow old *at all*. "Baby boomers literally think they're going to die before they get old," said a pollster, confirming Mabe's contention. A study done by the pollster's research firm found that baby boomers defined "old age" as beginning at 85, three years after the actuarial tables say the average American dies. When the boomers reach 85, we can only wonder where the concept of "old" will lie.

Most important for this book's purposes is that music played such an important, often defining, role in the baby boomer experience that the boomers never stopped listening. Where the boomers' parents might listen to Glenn Miller and get nostalgic, boomers go to see Creedence Clearwater Revisited and dance in the aisles.

"People like us, who grew up in the '60s, we took our music with us," said Allan Pepper, owner of the late, lamented Bottom Line night club in New York. "When our parents grew up, with big band music and Tin Pan Alley, they put the music aside when they got married and raised a family. My generation kept buying records and kept listening."

Beyond all else, baby boomers hold the economic reins in the U.S. (and around the world). There is no doubt that the approximately 78 million boomers still represent the 800-pound demographic gorilla. Demographer William H. Frey noted, "Now in middle age and their prime earning years, baby boomers' economic clout is reaching its peak and, as in the past, the group continues to shatter the precedents set by earlier age groups: boomers reinvent . . . lifestyles [and] consumer patterns."

This, of course, made the baby boomers a prime target of marketing and advertising, and what better way to reach them than via rock and its icons? So in 2005, artists of unimpeachable musical and personal integrity like Bob Dylan and Paul McCartney appeared in advertisements for Kaiser Permanente and Fidelity Investments respectively. In the meantime, the Rolling Stones, who had taken an alleged $15 million from Microsoft to appear in various promotions of Windows 95 (which in turn promoted the band's song "Start Me Up"), appeared in ads for Ameriquest Mortgage, who also sponsored the Stones' 2005–2006 world tour. The campaigns were, by all appearances, successful.

The baby boomers consistently bought more recordings over the past decade than their younger compatriots. In 2004, 40-year-olds and older accounted for over 37 percent of sales, versus a little over 30 percent for people 15–29 years old. In 1992, the difference was even more pronounced—boomers bought 42 percent of the music and 26 percent was bought by people under 20. This predates downloading from the Internet, and points to possible roots of the decline in prerecorded music sales. However, what happens when the music doesn't speak to us, when no music that we hear lures us into the record stores? Could it possibly be that the nearly 20 percent decrease in CD sales over the last decade has more to do with the fact that boomers have less to go to the stores for than it does their children (and them as well) swapping music files? "The older demographic is missing," Canadian Record Industry Association head Brian Robertson observed in 1996, "the one that has the most disposable income."

Over the past decade it hasn't gotten much better.

25

The Lost Audience
How the Music Business Broke Faith with Its Main Supporters

WHEN I WAS a kid (we're talking Bedrock here, folks: stone cars you drove with your feet, birds on perches using their beaks to play rock music on real rocks) I spent my "discretionary money" on two main things—guitar accessories and records. These were the black plastic kind that you could scratch and stuff. Oh, yeah— I also bought concert tickets. And snacks. . . .

I was the poster child for music business marketers. I heard a song on the FM rock station; it moved me. I cracked open the piggy bank, begged Mom and Dad for more money (piggy was invariably empty), and bought it. The record industry rose over the 1970s and 1980s because it was largely the only way for 12- to 25-year-olds like me to use our discretionary funds, money that ran into the tens of billions.

I have two teenagers now. I'm also in the music industry. I can get them pretty much any record they want by asking for it, and they know it. You know how many records they've asked me for recently? None.

For the music fans in my children's demographic, download-ing music has become de rigueur. Many 12-year-olds have never bought a CD. They think of music as a free commodity. This early branding could devastate the business, but if it does, the business deserves it.

During my childhood, and even for several generations before that, the music business owned the 12- to 25-year-olds. From Sinatra to Elvis to the Beatles, and even through Mötley Crüe and Bon Jovi, "the kids," as the music business liked to call its core customers and constituency, bought music at the rate of billions of dollars a year.

The record companies still see this 12–25 demographic as theirs, despite all the evidence to the contrary. They wallow in this particular fallacy, gearing their promotional dollars to radio stations focused on the "youth market," despite the increasing difficulty of getting music onto these stations' decreasing playlists. Yet they ignore folks like me, hard-core fans raised on records, in favor of a generation of kids raised on robbery.

How do you convince the record industry that this older demographic is the one more worth targeting? It becomes hard, because the business sees teens as a group that breaks into easy-to-reach monoliths: X percent listen to rap, Y percent pop/boy bands/girl groups, Z percent punk-pop/metal. It perceives the kids as easily swayed by peer pressure, so if their friends own a record, chances are they will want to own it as well. While this becomes less and less true every year, sales of Eminem, Nickelback, Destiny's Child, etc. show the logic can still work if enforced with a ramrod.

Conversely, the musical interests of 30- to 56-year-olds generally expand as they get older; travels through life and time expose these listeners to more and different sounds. Less influenced by others, these music fans develop their own, continually changing personal tastes. The teen who wouldn't listen to Sinatra, opera, or John Coltrane on a bet may count one or all as passions at 30.

Sure, peer pressure still exerts a subtle influence on adults, as the coolness factor still applies. One record exec explained this to me in terms of "the dinner party album du jour." The CD gets put on during dinner and everyone goes, who is that! The exec's example was Norah Jones, and this is how she gained the traction that eventually led to her eight Grammy Awards and sales of over 14 million albums.

However, you can no longer sell adults all the same things that their friends buy. Their diffuse tastes make the record companies less interested in this group as a whole. The reasons are obvious. To feed the behemoth that the business has become, conventional wisdom says a major label has to sell 250,000–500,000 copies of any given CD, just to break even (I've seen this figure cited as high as two million). This creates the alarming situation in which 5 percent of the albums the major record companies release support the other 95 percent. Unfortunately, for it and us, right now the major music business is retrenching. This happens in waves. A major one of these declining cycles happened in 1979. That lasted a few years, until the introduction of the CD pulled us out of it.

But this wave might just capsize the major record business. Not since the Depression have we seen 20 percent decreases in record sales. The majors seem busier looking for a scapegoat than trying to find an actual solution to this problem, save scaling back on employees and signees.

Independent record labels can create the music that will reach the rock-and-roll adult, and they already do. Putumayo does very well with its world music, making tidy profits on CDs that sell between 15 and 90 thousand copies. Concord, fundamentally a jazz label of long standing, has recognized part of this lost audience and risen to the occasion by signing artists like Barry Manilow and Ray Charles, who had fallen out of favor with the major labels they once supported. Barry sold 160,000 for Concord and Ray Charles did even better, selling in excess of three million copies and earning eight Grammy Awards in the process. With his momentum, Barry went back "home" to major label Arista and topped the charts.

So some music reaches this demographic, when the demographic becomes aware of it. The problem, of course, is that for every boomer buying Barry Manilow there are six that might like to burn it, for every buyer of a Putumayo world collection there are dozens who wouldn't let "that music" get played in their car, and for every fan of the Band there are a dozen groups on independent labels that they would love if only the label could get the music to them. The question becomes, how do you market to a diverse group that would sooner listen to "oldies" and "news radio" than any of the major-market stations? How do you get them to renew their passion for music? How do you reach a niche in a business that has a century old history of mass marketing?

Can the business create a promotional channel to reach adults, beyond R + P = S? Especially since, as we've seen, even getting pop product over the airwaves has turned into a fierce and bloody competition, taking no prisoners and leaving few survivors? The record business seems to have missed or misinterpreted the widespread changes in the symbiotic relationship between it and radio in its trip down denial. As we have seen, radio, once a beacon of media independence, now answers to central control, in large part, by four or five major media companies. Local program directors have less and less power over what they program. The days of the "local hit" dwindled to nothing some time ago. We have entered an era when local programmers hardly have any power at all. Where diversity once ruled, constriction has become the name of the game.

Ironically, as we have also seen, worldwide, centrally controlled stations may offer part of the answer to the dilemma of playlists controlled so tightly they can barely move. XM, Sirius, and digital cable radio reach out to the adult demographic, with centrally programmed channels, but hundreds of them, each speaking to a specific audience. Their logic, that only people in this demographic would likely spend the money on subscriptions to radio with programming diverse enough to speak to them, seems sound. Paid subscription radio reaches out to people with discretionary income who have become disenfranchised by radio in general.

Internet radio also has this chance, but the recent CARP (Copyright Arbitration Royalty Panel) decision on Web radio royalty rates sent a lot of Internet radio programmers reeling out of the game, and only recently have they started regrouping. Recognizing the viability of this medium, Artemis Records stated that it will issue free licenses to nonprofit Internet-only radio stations that want to webcast its music. With adult-oriented artists like Rickie Lee Jones and Warren Zevon on the label, that might be one of the smartest promotional moves of this young millennium.

The Internet offers other viable possibilities. Record companies could mine lists of fans of people who buy their music, creating opt-in direct e-mail marketing for music from a listener's favorite artist and other artists of the same ilk. A record company could send a song or a link to a song to likely listeners. This, of course, begs the question of how you find those likely listeners. The initial research would cost a fortune, though the Internet, again, might make it simpler. Information mining, if done right, could turn into a valuable ancillary source of income once someone figures out how to generate the mining stream in the first place. Once companies or artists figure out how to get the audience to a site, they have won at least half the battle.

THERE IS A WEB site called Pandora.com, for example. They use a proprietary database called the Music Genome Project as its core. Created by programmers and musicologists, it breaks songs down by hundreds of musical attributes and then matches up elements like melody, harmony, rhythm, orchestration, lyrics, and vocal style with other similar music. When you access the site, it asks you to input the name of a favorite band and starts streaming music by other bands with a similar "genome" that it thinks you might like. It even gives you the reason it thinks you might like it. If you do like the music, you give it a thumbs-up, and Pandora plays more in that vein. If you don't, you give it a thumbs-down, and it stops playing that song and adjusts accordingly. The technology rocks my world, and it's an amazing source of music I have not previously heard—and that, I humbly add, takes some doing. Now, what if the company could mine this information? Suddenly, it has a whole profile on me that it can sell to record company marketers about the kind of music I want to hear. Those marketers in turn could reach out to me with promotional offers to make me aware of their artists. And unlike some of the spam I now get, I might even *want* to hear what they have to offer.

Television presents another possibility for reaching the "lost audience," especially as two things happen: Web technology and television start to converge and niche cable/satellite networks continue to spring up like crocuses in spring. Broadcast advertising costs a fortune, but cable advertising costs less—still pricey, but you can buy 30 seconds in the wee hours of the morning on some cable stations for under $30. Sell a handful of CDs, bring people to your Web site, get the word out, and you could reap some return on investment.

Of course, there's the old standby, print. Especially in these post–September 11 days, when print ad revenues have fallen through the floor, magazines, newspapers, and zines certainly remain the most cost-effective advertising vehicles. And even if a musician or record company trying to reach this audience lacks an advertising budget, a good PR campaign with the correct hook can get people onto the Internet or into the record store.

Perhaps the record business is beginning to get it. In 2003, a terrible year in general for the record business, CD purchases actually went up by 6 percent among consumers between the ages of 55 and 64. Analysts credited the phenomenon of Norah Jones, and Rod Stewart's *Great American Songbook*.

The early years of the new millennium have seen many businesses go through cataclysmic changes. People who continue to do business as if nothing has changed in the last 20 years will get left in the dust eventually. That's just the nature of things. Ironically, as things in the music business change, the landscape begins to look more like it did 50 years ago, with many small companies in the early stages of reaching, or at least reaching out to, their niche audiences and making a living by doing so. Of course, the methods of marketing are very different now, and my suggestions offer just the sketchiest outline of how to approach this. I'd be marketing right now instead of writing this book if I knew definitively how to get it done. The person who gets this to a science might become the wealthiest person in the forthcoming economy, at least as far as the record business is concerned. The audience is out there, just waiting to be reached.

26

An Embarrassment of Riches
Entertainment Options Today—
"Hey, Kid, Wanna Buy a Record
or a Video Game?"

THE MUSIC BUSINESS still counts on "the kids." That phrase has been on the lips of every record executive for at least as long as I've been in the business: "We're putting out music, and we're doing it for the kids." Thanks, Dad.

"If kids aren't clamoring for music," said Russ Crupnick of the market research company NPD Group, "not only do we lose sales to younger consumers, but also parents will be less likely to shop the music section on behalf of their children."

These days, youthful dollars inspire heavy competition. The number of leisure-time options on which 8- to 25-year-olds can spend their money has risen exponentially since I last personally inhabited that demographic. My teens would rather play video games than just listen to music—and the younger aspires to a career as a musician. The boys also spend a lot of time on the Internet. They rarely listen to music when they surf. They download music even more infrequently, although they still do it (and considering who dad is, maybe I just don't know about the number of songs on their hard drive . . .), and certainly don't have much in the way of hard good music CDs that I either got them or they went out and bought. And according to statistics, they're pretty average in terms of media use—if every teen with Internet access only downloads "a few" tracks, that still amounts to a lot of music.

A report by DFC Intelligence claimed that by 2010, the worldwide interactive entertainment market—which includes console video games, games for the personal computer, online games, and portable gaming systems—would equal or eclipse the music business, with gross assets of over $40 billion dollars.

To put that into perspective, the RIAA reported that in 2004, the record business sold a bit over $12 billion dollars worth of goods, a mild upswing of 2.5 percent over 2003. The video game business, meanwhile, had sales of $7.3 billion, a 4 percent rise over the previous year. And while CD sales have risen almost imperceptibly since 1996, video game sales have doubled. It doesn't take an abacus to figure out that *maybe* there's a connection.

Video games are but one of the hellhounds on the record business's trail. According to a report by the National Association of Record Merchandisers, college students spend more on video and cell phones than they do on music. The average college student purchases but one CD a month. (This might bode worse for the retail business than music or even the record business in general, as some of the money students used to spend on CDs now goes to devices for portable "digital content," some of which is likely to be music.)

Recent data on younger consumers by several reputable research organizations (Kaiser Family Foundation, Forrester Research, Alexander and Associates) revealed a ton of interesting information on the way younger Americans use entertainment media:

Television

- ➤ 99 percent of U.S. children between the ages of 2 and 18 lived in homes with televisions.
- ➤ 60 percent had three or more in the home.

➤ Over half had a television in their bedroom.

➤ Television accounts for more than 40 percent of media exposure for the 8–18 age group, over half if you factor in movies and other videos.

Video Gaming

➤ 70 percent of U.S. youth between 2 and 18 had video game consoles.

➤ 55 percent of boys would rather play games than watch television.

➤ Males spend an average of 12 hours a week playing video games.

➤ 25 percent of a gamer's leisure time is spent playing video games.

PCs

➤ By 2005, 86 percent of U.S. homes with children between the ages of 8 and 18 had PCs.

➤ 74 percent had Internet connections.

➤ Americans spend an average of three hours a day online.

➤ Instant messaging has become the most popular online activity among 8- to 18-year-olds.

➤ 87 percent of teens 15 and older, and 83 percent of the broader 12-to-21-year-old age group use IM (as opposed to 32 percent of adults).

➤ Over 25 percent of 12- to 17-year-olds said they could not live without their PC, twice as many as those who couldn't live without their mobile phones.

➤ Young people between the ages of 12 and 17 spend an average of between 11 and 20 hours per week online.

➤ 8- to 18-year-olds consume about six hours of media daily, unless you count double for the 16 percent of the time they use two media simultaneously. Then it rises to eight hours.

Cellular phones

➤ Nearly 50 percent of 12- to 14-year-olds have mobile phones.

➤ Active mobile phone users spend 13 hours a week on their phones talking and four hours a week using data services.

➤ Young females spend 23.5 hours per week on their mobile phones, more than the 20.9 hours a week they spend watching television.

➤ 21 percent of teens downloaded at least 10 ringtones in the three months preceding the survey.

➤ 60 percent of all people surveyed said they paid for text messaging; 48 percent for custom ringtones; 22 percent for games.

➤ 18 percent of active gamers have downloaded a game to their cell phone.

All this is to say that the modern consumer faces an unprecedented number of choices for his or her entertainment and media dollar. And this doesn't only affect the youthful dollar. According to the Entertainment Software Association, the average video game player is 30 years old and has been playing for a dozen years. Around 20 percent of Americans over 50 years old play video games, and women comprise 43 percent of video gamers. Indeed, women over 18 years old represent a bigger share of video game players than boys between 6 and 17 years old. "We'll see a time," said Rob Smith, editor-in-chief of *Xbox Magazine*, "maybe not in eight years, but in 12, where we'll have someone in the White House who grew up playing [video] games."

The music market has stagnated in the face of the other draws on discretionary entertainment income. Part of the reason why has to do with perceived value. While a new video game can cost perhaps twice or three times what a CD sells for, it offers between 20 and 40 hours of game play, and the experience often bears repeating. I know my family have all played pretty nearly every game in Nintendo's Legend's of Zelda franchise several times, and Mario is timeless.

In addition, the perceived value of prerecorded music itself has changed since Robert Shelton compared the cost of one minute of music on LP to one minute on glass and lacquer in the 1950s. Now, fifty years down the road, economist Barry Ritholtz sees that DVDs are a far better investment than CDs:

> It's pretty obvious to any intelligent consumer that CDs are a lousy deal. For $18 suggested retail price, you get about 45 minutes of pre-recorded music. Sometimes, you even get more than a page of liner notes. It comes in a cheap jewel case which is all but certain to break eventually. . . . Now, compare CDs with DVDs. For about the same amount of money—and often less—a DVD delivers:
>
> ➤ Two hour+ feature of audio and video;
> ➤ Gorgeous video quality;
> ➤ An informative booklet and/or decorative case;
> ➤ Pristine audio;
> ➤ Extra features, outtakes, deleted scenes, "making of the film" documentaries, interviews with director, actors, writers.
>
> So for your entertainment dollar, what delivers more bang for the buck, the CD or DVD? . . . The "central planners" of the music [business] failed to recognize that their oligopoly was not impervious to economic pressures.

Of course, the record industry would argue that a CD delivers an experience that people often want to repeat on a daily basis—people play their favorite music over and over, something they might not do with a piece of media as linearly demanding as a DVD, especially of a movie. However, in 2003, as the record business sagged like an aging weight lifter, Adams Media Research reported that consumers spent $14.4 billion on movies for the home (exceeding the gross take at theaters and rental shops by five billion dollars).

The record business is keenly aware of its losses to all these sources, but it has just started to twig, over the past few years, how to join 'em since it can't beat 'em. The record companies and the video companies, after all, are gunning for the same demographic—people with disposable income that they want to spend on entertainment. In that time, video games have benefited from the record industry's willingness to license songs. And record companies have benefited from the extra exposure. My 14-year-old son was singing along to "That's Life," to the astonishment of both my wife and me. He told us he had learned it from *Tony Hawk Underground 2*. That game also features the Doors' "Riders on the Storm." "Our central strategy," said EMI Music EVP Adam Klein, "is to get music to where people are and, in that sense, video games are a key part of our strategy."

"The impact of musical introduction that MTV and radio have had," added Steve Schnur, a music executive at video game publisher Electronic Arts, "video games have now."

Record executives bemoan the fact that they have failed to teach "the consumer the value of the CD." However, as *Billboard*'s Ed Christman pointed out, "Maybe I'm slow off the mark, but it seems to me that what is going on in the pricing of other entertainment formats matters more to the consumer than label executives' justifications for the current CD pricing structure."

Part VI | **Money**

27

Music Education

Buddy, Can You Spare a Dime?

IF A PERSON EATS only swill, then the only judgment he can make is what kind of swill he likes. If a person only hears the music that's played on the radio, she is only exposed to that small portion of a much greater musical spectrum, and can only make judgments based on that small universe of music she hears.

Now, the record business, especially the major companies, counts on this. In a way, radio stations have done the business a favor by limiting the amount and kinds of music they'll play. As much as the record companies bitch and moan about limited playlists, it allows them to limit the kinds of music they try to bring to market. And as radio's musical content grows more uniformly banal, the gravitas of the artists on the radio—the same artists who will receive the marketing dollars from the record companies—continues to diminish.

Sure, the major companies continue to pay lip service to their marginal divisions. All of them have a classical department and a jazz department, but they never count on them for sales, and consequently the budget behind the entire jazz and classical divisions of most major record companies might equal the money they put behind one highly touted pop recording. That's good business but it's bad music.

Avril Lavigne and Kanye West, while fine pop performers, do not represent the apex of musical creativity. But because of the limited exposure to other sounds, an entire generation has come up thinking they do. Very few have heard of the likes of Karlheinz Stockhausen or Ronnie Gilbert or Sonny Rollins.

Where does one gain such exposure? Well, like sex, you can learn it at home, you can learn it on the street, you can learn about it from friends, or you can learn it in the classroom. However, unlike sex, there's no guarantee that anyone will necessarily learn anything about music at all.

Sadly, government money to schools has started trickling down, as opposed to flowing. You can't spend the same dollar twice, and the U.S. dollar has other places to go. To fund the once-more-expanding military-industrial complex (now there's a phrase redolent of nostalgia and terror), funding for nearly every human service in the federal budget, including music education, has plummeted, though the Bush administration prefers to call it "modest reductions in the rate of growth." Compound this with a reduction in arts funding nearly to the point of nonexistence, and the prospect for cultural deprivation lurks around the corner. And as the Residents used to say in one of their posters, "Ignorance of your culture is not considered cool."

The loss of music education deprives students of other benefits as well. When I was a substitute science teacher in a Bronx grade school, I would bring in my guitar and explain the mathematics and physics of how strings work. Because the guitar is fretted based on mathematics and physics, this is fairly easy and allowed me to introduce concepts like fractions and how sound travels through the air in a way that stuck with the kids. "Music is a specialized science which deals with the quality of sound, acoustics, and timbre," said educator William H. Yoh.

> Extensive training is given to the aural discrimination between like pitches and those that are different. . . . Although it is a simplified form of arithmetic, counting in groups of two, three, four, and higher are used consistently in all music repertoire. When teaching the values of rhythmic notation, we develop and reinforce the concepts of addition, subtraction, multiplication, and division.

This effect is not necessarily a conscious phenomenon, either. In a study of first and second graders in a Rhode Island school district, they performed better in reading and math when their curriculum included just an hour of music and an hour of art a week. There was a 22 percent difference in test scores between the students who enjoyed this exposure to music and art, and those who did not receive it.

According to a profile of SAT Program test takers:

> Students with coursework/experience in music performance and music appreciation scored higher on the SAT: Students in music performance scored 57 points higher on the verbal and 41 points higher on the math, and students in music appreciation scored 63 points higher on verbal and 44 points higher on the math than did students with no arts participation.

Schools that produced the highest academic achievement in the United States spent 20–30 percent of the day on arts, with a special emphasis on music. A parochial elementary school in the Bronx that was about to lose its accreditation implemented an intensive music program into its day. Within eight years, 90 percent of students were reading at or above grade level.

And finally, the Texas Commission on Drug and Alcohol Abuse noted that "secondary students who participated in band or orchestra reported the lowest lifetime and current use of all substances (alcohol, tobacco, and illicit drugs)."

So we should all agree that music education is important, perhaps even vital—and most of us do. In a 2004 Gallup poll, 95 percent of the people questioned felt that music was essential to education. Of those who answered the nationwide survey, 80 percent responded that music education made a child smarter. So the question becomes, do we want a nation of dumb kids?

School systems find themselves between a curricular rock and a budgetary hard place when it comes to music. Said one California school superintendent, after effectively eliminating music from his system's program of study, "The other choices were worse: cutting reading teachers, closing schools, or (cutting back on) class size reduction."

The *Pittsburgh Post-Gazette* reported that schools in California had a 50 percent decline in the number of music education programs because of financial constraints. In Wisconsin, teachers claimed the No Child Left Behind law foisted on the nation is threatening music and art programs throughout the state: "School districts statewide are slashing the music and art programs in order to reduce the budget. They feel pressured to cut these programs first, because unlike math, writing, and reading, music and art are not government tested."

One of those Wisconsin schools might actually have to return funds from VH-1's Save the Music program because it doesn't have a full-time music teacher to supervise the piano lab set up with the cable network's $25,000 grant. It could buy the instruments, but once it had them, it couldn't afford to hire anyone to use them.

One music teacher noted that as time went on, student attendance at events like orchestral concerts and ballets had dwindled. "The reason for that," he pointed out, "is that they are not receiving that kind of education in schools. I'll bet that nine times out of ten, if you asked those who do attend a concert they will say, 'Oh, yes, I had music in school.'" What to do to save some semblance of music education in our schools, as the federal government "modestly reduces the rate of its growth" and through legislation forces state and local governments into a "Sophie's

Choice" between meeting federal testing standards and actually enriching their student's cultural education experience? Well, there are sources for grants, like the aforementioned Save the Music program. When the National Academy of Recording Arts and Sciences collects dues, and license fees for the annual telecast of the Grammy Awards, it channels some of the money into grants for music education. Even Paul McCartney has gotten involved; via his previously mentioned relationship with Fidelity Investments, he formed the Music Lives Foundation, although the bankers seeded it with a mere million dollars (they probably found it between the cushions of their couch). "After years and years of playing in a band and making a living doing what I love," Sir Paul said, "I can honestly say: where would I be without music?"

"Children in the vulnerable age bracket have a natural love for music," Frank Zappa said in his testimony before Congress.

> If, as a parent, you believe they should be exposed to something more uplifting than "Sugar Walls," support music appreciation programs in schools. Why have you not considered your child's need for consumer information? Music appreciation costs very little compared to sports expenditures. Your children have a right to know that something besides pop music exists.

Members of Congress have vilified spending money on the arts, claiming it funds degenerates who think putting crosses in bottles of urine is uplifting. But art does not necessarily need positivity to inspire or edify. And a government frightened of edifying its people has something serious to hide.

Music and art in general are hallmarks of civilization. When did *Homo sapiens* make the break that made us sapient? Some say the break came when we could not only use tools (many other species use tools), but also start creating things for the sake of creation. For a lack of money, will we allow civilization to devolve?

Education in the humanities, meaning those things that make us uniquely human, has started to fall by the wayside in favor of math and science. Math and science are, of course, exceptionally important. I have a child who is studying to be an engineer. But he also has attended philharmonic concerts and the opera, can sing Gilbert and Sullivan, plays a little brass and a little bass. He reads for enjoyment, and his love of manga and anime has started him learning Japanese. In other words, it takes more than leaving no child behind in math and science to educate him or her; it takes more than just teaching what words look like on paper to instill a love of reading into a child. It takes more than academics to make a well-rounded human being.

Eliot Spitzer seems to recognize this. The settlements from his payola investigations—over $30 million as of this writing—will go to a nonprofit organization supporting art and music education. By doing bad, it would seem the major record companies did good.

28

The Orlando Phenomenon
Boy Bands and Bad Girls Made to Order

SINCE THE DAYS of Sam Goody and long before—since the days of Gilbert and Sullivan, of Johann Sebastian Bach, of the traveling minstrels, of the Greek theater—music has been a commodity as well as an art. For the professional musician, singer, or composer— or the wannabe—the trick has always been to find the balance of art and commerce that you can live with. It turns into a sort of yin-yang exercise.

There have always been musicians, too, who took no part in this balancing act, who either accepted their roles as products or were simply treated as such. However, as music became more and more commodified during the era of corporate co-option, the performer as product has become an increasingly common phenomenon. And in the future the pop-as-commodity will consume more and more musicians.

For example, in 2005, the London-based ad agency Saatchi and Saatchi set out to find a way of reaching people in their teen years and early 20s. It did this by creating its own all-woman hip-hop group, making them employees of the agency, and offering their services to advertisers as a sort of human billboard. The client got to brand the group and have its products seen or used or worn on stage and in videos, and—for a few dollars more—mentioned in the song lyrics. TV marketing guru Cynthia Turner wrote:

> The band made its first appearance last evening at Saatchi & Saatchi offices, and unless you knew any better, you'd never

know it was a marketing device. The agency calls this Branded Entertainment, and finds masking advertising within entertainment is a better way to reach this tough young demo. Also coming . . . commissioned entertainment for other media including TV, film, cell phones, and video games.

The Saatchi and Saatchi idea builds on an even older record business warhorse, the made-to-order pop star. It dates back at least to the days of *American Bandstand*, when producers would take kids off the street and out of the schools and turn them into stars. Bob Marcucci was the acknowledged expert during the 1950s and early 1960s, the inspiration for the 1980 film *The Idolmaker*. His first project along these lines had taken trumpet prodigy Francis Avallone and turned him into singing teen idol Frankie Avalon. He figured that if he'd done it once, he could do it again, and he did.

Marcucci recounted the experience:

> I decided I needed a star like Presley. Frankie wasn't that star. He didn't have that kind of look. He wasn't in that genre. Ricky Nelson was very hot. Sal Mineo was very hot. I did a search throughout the country. Big search. I had disc jockeys do promotions. I asked for people to send me pictures. But I couldn't find him. . . . One day, I'm driving home, and I go past the street where my best friend lives and there is a big . . . police ambulance in front of my friend's house. Turns out the ambulance was for the house next door, and out walks Fabian. He had the look. I went up to my friend and asked him if he knew whether that guy could sing. My friend said he had no idea.

It turned out the ambulance was for the guy's father. The guy, Fabiano Forte, picked up the story: "The strategy was for me to be a male teen performer. . . . They said, 'You're going to have a pompadour, and . . . you're going to dress in a certain shirt and pants.' . . . Bob would say, 'Move this way, move that way,' until it became second nature." Fabian had never even thought about being a performer until Marcucci approached him. He was molded in Marcucci's musical image.

Thus the prefabricated pop star became something of an insti-
tution. Reviled by people who still think popular music should
have some integrity and credibility (predominantly musicians, critics, and serious fans), the manufactured performer remains a fix-
ture on the pop music landscape.

As prevalent, the crossover pop star continues to have enormous appeal, and with current technology—from television to the
Internet—and a little luck is even easier to manufacture. Marcucci
had his finger on this particular pulse as well, when he mentioned
actor-turned-singer Sal Mineo. An actor who can sing, a singer
who can act, or an actor who can carry a tune well enough that
studio wizardry like the autotuner (which takes out-of-tune vocals
and puts them into key electronically) has a big advantage over a
person who only acts or sings, as working in several markets can
have a synergistic effect on his or her career. Several 1950s actors
like Ed "Kookie" Byrnes had their one hit record. And the *Mickey
Mouse Club* spun off TV stars from Annette Funicello to Christina
Aguilera. Not to mention the media phenomena that are Jessica
and Ashlee Simpson—the latter of whom was embarrassed in
front of a live, national TV audience when she tried to lip synch
to the wrong track on *Saturday Night Live*. Oddly, it didn't seem
to hurt her career too much—being the butt of jokes kept her in
the spotlight. Her sister stayed there as much due to her talent
(and other assets), as to her tabloid-worthy exploits and relationships. The more media they can hit, the more marketable they
seem to become.

Actors who can sing became extremely important to both television and records as the rock era took hold. With the success of
the Beatles in 1964, both on records and in the movies, and especially with the ratings they drew on *The Ed Sullivan Show*, naturally TV sought to bring them to their audience in an effort to
garner those kinds of ratings on a regular basis. When the Beatles wouldn't commit to doing a television show of their own, TV
producer Bob Rafelson took a page from Marcucci's playbook:
he recruited four young actors who could sing and turned them

into the Monkees. Rafelson then enlisted music publisher Don Kirshner to give the band a musical identity. Paired with some of the best songwriters of the day (Neil Diamond, Carol King, Jerry Goffin, etc.), the actors became a pop phenomenon almost on par with the band they emulated.

This led the producers of an animated series based on the long-running popular comic book *Archie* to call on Kirshner to supply music for the cartoon's fictional teens. The Archies revealed something that independent rock and roll knew but the corporations were still clueless about: 8- to 11-year-olds liked popular music.

Although the musicians who played and sung as the Archies were not kids themselves, they definitely appealed to kids. Their song "Sugar, Sugar" sold 3 million copies, and *Billboard* named it the #1 single of 1969. Not bad, considering "real" groups like the Beatles, the Rolling Stones, and the Temptations all topped the charts that year, too. Not bad, also, for a group that didn't actually exist.

This led to an entire movement in popular music geared toward the demographic that has come to be called the "tweens": 8- to 12-year-olds. Its songs became known as "bubblegum music," because they were a favorite confection of the tween audience and because they were sweet and sticky and ultimately insubstantial. Many of the bubblegum bands originated on television shows—the Partridge Family, the Banana Splits, and Lancelot Link, a band made up of lip-synching chimpanzees (Ashlee Simpson, anyone?). Of course, there were real studio performers behind them. While it didn't exactly rule the charts, bubblegum had a substantial sales impact and made people like Artie Ripp, whose Kama Sutra records (despite the—*ahem*—adult connotations of its name) sold millions of singles to kids through the late 1960s and early 1970s.

"The incredible thing is," noted Artie Ripp, "the majors at the time—Columbia, RCA, Decca—were not in the business of selling music by kids to kids. The independent guys, like [Ripp's mentor] George [Goldner], discovered kids actually had creative value. And what's more, you could put that value on record."

Bubblegum also had built-in promotion that could completely change the labels' relationship with radio. Television made this music popular, and radio actually had to come to the record companies for it because people wanted to hear it.

By the 1980s, this relationship became more codified, albeit more subtle. The performers got on TV and became popular. The 1981 advent of MTV certainly accelerated this process. One of the biggest stars to spring forth from MTV's copious navel was Madonna, who promoted an image at the time that was safe enough for TV yet sleazy enough to make parents of young women look twice before their girls went off to school. This became the way, the Zen of pop star development.

Nowhere was this effect more evident than with the *New Mickey Mouse Club*, which turned out two of the hottest female performers in the record business, Christina Aguilera and Britney Spears. Both bounce around between a bad-girl image, a stab at "artistic integrity," and even occasional moments of quasi-humanity (Britney posing naked and pregnant). The teen idol had transformed.

In the wake of the success of young hip-hop groups (some called them "bubblegum soul") like New Edition (Bobby Brown's first recording group), came the pop phenomenon New Kids on the Block. Produced by Maurice Starr, who had also done the honors on the New Edition albums, and managed by Johnny Wright, between 1986 and 1994 the band managed to land two chart-topping albums and three #1 singles, selling millions of records.

This impressed Lou Pearlman, who took note of the group when he booked them a private jet through his company. Amazed at what looked like a billion-dollar business built around the New Kids on the Block, Pearlman called his cousin Art Garfunkel to confirm it. "Artie told me, 'You're in business; you like music. You should do something like that.' So, as a weekend goof, we decided to do a little audition, and one thing led to another."

The main thing it led to was a group of Orlando kids he dubbed the Backstreet Boys. Breaking them in Europe before unleashing them on America, Pearlman discovered the formula alchemists had been searching for since time immemorial—he turned dross into gold . . . and platinum. Continuing to draw from this Orlando talent pool, many members of which had performed at the theme parks (Justin Timberlake of the Pearlman creation *NSYNC had once played Frankenstein's monster in the Monster Revue at Universal Studios theme park) and—like Spears and Aguilera—in Disney properties like *The New Mickey Mouse Club*, Pearlman's Trans Continental Entertainment became a teen pop factory, and remains one as of this writing.

"The *Mickey Mouse Club* was a big source for a lot of big things," Pearlman said, "and we're going to help keep cultivating talent. . . . A lot of people want to be singers but can't without the right help." Again, Pearlman recognized the advantage of momentum: keeping something rolling takes a lot less effort than getting something rolling. By using former *Mickey Mouse Club* stars, he already had traction and recognition among the target demographic. It cost less to realize more.

Pearlman has fallen onto a basic, even open secret that Marcucci, Ripp, Kirshner, and so many others have known but guarded: teen pop idols will not go away, at least, as Pearlman is often quoted as saying, "until God stops making little girls. . . . These kids, they're fanatics. We don't have any fans. We have fanatics. They'll buy anything that has to do with the band or their picture on it. And they have loyalty. If they love somebody, they'll stay with them."

The idol phenomenon took on a new dimension in 2001, however. A former Chrysalis Records A&R man and artist manager named Simon Fuller took the concept out of the exclusive purview of teens, with the ITV show *Pop Idol* in the UK. The show, a riff on the old talent-show formula that dates back at least to the *Major Bowles Amateur Hour* in the 1930s, had singers competing for a recording contract. It became such a phenomenon that

Fox TV signed it and Fuller to duplicate the show (and hopefully the success) in the U.S. *American Idol* debuted in 2002, and became every inch the spectacle that it was in England, making a pop culture hero of the "nasty" judge, Simon Cowell. Nearly 35 million people tuned in for the premier season's finale, more than had watched the Oscars.

"*American Idol* amounts to much more than the aggregated neediness of its most eager participants," Simon Dumenco observed in *The New Yorker*.

> As a mass phenomenon it suggests multiple, intertwined orders of psychopathology: The culture at large gorging on hordes of fresh "talent." A populace parodying the idea of democracy by choosing exactly the entertainment it wants (and deserves). And, perhaps most pointedly, the fame factory engaging in a sort of ritualized cycle of binging and purging. . . . The core product itself not only shows every sign of being unstoppable, but may just permanently alter the way the music industry molds and markets talent. . . . *American Idol* . . . harnessed the reality TV genre to show the fast-fading recording industry a new path to riches, turning poorly paid nobodies into overnight pop-cultural icons, with virtually none of the usual behind the scenes primping and preening. Turns out the record industry's star-making machinery becomes entirely irrelevant when you really let the market decide.

For the winners, and even the runners-up, it gave the artists the sort of toehold that television had given the Archies or the *Bandstand* boys or the Monkees or Christina and Britney. Of course, "the record industry's star-making machinery" becoming "entirely irrelevant" is what many in the record business feared. They liked to think they owned the machinery behind the popular star. It has long been their be-all and end-all, with "talent" being disposable fodder for the star-making sausage mills. Letting television create the demand, and worse, letting the people pick their personal performers seemed to violate business as usual—until the actual albums by the performers came out. Then the record companies had to remind the fans who these performers were and why the fans should care, allowing them to pump them through their own star-making channels, albeit more for a refresher than trying to cut a gold record out of whole cloth.

To the disenfranchised music fan, *American Idol* and its ilk represented the final betrayal, the last word in processed pop music. "The industry is only interested in prepackaged goods," said English technologist Gavin Alexander, "there's no room for development or growth if you're an artist."

This leaves fans of more organic music—music that relies on the sinews, brains, and talent of the performers; music that says something to us, that *dares*—feeling like whole-food devotees at a McDonald's every time we turn on a radio or walk into a record store. It also makes Lou Pearlman and Simon Fuller the reigning Ray "McDonald's" Krocs of contemporary pop.

But the boy-band mills and the ready-made pop stars feed many of the major record companies' needs. They ensure a quick profit, bringing up the numbers on the investor's quarterly corporate reports. They keep CDs pumping through the distribution hubs. They keep product on the shelves for the young people who actually deign to purchase records. But, while a major commodity, this type of popular music has proven time and time again not to be a lasting one. For an industry that relies on its catalog, where will the catalog come from 10 years from now?

29

Breaking the Star = Breaking the Bank

ONCE UPON A TIME there was an artist named Bruce. He was signed with great fanfare to a major record company. He had a tremendous reputation up and down the mid-Atlantic Coast, concentrated on his home turf in New Jersey, as an amazing live performer. He got a tremendous buildup by his record company as a brilliant songwriter, the second coming of Bob Dylan (which was strange, as Dylan wasn't—still isn't—quite through with his first coming). His first record sold only 23,000 copies in its first year, and even after he was proclaimed "rock and roll future" both his first and second albums together didn't reach 200,000.

Now, if Bruce were recording today, chances are he wouldn't have gotten a third chance (at least at that record company). In fact, chances are he wouldn't have gotten a second chance and would have been cut loose after the disappointing sales of his first album. He would not have gotten the opportunity to redeem himself with his breakthrough third album (indeed, one of rock's greatest albums, period), *Born to Run*. Yes, that Bruce.

The record company did a lot of work to build Bruce Springsteen into a success, just as record companies did for countless other artists that made it (and didn't) throughout the first three decades of the rock revolution. These days, that work either doesn't get done, or is done before an artist signs to a record company. With a little over a thousand albums accounting for more than 50 percent of all records sold, and perhaps only 150 new ones making money during any given year; with the actual costs involved in the creation, manufacture, and promotion of the recordings; and with companies now responsible to stockholders and business conglomerates for their bottom lines, the stakes have made that kind of long-term effort impossible. Today's artists must create music that will reach a maximum number of people in the minimum amount of time, or scale back the expectations of their careers. Today's record companies have to struggle just to get the music in front of potential fans.

As we've seen, the conventional way to reach an audience has long been radio, to the point that payola has become institutionalized. These days getting an artist onto the charts, depending on what kind of music the artist plays and which chart the record would get on (many get on "genre charts" like R&B/Hip-Hop, Country, or Dance before they get onto the Hot 100) could cost from $100,000 up to a quarter of a million dollars. That's just for one song.

Take the admittedly extreme case of Carly Hennessy, signed by MCA to compete with Britney Spears. Her debut album cost nearly a million dollars to make, and over $1.2 million to promote. After three months, the album had sold fewer than 400 copies.

"We've never been one to spout that major labels no longer practice artist development," wrote *Billboard* columnist Melinda Newman, "it's just that they now limit it to acts that they believe (and hope and pray) can turn into huge moneymakers down the line. And that line is getting shorter and shorter."

Much of the work that used to go into artist development would seem to have fallen to artists' managers or even the artists themselves. "Labels used to thrive on demo deals and development deals but the machine is not what it used to be," noted music business veteran Jack Ponti of the Platform Group. "Managers of any worth or stature also want to see/hear a developed act before they commit."

Of course, while it used to fall to the record company to groom the artist during and after recording the demo, that whole process has fallen to the manager. A developed act in terms of having songs and beginning to develop a following has to be further groomed for success in the mainstream of the record business. This aspect of bringing an artist to the fore makes or breaks both the artist and the manager in the current record business environment.

"I'd say managers do most of the artist development these days, if not all of it," Barry Bergman, president of the Music Managers Forum–US, stated. "It's not that the record companies want a readymade product. They want an artist that can sell tickets, they want an act with a following, they want it on the radio somewhere. There has to be something going on. Or you have to be an act that's selling a lot on your own."

Of course, taking on the task of developing an artist involves enormous potential risks. This was hammered home for me not long ago when it nearly killed a friend of mine, now a former artist manager. One evening, we sat down to drink and enjoy one of his bands at a New York City showcase dive called Arlene's Grocery Store. After his band finished up, we thought about moving on to another, quieter venue to continue our imbibing and talking, when the next band came on. They were brilliant—a group, as it turned out, that included two former members of a gold-record band on a major label that had broken up about six years earlier.

I kidded with my friend that he should see if they had a manager. He took me seriously, approached them, and discovered that although they had this pedigree and had won a radio station's "best unsigned band" contest, they still had no management. It took him six months, but my friend convinced them to let him and his partner do the job.

Now, most managers limit the amount of money they will put into a band. While this investment, like most things in the record business, is recoupable by the manager from the band, most managers just don't have pockets that deep. My friend and his partner put nearly every penny they had into this group, paying for pictures, press kits, CD duplication, studio time, the works. And they actually got the band an offer, not from a major, but from the closest thing in the independent record world to a major—the record company arm of one of the world's largest independent distributors. However, having already recorded for a major, the band regarded this as a step backward. They severed relations with the management company. As far as I know, the legalities are still pending.

In the meantime, my friend lost his wife, his family, and his house. He called me up one evening in the throes of what sounded very much like a heart attack (turned out to be acute angina). He bailed out of the music business and got back into software sales. Last I talked with him, he seemed a lot happier.

One thing that many managers seem to have discovered in this process is that downloading files may not be the bogeyman that they've feared for the past decade. It can actually eliminate the need for the hundreds of thousands or millions of dollars that it traditionally has taken to break an artist. And as music consumers begin to veer away from "hard product," there are ancillary consumables that they crave.

Ed Majewski of Majic Management said:

> The group I am managing are on MySpace. In less than eight months, we have over 13,000 friends, almost 52,000 plays and close to 50,000 views. . . . What I have learned through this is the voice/opinion of the kids out there today. Many, many e-mail me on the page, "How come we can't download your music?" We are on the cusp of saying, "Why not?" This may go against everything that has been believed in the industry thus far, but we all do realize that the game is changing.

So what are artists to do while they are "developing"? Beyond burning the candle at both ends and working a day job while playing at night, how can an artist make a living if not through selling CDs to fans? If some are just going to download and not buy—though, as we've seen, the most avid downloaders are also the biggest paying consumers—how does an artist pick up the slack and shortfall? "Fans cannot download a T-shirt, hoodie, coffee mug, poster, or whatever else you can market," Majewski said.

When we were young, we used to brag about our record collection. For me, before I was 21, 1982, I owned over 1,000 LPs. It was a status symbol. My collection kicked ass! Today, it may be different. It may be "I have this shirt, you don't." I wonder if kids wearing/owning something you can't download may be the new status symbol?

To survive, the record business will have to either get a grip on the new technology and the new ways consumers actually consume music or succumb to artists owning and exploiting their own intellectual property, in essence becoming their own record companies. Then they would outsource the services the record companies traditionally performed, like promotion, publicity, marketing, and hiring experts to do that one thing the record companies allegedly do best—promoting and creating a brand name around an artist. These independent contractors would find the artists' unique selling point and exploit it for the benefit of the artists (and likely the managers who will wind up footing the bills for this service initially), who would reap the kind of financial rewards outlined in chapter 9, obviating the need for the major labels. Some see the failure to develop artists as a symptom of the modern record companies' size and scope. When dealing with business on a macroeconomic level, a lot of the nitty-gritty things that used to happen every day have fallen by the wayside. "Major labels can't afford to do artist development because they can't scale down enough to do so," Ponti said. "The indie model is total artist development but they have no idea that that is what they are actually doing."

Clearly, in a changing business, the big question becomes how to get artists in front of people who might love them, pay to see them, pay for the T-shirts so they can become walking billboards for them, even perhaps buy a copy of the CDs to go with the files they already downloaded. For the 93 percent of recording artists selling less than a thousand copies of any given release, what do they really have to lose by getting themselves in the public eye in any way possible?

Of course, one of the words for this is promotion, and promotion costs money, potentially a lot of it. Especially for artists or managers not able or inclined to do some of the expensive stuff themselves, like building Web sites, putting together and mailing out press kits, and the like.

Beyond that, developing an artist means helping to find the thing that makes recording artists *artists* in the first place, the thing that makes each of them unique, good for more than a few seconds' pleasure; the thing that helps them stand up to repeated listening, inspiring people to go out and buy their art and develop an attachment to it and to them. Very few artists can find this by themselves. In the past mentors, teachers, friends, even competitors aided in this development. In the professional recording and record company world, when demo deals allowed artists to discover elements of this unique voice—to do their own thing and be known for themselves—artists could nurture and communicate those elements that made them special, the thing that made what they did art.

Late soul singer Lou Rawls explained it this way: "People want something that they can put into their hip pocket and say, 'Yeah, this is going to last.' Something I can pull out my pocket two weeks from now and still like it."

Certainly there was, as there is now, a truckload of disposable pop, of performers not up to the task of making a lasting contribution. But at least the environment once offered artists the opportunity to get there and try. Now, often no one will take the chance because the risk is so great.

30

The Video Revolution
Looks Aren't Everything;
They're the Only Thing

JOE JACKSON, one of the performers from the class of '77, became a punk (actually, he called himself a "spiv rocker" back then) out of the conservatory. He went on to have a long and varied career, but as he aged (and lost his hair), he faced the decision of whether he wanted to undergo cosmetic procedures so that he could continue to make pop hits and videos. When he decided "no," he effectively gave up playing rock for money.

He did try one last rock hurrah, signing with Virgin. At the time, pretty nearly every Virgin artist had a video budget—it was one of the label's prime means of promotion. Joe had not made a clip in six years, but Virgin coaxed, cajoled, and cudgeled him into doing a couple.

"He said, 'I don't mind doing music videos if I can give MTV the finger,'" recalled director Marcus Nispel.

How an artist looked was starting to take precedence over how an artist sounded or the quality of an artist's songs. This caused Joe Jackson to, for all intents and purposes, abandon pop:

> Things which used to count, such as being a good composer, player, or singer, are getting lost in the desperate rush to visualize everything. It is now possible to be all of the above and still get nowhere simply by not looking good in a video, or, worse still, not making one.

Jackson put his finger on an attitude that has led to a marked fall in the quality of music. He quit playing rock at one of the peaks of importance for music videos, when the conventional wisdom said you couldn't have a hit without one.

Fortunately, he had his conservatory training to lean on, and he started making composed albums of postmodern "classical" music with rock instrumentation, winning a Grammy for his 1999 *Symphony 1*. The classical albums didn't sell the hundreds of thousands that *Look Sharp* or *Night and Day* sold, but he maintained a career, and he didn't have to do videos.

WHILE IT MIGHT be a chicken-or-egg situation, in 1981 only 23 percent of the singles in *Billboard*'s Hot 100 hit singles had accompanying videos. By 1986, that number had risen to 86 percent. By 1989, fully 97 percent of the Hot 100 hits had a video version. The record companies regard music video as essential, and it becomes a huge draw on their assets. Even an inexpensive music video costs thousands of dollars, which, as we've seen, very few records make. The ideal recording artist, from a music video standpoint, is an underwear model with a great voice, but some very talented musicians just aren't very attractive. Some just look awkward. Would Janis Joplin or Joe Cocker even stand a chance in today's marketplace? Would anyone download their clips to watch on their video iPod?

"I have two bands that I'm managing now that would have been signed four years ago," manager Larry Mazer complained in 1990, "Now, nobody will commit. The labels tell me they won't get on MTV."

"There's a band from Chicago called Rebels Without Applause that I did shows with when I lived in the Midwest," said Jason Lekberg of the band Wraith.

> Mudvayne, SOiL, and many of the bands that got signed from the Midwest opened for them yet they never got a deal. Greg, the singer, and I talked about it and he didn't really go into too much

detail, but I know they had meetings with a few labels. The problem is, he's a very large black man. Unfortunately, I think the shallow industry couldn't see past it.

Conversely, being videogenic has made many careers. Grace Jones was a model before taking the mic. Madonna became the original video diva, her career kicking off and growing up alongside MTV and the "video revolution"; her videogenic appearance has allowed her to slip in and out of personas. Paula Abdul was a dancer and choreographer before releasing a slew of hit records.

Some years back, on the strength of her kinetic video personality, Abdul was hired to do a commercial for Diet Pepsi. When the ad came on the radio one afternoon as we were driving, my wife asked me, "What is that on her voice?"

"What is what?"

"Her voice. It never sounds natural."

"Ah, that's called gated reverb. It gives her voice more presence in the mix."

"In other words, she really can't sing."

"Well, yeah."

"Then why is she such a big star?"

The answer, of course, is that she looked so good on MTV, and was packaged so well.

Some artists took this audio manipulation to the extreme. The actual voice of the dance groups C&C Music Factory and Black Box was Martha Wash, one of the Two Tons of Fun/Weather Girls and a studio vocalist of some note. Although Wash's soulful alto rattled the walls of dance halls and rang out of radios everywhere, commanding "Everybody Dance Now," the slimmer Zelma Davis lip-synched the lines in the group's videos.

Milli Vanilli was a group made for video in the same way that the Monkees were made for TV. The main difference is that all of the members of the Monkees could, to one degree or another, sing. After Milli Vanilli won a Grammy Award for Best New Artist in 1990, it was revealed that neither of the two fronting members of the group had that skill. They were forced to give the award back. The scandal eventually drove one member of the duo to suicide.

This obsession with appearance is not solely an issue in popular music. Opera singer Deborah Voigt claimed that she was dismissed from a production at the Royal Opera House in London because of her weight. Conversely, young, photogenic Scottish violinist Nicola Benedetti got a one-million-pound contract from venerable classical label Deutsche Grammophon at the age of 17. Said Welsh broadcaster and singer Beverley Humphries:

> I'm very uncomfortable with the way that we've gone down the avenue of believing, or being led to believe that physical image is more important than talent. It takes years of working on your instrument to become a great musician. The danger of singers and musicians being taken up because they look good—and making them an immediate, overnight success—is that it demeans and reduces the true greatness of performers.

The reality is that in the past two decades, video has become a major part of the promotion and artist development process. "We want to break new acts and sustain important artists," noted MTV's COO and president Michael J. Wolf in 2005. "MTV is a juggernaut. MTV today is different from MTV 36 months ago."

Despite this ever-changing landscape, MTV has consistently helped to sell records. In its early days, it built the careers of unknowns like Duran Duran, Madonna, and Cyndi Lauper. During the days of the "Buzz Bin" in the early 1990s, careers of acts like Jane's Addiction and the Red Hot Chili Peppers were made by MTV. Temple of the Dog sold over a million copies of its album two years after its release, due to delayed video exposure. The band's record company attributed most of the album's success to MTV. Bottom line—an artist that can look and sound compelling on MTV will sell records.

Note the artist does not necessarily need to look *good*, just compelling in one way or another. No one would call Kid Rock one of the beautiful people, but he has a persona that translates very well into video. Billy Joel's older clips and even Elton John's more recent videos remain stalwarts on VH-1, MTV's sister channel, capitalizing on their long careers, and established personas.

However, there came a time when videos alone could not bring in the increased ratings MTV needed to sustain the business. So the channel split into several channels. Now there's the original MTV, which has become more of a lifestyle channel than a music channel. There's the aforementioned VH-1, which skews toward the aging original audience of MTV, as MTV still stays targeted at teens and tweens. MTV-2 picked up the musical slack. In all, many cable and/or satellite systems have half a dozen music channels associated with MTV, and several independent, more specialized video outlets like Fuse, CMT, and Much Music. MTV may no longer directly stand for Music Television, but a dozen other channels continue to rely on videos for their core programming, and the record companies continue to fund the creation of the clips that feed them.

As MTV became the "juggernaut" Wolf describes, if an act had any chance of achieving any kind of buzz, it had to have a video. After payola, this is one of the most expensive lines on most artists' ledgers, including indie artists. The budgets of the videos tend to reflect their importance in the artist's overall financial picture, a cost-to-reward ratio that, if not necessarily scientific, is the result of experienced intuition on the part of the record company. An independently distributed heavy metal act might have a budget of between $2,500 and $6,000 to spend on a video. A video for a large-budget album or major-selling artist could still cost upwards of a million dollars, although as the record business has contracted so have the budgets.

In 1981, a major video might have cost $15,000. By 1984, as MTV became a proven selling tool and the stakes got higher, so did the video budgets, which averaged out at about $50,000–$60,000. Four years later, that range had risen another $10,000, and through the 1990s, that generally fell in the $60,000–$80,000 range. These days, a video for a major record company might run anywhere from $10,000 to $250,000; the average is around $40,000.

This cut in available funds is a circumstance that some directors find very frustrating. "You do music videos, you deal with certain budgets," Nispel said. "Usually they don't allow you, at least the budgets that I'm still having, to go over two days of shooting."

Of course, some artists don't need video exposure, feel they don't benefit from video exposure, or have record companies who choose to limit the expense of video exposure. "Certain artists with less of a video audience," said video producer Lara Schwartz, "like Clapton or BB King, make less videos and for a lot less money than other pop artists who rely heavily on videos, such as Madonna or Kanye West or Britney Spears."

As with so many recordings, many artists are taking the do-it-yourself route for video as well. One of the pioneers of this concept (and music video in general) was Todd Rundgren (him again?), who helped develop desktop video editing and effects in the early 1990s. His video for "I Can't Change Myself" was "all done on desktop computers; it wasn't done with any expensive mainframe equipment," he said. "As a matter of fact, I bought all the equipment and produced the piece within what would have been a relatively slim video budget. This kind of stuff can be done by anyone if you have the perspicacity to undertake such a thing."

A little less than a decade later, Pete Townshend was just amazed by what a person could accomplish with a digital camera and a desktop computer. "From now on the whole thing is going to be movies," he said.

> Music is going to disappear. Everybody is going to become a filmmaker. You know, anybody that's got an iMac, they're away! They're going to be making movies. A musician today has to be so visually oriented. So, there's going to be an explosion of that. My kid, Joseph, got an iMac for Christmas. He's ten. He made his first proper skateboard movie, just like the ones that come out of Seattle. He spent an afternoon doing it with a friend.

By capturing video directly to the hard drive of a laptop, and using the artist's apartment as a set, director Jacob Rosenberg created a professionally crewed video for L.A. singer/songwriter john gold to promote his DIY album *the eastside shake* and the lead track "Cactusflower." Using a borrowed Panavision camera (ostensibly so they could demonstrate the viability of recording direct to computer), professional lighting, and ultimately, special effects, they made a video that would not seem out of place on MTV for literally next to nothing.

While the DIY videos might not get on MTV, much like the DIY records, that's sort of the point. They have a different target. The videos do get used in clubs, on local channels, even in clothing stores. Nor are they free. The equipment costs money. If you don't have to necessarily hire a crew (e.g., you have friends shoot the video, take care of the lighting, etc.), you at least have to feed them. Then there's the time it takes to do a DIY production, a heavy investment, although not directly a monetary one.

If the tightening of radio had started to commoditize music, MTV finished the job. "Videos are nothing but commercials," said Nispel. "The only difference is you have a product that sings and dances if you're lucky."

"You're making a three-minute marketing tool," agreed a vice president of video at Warner Brothers Records. "It's like designing an album cover. We're not making *Gone with the Wind*."

However, as the Internet has started to change the average person's access to any kind of music he or she can imagine, and as the bandwidth constraints become less and less of an issue in most of the industrialized world, visualized music has found a second life. Internet sites like Launch, You Tube, and AOL, to name some of the largest among dozens—perhaps hundreds—that stream music videos on demand, have become an exceedingly important part of the video promotion mix. Add to that the advent of the video iPod, Pocket PCs with the power to play videos, and even cell phones with video capacity, and people have begun to pay $1.99 or more to download their favorites. Townshend seems to have once again predicted the future—everything is movies.

In fall 2005 iTunes began selling music videos, and by mid-December 2005, MTV had arranged with Microsoft to integrate a new service into the popular Windows Media Player that would offer downloads of music and videos. Thanks to the technology that the record business spent so much time resisting, what once was a promotional expense has become a potential source of revenue. Provided anyone wants to pay to see it.

31

Contacts and Contracts

Why an Artist Can Go Gold One Day and Be Flipping Burgers the Next

"TODAY I WANT to talk about piracy and music," Courtney Love told the industry-ites, artists, and computer music gurus at the Digital Hollywood Online Entertainment Conference (ironically, held in New York City).

> What is piracy? Piracy is the act of stealing an artist's work without any intention of paying for it. I'm not talking about Napster-type software. I'm talking about major label recording contracts.
>
> Artists want to believe that we can make lots of money if we're successful. But there are hundreds of stories about artists in their 60s and 70s who are broke because they never made a dime from their hit records. And real success is still a long shot for new artists today.

Hank Shocklee had similar things to say. The producer of albums like Public Enemy's *It Takes a Nation of Millions to Hold Us Back*, Shocklee took a position as the senior VP of A&R for MCA Records. Then after a few years he left the post:

> I got tired of signing these kids, watching them make the record, then start taking limousines and stuff on the record company's dime, forgetting that it was getting billed back to them out of their royalties. Six months later, they'd be sitting in my office saying, "Yo, what the fuck is up with this? My record went gold and I'm back flipping burgers."

It all comes down to the contract, the holy grail of so many unsigned musicians. Many younger, less experienced artists get slammed here. Shocklee himself recalled getting grossly underpaid by the standards of the day for his first production. But it was a short-term contract, and he could regard it as a learning experience in his career. A recording artist's contract can last seven years or longer, which doesn't allow for much of a learning curve if the artist expects to earn something from recording, even a name.

"One has to be very careful in contractual arrangements," warned veteran music business attorney Jeffrey Jacobson. "Little provisions like mechanical royalties [the money paid to songwriters for every song on every album sold] not being subject to recoupment [of advances] can result in significant income to the artist. Cautions in these seemingly minor provisions can enable the debut artist with sales to eat."

"Signing isn't trivial," added English music business visionary Rob Cumberland. "It can tie up your songs, your recordings, and your band (or you) for years if you get it wrong."

For most artists, getting offered a contract is like a ballplayer making it into the big leagues. It tells artists that after however many years of struggling, honing their craft, finding their voice, someone wants to help them get their art to the masses, someone with the proven ability to do so.

What might not occur to the artist is that the only reason for a record company to sign an artist, from the days of Enrico Caruso, the first artist to demand and receive royalties in the early 1900s, until noon tomorrow, is that the record company is convinced it can make a profit. Record companies, like art galleries, are not in business for the art. For them, a contract has to make sense from a financial standpoint. Since many artists don't think in terms of a financial standpoint, the contract is a means to an end. Sometimes, their end.

The following contract came into my possession along with a box of other legal papers when I did research for another project.

It has haunted the artists who signed it for the rest of their careers. While we've discussed the economics of being a recording artist, here we're going to get down and funky, digging into the potential practical pitfalls and pratfalls inherent in signing a recording contract. I'm going to walk you through some of the contract's most notable elements, both common and unusual. These pieces of paper and ink can, as Jacobson noted, determine whether artists get to develop their art, reputation, and bank accounts.

When I first went through the specific document we'll be looking at, I couldn't believe the terms. I sent it to Jacobson just to confirm that it was as bad as I thought it was. He read it over and told me, "This is the Steven King novel of recording contracts. It made the small hairs on the back of my neck stand up it was so scary."

The names, of course, will be changed, but the essence will be in there. Suffice to say, the artists that signed it were huge, and despite not having played together for a while, they continue to enjoy a massive following. It's one of those groups that some radio station somewhere will have on the air every moment of every day. Yes, it's an older contract, and today a record company might not be able to get away with a lot of the terms, at least not all of them in a single document. But it might, for two reasons: the artist might sign without benefit of legal counsel (a foolish move under the best of circumstances), or the artist might just not care so long as a record comes out (a shortsighted move, but one many artists make).

Even getting legal counsel sometimes isn't enough. Cumberland reminded the artists who would learn from the past that "your lawyer doesn't sign the contract, you do. Your lawyer doesn't sit at home for seven years while a bad contract runs out [or as we'll see in this case, doesn't run out], you do. Your lawyer doesn't work for nothing if he gets it wrong, you do."

As with so many music business contracts, the artists and record company agreed to and signed this one in California. In answer to the days of the motion picture studio system, when the major movie companies put actors under contract and kept use of their services forever at a pittance compared to what they made the studio when they became stars, California instituted a statute saying that a personal service contract (like a recording or movie studio contract) can last no longer than seven years. However, this contract devised a way of circumventing that law, by starting with the phrase, "The Artists agree to record for the record company a minimum number (as hereinafter set forth) of masters (as hereinafter defined) embodying performances by the Artists . . . in each year of the term hereof."

By the definition of the contract (found some 22 pages later) a "master" is five and a half minutes of recording, basically the maximum that would fit on a 45 rpm single, an anachronism that, like so many provisions in contemporary contracts, remains part of the boilerplate. According to the terms of the contract (this located 16 pages after the referring paragraph), the artists had to put out:

➤ 12 masters a year for the first two years, for which they received the princely sum of $100 each as an advance royalty.
➤ 24 masters a year for the next two years, this time for $200 each.
➤ 24 masters a year for the next two years at $400 each.
➤ "such additional number of masters (not to exceed ten (10)) as the record company may elect upon written notice to the artist no later than three (3) months from the end of each year in which such election is made by the record company, and such additional number of masters shall increase the minimum number of masters as required."

Now, if you do the math on this, the artist must record between 120 and 180 masters, depending on if the record company notifies them for the extra 10, to satisfy this provision of the contract. While pretty onerous in its own right, it gets even more interesting about seven pages on, under the heading of "Failure to Perform": "The record company, in addition to all other rights and remedies available to it, shall have the absolute right in its sole discretion to extend the then current year and/or the term of this agreement until such failure to perform is so corrected."

Therefore, if the artists don't record and release those 120–180 songs in the course of six years (an average, then, of 20–30 songs a year), the clock stops. A contract that legally cannot run for more than seven years can go on until doomsday.

Nor does it matter *why* they could not record:

> The cause of such failure, whether caused by sickness of or accident to the Artists or any of them or due to any delay or impossibility or commercial impracticability because of any act of God, fire, earthquake, strike, civil commotion, act of any government or any order, regulation, ruling or any action of any labor union or association of artists affecting the Artists, the record company or all or any portion of the phonograph record industry generally or specifically, shall not affect the applicability of this Agreement.

So, in legal terms, the contract could go on *beyond* doomsday. Like so many things in this contract, the provision does not cut both ways. While the record company could obligate the artists to record as many as 180 masters,

> nothing contained in this agreement shall obligate the record company to record the minimum number of sides or masters specified herein or to make or sell records manufactured from such masters. The record company shall fulfill its entire obligation as to unrecorded masters by paying the Artists the amount specified under the terms of this agreement for such masters, even if such masters are never recorded.

In other words, if it wants to cut the artists loose, the record company has to pay the $100, $200, and $400 per master for which it contracted, which amounts to $31,200. Then buh-bye.

"It's the story of the recording industry over the past 100 years," Cumberland said. "Labels can't make commitments to their artists, but the artists make exclusive commitments to the labels."

Even if they do record, "all material recorded by the Artists shall be selected mutually by the record company and the Artists, and all masters shall be subject to the record company's approval as commercially satisfactory." So if the record company doesn't think it can sell the record, the company doesn't have to press it and it doesn't count as one of the contracted masters.

Of course, the artists have to pay to make the record, albeit not directly:

> All recording costs incurred by the record company under this Agreement with respect to masters as to which royalties are payable (or the proportionate share of costs allocable with respect to masters embodying the performance of the Artists hereunder and the performance of other artist or artists) shall be charged against royalties, payable hereunder. All advance payments made to the Artists by the record company under this Agreement shall also be charged against royalties hereunder."

So, as we've already seen, any costs the artists incur in making their "masters" get charged back against the artists at the rate of the royalty.

The document I have, bad as it seems, is actually a renegotiated contract made after the artists became a mighty force in popular music. This made deciding the royalty rate a somewhat contentious issue. What the parties ultimately agreed to is actually pretty interesting. The earlier contract had had a sliding scale, and all music recorded before the new contract was signed and for a year afterward still fell on that scale, which started at 10.5 percent and went to 12 percent. However, all music that was recorded after that time gave the artists "a royalty of twenty percent (20%) with respect to so-called singles and a royalty rate of eighteen percent (18%) on albums, except the royalty rate on sales of albums subsequent to [the theoretical expiration date of the contract] shall be twenty percent (20%)." Of course, albums that combined music recorded before the agreement accrued royalties at the old rate of 10.5–12 percent. Since the band broke up not too long after the 20 percent rate kicked in, they didn't get to enjoy that greater rate for very long.

Now, one of the things I found most interesting about this contract is that it paid the royalty based on 100 percent. Back in the glass-and-lacquer days, only 90 percent of any given shipment actually arrived in sellable condition, so royalties were generally calculated based on 90 percent of sales. Long after the glass and lacquer disappeared from the recording scene, and even into the days of plastic-coated aluminum (i.e., CDs), that 90 percent figure continues to appear in contracts. So that 100 percent seemed like a bright spot in an overwhelmingly dismal contract until I read a few words further. Where most contracts say that they pay based on the domestic *gross* sales, this one paid on domestic *net* sales.

Now, in Hollywood, they have a phrase for percentage points paid on the net. They call them "monkey points," because you'd have to be a monkey to take them. A careful accountant can make sure nearly any but the most profitable projects doesn't show a net profit.

Beyond this, there is a grocery list of things on which the record company will not pay royalties:

➤ "No royalties both for records and publishing shall be payable on sales of promotional records."
➤ "No royalties, both for records and publishing, will be paid by the record company on records given to distributors in the ratios of the normal industry practice on one hundred fifty (150) 'free' records with every five hundred (500) records purchased."
➤ "No royalties . . . shall be payable with respect to records given away or furnished for promotional purposes on a nonprofit basis to disc jockeys, radio and television stations

and networks, motion picture companies, distributors, reviewers, customers, and others."

➤ "No royalty shall be payable with respect to records given to members of record clubs as bonus or free records as a result of joining clubs and/or purchasing a required number of records."

This last one is particularly telling. One of the first things most artists do when they have the clout to renegotiate their contracts is to get that clause out of there. For example, Hootie and the Blowfish's major label debut *Cracked Rear View* sold 16 million copies or so. They never made a cent from at least three million of them that were sold through record clubs because they had this clause in their contract. It was removed before they released their sophomore effort.

Nor does the artist always get a full royalty:

As to sales of prerecorded magnetic tapes . . . the royalty payable to the Artist shall be one-half (1/2) of the royalty rate applicable in the respective period to sales of phonograph records. . . . As to any device utilizing a new medium of sound and/or sight and sound reproduction, the royalty payable the Artists shall be computed in the manner hereinabove provided for prerecorded magnetic tapes.

Now, when they drew up this contract, the compact disc still had not come to market. That would make the CD "a new medium of sound and/or sight and sound reproduction." The artists in question continue to sell hundreds of thousands, or even millions of CDs a year. While they have since made concessions, giving up certain rights that the company let them retain and renegotiated that point, for quite some time they received half royalties on CDs.

The 50 percent royalty also applies to "all sales outside the United States, its territories and possessions, and Canada." This, too, is not an unusual clause.

Another common clause involves who owns the actual recordings, or masters:

All recordings made by the Artists or any of them during the term hereof . . . and the copyrights and/or copyright renewal rights therein and thereto shall be entirely the property or the record company, free and clear of any claims of the Artists. . . . The record company shall have exclusive and perpetual right throughout the world to edit, cut and otherwise control such masters and recordings and performances and may manufacture, advertise, sell, lease, license, or otherwise exploit the same.

Some artists manage to hold onto their masters and lease them to the record company—Frank Zappa (and his estate) and David Bowie notably retain these rights.

Some of the conditions of the contract are almost laughable. For example, under the heading of "Advertising": "The rights granted under this section shall include any professional name by which the Artists are or may be known and shall allow the record company to fictionalize any biographical material to the extent that the record company so desires." The artist is a mutant Venusian come to Earth to make it safe for sound.

However, most of this contract is no laughing matter, particularly this passage:

Any and all original musical compositions, and original arrangements of musical compositions in the public domain, including the title, words, and music of such compositions authored, co-authored, composed, or co-composed by the Artists or any of them . . . hereinafter shall be the subject of a copyright and shall be assigned by the Artists and/or any publishing affiliate of the Artists or any of them to any publishing company or companies designated by the record company, with statutory fees applying.

What just happened in that paragraph is that the artists gave away their publishing rights. The relationship between the composer and the publisher generally calls for a 50/50 split of the revenues. Mechanical royalties get paid directly to the publisher (in this case, the record company pays mechanical royalties over to its publishing division) and the publisher is responsible for paying the songwriter it represents. The performance royalty organizations (ASCAP, BMI, and SESAC in the United States) pay equal amounts to the publishing company and the composer. However, many composers retain all or a portion of their publishing, cutting out the outside publisher, as an added stream of income. They can have a publisher administer the songs through a subpublishing deal that earns the subpublisher a cut of the publishing in exchange for doing all the paperwork, collecting foreign royalties, and trying to exploit the copyrights. After signing this contract, these artists no longer had that option.

Again, this is not an uncommon ploy for record companies, especially independent ones, to attempt. In the same way that the songwriter might want to form her own publishing company to get both the songwriter's share *and* the publisher's share of the royalties, the record company wants to hold onto the stream of potential income these rights offer:

> All recording costs incurred by the record company under this agreement with respect to masters to which royalties are payable . . . shall be charged against royalties, payable hereunder. All advance payments made to the Artists by the record company under this Agreement shall also be charged against the royalties payable hereunder.

These royalties include the mechanical publishing royalties that Jacobson mentioned earlier, so the move to retain the publishing covers the record company's financial assets against the liabilities of records that sell too little to recoup on their own.

Sometimes even the extra stream of revenue from the publishing royalties against the advance is not enough, for either party. Certain well-established bands have tried to create a new model for the relationship between the record company and the artist, with EMI leading the way for the record companies. As of this writing, EMI's most recent deal was with the hard rock band

Korn. The artists received a $25 million advance, far larger than most. More than just a piece of the publishing, this large advance gives EMI's Virgin Records imprint a 30 percent stake in everything Korn makes—touring, licensing, merchandising, publishing, endorsements, the works—over the course of two albums and two tours. *Billboard* estimated that it would take $84 million in gross profits for the record company to break even.

Dave Marsh, however, wasn't so sure EMI got a bad deal:

> Korn not only loses economic independence, its revenue streams are further compromised by the specter of what's known as cross-collateralization—the lumping together of all an artist's royalty income on a statement. Imagine that Korn's last album on the deal sells so few copies that the band is now $3 million in the red on its record royalties. But its worldwide concert tour associated with the record has a profit of $6 million. Of that, the record company is entitled to something more than 25 percent, that is, at least $1.5 million. Doesn't the $3 million in record royalties come out of the $6 million, too? (Why else would the label make this deal?) $3 million plus $1.5 million is $4.5 million, plus a bit more—that is, the company keeps almost all the money from the tour plus all the money from the record sales. . . . It's even a good deal for Korn, presuming they break up quickly enough.

While the stakes are higher, it bears a striking resemblance to the reason the record company in our contract wanted to maintain control of the artists' publishing.

Pretty much the polar opposite of this strategy is the one used by label Fake Science. With 15 bands on its roster, this Oakland, California–based company offers artists production, engineering, and marketing. The artists get 60 percent of the revenue from all songs downloaded from the Fake Science Web site, and keep the rights to all their material, both the songs and the recordings that Fake Science funded. Basically, the label puts the band at no financial or creative risk. That said, no one involved—not the artists or the label's owners—seems to have given up his or her day job.

But then, Fake Science has the luxury of their day jobs. To them, the label is a flyer, something they do because they can, a hobby, even. Virgin Records is a full-time record company, and as such needs to make a profit by selling records and any other way it can within its purview. You see, unlike with so many of the "dirty little secrets" we've uprooted, the reason why the record company would want to foist a contract like this onto its artists should not seem mysterious. When only 5 percent of the records released make a profit, the record company needs every edge it can get. However, the music business, as we saw right up front, begins with the artist. Without the artist, why make records in the first place? And if it all begins with the artist, doesn't it make sense to look after and develop that investment? The contract is a crapshoot. The artist can be eternal.

Conclusion

The Bilious Stew of the Music Business at the Turn of the Millennium—and Hope for Deliverance

"THE RECORD industry has come back, bigger and better than ever. . . . It has been on the verge of disaster . . . but each time the sobbing requiems were premature." It sounds like something someone could have written in 1983 or the early 1970s, or even last week, but actually it comes from a *New York Times* article circa 1942. People have predicted the death of the record business since its formation. And it's been true every time. The music business consistently demonstrates the resilience of Mr. Bill or Gumby—you can crush it, reshape it, twist it, but somehow it always manages to survive, largely due to one truism: music is not going away. People will always want music, and they will get it, whether it involves commerce or not.

The record business is *not* the music business. People made money with music thousands of years before Edison conceived of storing sound, and will continue to make money with music thousands of years hence, until the concept of money itself becomes quaint (come the grand and glorious revolution). And considerably more will make music just for the sheer pleasure of it, as they've done pretty much since humankind could call itself that. It bears repeating: music is one of the hallmarks of humanity.

I suspect, however, that until the revolution comes and money becomes irrelevant, people will continue earning money by making and marketing music, one way or another. In the short term, this will require making music better or marketing oneself better or just, for whatever reason, being more appealing to a wider audience. The good news for musicians and audiences is that the potential for more people to make a living appealing to their own niche is greater now than at any time before. Thanks largely to the rise of communications technologies that allow instant access to information from anywhere on the planet, we grow closer and closer to Marshall McLuhan's "global village" with every passing day. Musicians and marketing people are beginning to use these resources to reach their audiences, thinking locally, but also thinking globally. With over six billion people on the planet, finding 60,000 or 600,000 or even six million who like a particular sound shouldn't be that hard. However, as the technology exists today, audiences still have to meet them halfway.

This is a problem, as audiences have become spoiled. In this era of fast food, instant access, and media on demand, people have gotten used to having music dropped into their lap by radio, MTV, friends' recommendations, etc. Musicians and marketers need to figure out ways to painlessly bring the music to this audience that don't involve the traditional mass methods of dissemination that have simply stopped working efficiently. The process has already begun, and I expect it to snowball as more and more people invent newer and better methods for getting music to the people who need to hear it.

More years ago than I care to think about, my buddy and colleague Dave Sprague told me that rock was dead in the same sense that jazz was dead: both have broken off into offshoots and mutations. It's all a bunch of hybrid styles or substyles—punk rock, emo, jam band rock, electronica rock, death metal, heavy metal, hard rock, folk rock, Lilith rock, etc., etc., ad nauseum. In the process, the focus and the music may have improved, but the artists creating it have limited their audiences. You can't generally consider it a mass media anymore, because there's neither a monolithic jazz audience nor a monolithic rock audience anymore. It's part of the process of the music developing, of feeling itself as an art rather than a product. Being better than everything else on the charts doesn't matter when it comes to art. The charts deal in commerce, not quality. They don't measure what sounds the best (as if such a thing were possible), but what *sells* the best.

So, as I stated in the introduction, probably more great music—music that *you* will like—is available today than at any other time. Surely *something* released among the over 60,000 albums that came out the year before I wrote this will appeal to you, even if you're just one of 50 or 100 people who appreciate it. The difference between now and a quarter century ago is that now the audience has to find the scent, hunt for it, and perhaps even dig a bit. Unfortunately, a business geared around selling millions of a thing to make a profit requires that the thing be easily accessible.

I run into people every day who would love to sell a gazillion records. The hip-hop artists still have an audience they can tap, and, for the time being, enough of a monolith to mass market. And there will always be pop stars who, for whatever reason, incite enough excitement to become mass merchandise. But others have started to become more realistic about the times. With little that can be considered monolithic in music any more, music becomes difficult for the behemoths to market. I think the fact that only 32 albums went platinum in 2005 points to that. With radio cutting back on the amount of music it plays, narrowcasting, and programming to a lower and lower common denominator, less gets heard via that traditional avenue of musical promotion.

I visualize the current landscape as a large, sticky funnel—anything of substance sticks to the inside walls, leaving only the thinnest, slickest stuff to find its way out, sometimes taking with it the odd, occasional glob of something substantial that just happens to work its way through. The rest of it doesn't come out through the narrow end of the funnel. To get to it, you need a spoon.

The situation the record business finds itself in is not without precedent. Media columnist Michael Wolff sees parallels between the contemporary state of the record business and the earlier days of the book publishing business. In the 1930s, young, creative communicators aspired to write the great American novel; now they aspire to record the next great international-hit album. Wolff pointed to a time when Hemingway was Kurt Cobain (right down to the shotgun), John Steinbeck was Bruce Springsteen (and now Bruce is returning the favor—more than one person has referred to him as Steinbeck with a guitar), and Norman Mailer was Eminem (language, boys, language). "They made lots of money, they lived large (and self-medicated). They were the generational voice."

Rock stars, Wolff wrote, once would only be happy if they sold hundreds of thousands or millions of records, but as in the book business, those days are waning. "Soon you'll be grateful if you have a release that sells 30,000 or 40,000 units—that will be your bread and butter. You'll sweat every sale and dollar . . . it will be a low-margin, consolidated, quaintly anachronistic business, catering to an aging clientele, without much impact on an otherwise thriving culture awash in music that only incidentally will come from the music industry."

As we've seen, a lot of this has already begun to happen. As early as the 1990s, baby boomers bought more CDs than their kids, the graying population forming the record business's key clientele, whether catered to or not. The low margins have made record retail as it has existed for half a century almost untenable today. Consolidation has affected nearly every aspect of the business, from retail to radio to the record companies themselves. If only 0.35 percent of all records sell more than 100,000 units and 96 percent sell less than a thousand copies, the day is swiftly coming when an artist will be happy with a CD that sells 30,000 copies, especially on an independent label.

The vertical integration of the record business has been breaking down for years, but the business would seem to have become aware of the rust and wear on the chain only as the links started to fall apart. The process was gradual and subtle, but eventually the chain has to break.

The main links, the symbiosis between the radio business and the record business, continue to break down. Radio getting free content in exchange for giving that content free promotion had become a public canard by the late 1950s. Nothing is free. The music business has paid for play since long before the days of payola, perhaps even before the days of the song plugger. The business's own organ, the RIAA, hinted at this when it tried to justify the cost of a CD:

> Marketing and promotion costs [are] perhaps the most expensive part of the music business today. They include . . . promotion to get the songs played on the radio. When you hear a song played on the radio—that didn't just happen! Labels make investments in artists by paying for both the production and the promotion of the album, and promotion is very expensive.

Some estimate that the record companies spend more than twice as much on promotion as they do on actual recording costs.

That recording costs have remained static for the last two decades has put the recording studios' balls into a vise. Squeezing from one side are the rising costs of competitive technology—96- and 120-track consoles and "studio quality" digital recording systems. Squeezing from the other side is the falling cost of competing technology, the computer-based home digital recording studio. Turning the handle is the falling revenue of the record companies.

It all boils down to this: the record business reached a tipping point, probably somewhere in the 1980s. It became just too large to support itself, but also too large to realize how close it was to collapsing in on itself like a black hole. The CD saved it from having to face this realization for another decade and a half. However, it seems slowly to have arrived at a place where expectations exceed reality, where an album that sells 10 million copies isn't regarded as an anomaly but a benchmark, and everything else the artist does subsequently needs to reflect it. So when an artist that sells 14 million of one album "only" sells two or three million of the next, the record business is disappointed, at best. At worst, the company has geared up with the anticipation of huge sales that didn't happen. That record causes massive layoffs, and other artists suffer from lack of resources due to the marketing and promotional priority given to the star.

The record industry's current problems started with consolidation and corporatization. At one time, radio, retail, and even, to a certain extent, the record companies themselves were mom-and-pop operations. Chess Records passed from father to son; Atlantic was started by a pair of music-loving brothers; Vee-Jay was owned by a husband and wife who got the name from the initials of their first names—Vivian and James.

Similarly, before the ownership rules were all but removed, many radio stations and even small chains of radio stations were family owned. As corporations consolidated ownership, they consolidated programming methods and even content. The stakes became too high for the possible eccentricities of individual programmers (i.e., DJs), giving way to programming by computer. Some stations—Internet, cable, satellite, and even broadcast—have given up on on-the-air talent (formerly known as the disc jockey) altogether.

The mom-and-pop independent record store still exists, but more as the exception than the rule, a business that has discovered a way to draw consumers that the big stores or chains don't—by specializing in a particular genre, or used and out-of-print records. Even many of these stores, like show-music specialist Footlight

Records, have decided they can better serve their audience and themselves by giving up their physical space for cyberspace.

As the record business got sucked into the vortex of larger and larger companies, as, more and more, a certain level of commercial performance became expected and mandated, it ultimately reached the point of diminishing returns. Reflecting the way contemporary society as a whole reacts in times of stress, the industry took no responsibility for these diminishing returns, preferring to blame its customers. When it came to people taping their records for use elsewhere, or even for friends, the record companies started a campaign about home taping killing the record business. People laughed.

Then came file sharing, and lawsuits, and suddenly no one was laughing anymore. To date, the record industry, via the RIAA, has sued over 16,000 customers—some say they might be (or might have been) their best customers—for trading songs online. So far 3,000 people have settled the suits for in the neighborhood of $5,000 each. One New York woman has spent $22,000 in legal fees; she's one of the few people actively challenging the deep legal pockets of the RIAA. "The recording industry," said a staff lawyer with the Electronic Frontier Foundation, "has basically been able to run this operation like a shakedown."

The RIAA has compared the practice of downloading songs "without permission" to shoplifting, but whose permission do the downloaders need? Many artists, including stars like Courtney Love and Pete Townshend, are happy to have people downloading songs if only to keep people listening—to use downloads, as Wharton School of Business's David Fader described it, the way the movie business uses film trailers: as a preview of and promotion for their music.

Unfortunately, contractually, the artists generally don't own these tracks. The entities whose permission the downloaders require are the record companies themselves, and they are generally so scared of the new technology they didn't invent and do not control that they won't even consider it. "Part of the reason for the major label decline is that there are a lot of old-school people still running the show," noted manager Ed Majewski.

> I think their train of thought is they will/can run the system to the ground. Basically, they are still going to do business like it was in the '70s. But the business has changed. One would think that they should change with the times. But why? Their mindset is, even if they run all the bigs right into the ground, they still can't lose. If the big labels all were to be out of business next week, what upstart "new model" wouldn't want to hire a Clive Davis or Donnie Ienner as a consultant? So there are people in power who know, no matter what happens, their ass is safe.

So if things go the way Wolff sees them, the way of the book business, can the record business scale back to a place where it can sustain itself on sales of 30,000 and 40,000 and the occasional bestseller? It would certainly take a good amount of the romance out of it, make the record business, like the book business, only marginally sexy. It would also require a major downsizing in the record companies, both in actual manpower and in clout. As in the days before the corporations descended on the record business, the independent companies would have a bigger piece of the pie. And due to the advances and changes in technology, in both the production and the distribution of music, DIY artists would likely have a much better shot at making a living with their music and reaching the fans who actually like the kind of music they make.

"Henceforth," Todd Rundgren said when he announced his A2P (artist to public) Internet subscription service, "I'm creating at the mercy of kindhearted fans." Of course, Rundgren realized that he'd been at the mercy of his fans for the previous two decades anyway. He now just has the means to rely on their mercy (and patronage) more directly.

Many more artists are seeing the advantage of owning their means of production. This doesn't just mean the custom label deals like Madonna's now-defunct Maverick Records or the Isley Brothers' T-Neck Records, which affiliate the artists with a major while giving them the illusion of autonomy. The new artist-owned and -operated labels are often companies either for artists who have developed a following on their own through touring and can sell CDs regionally or directly to fans along with T-shirts and other swag at shows or on their Web site, or for the artist who has previously developed a following via releases on a major label, and can capitalize on that following with their own label. We've done the math on this and seen that they can do very well for themselves selling a fraction of what they sold via a major label, because the margin of profit is so much higher.

For example, the band Hanson had a massive, chart-topping hit with "MMMbop" in 1997 from its major label debut on Mercury Records, but by the time it came to make a third album for the label (actually for Island/Def Jam, as Mercury effectively ceased to exist in one of the Universal Music Group consolidations and reorganizations), the group parted ways with UMG and formed its own independent label. This was not unknown territory for Hanson, which had started out recording for its own DIY label some seven years earlier. The new album, *Underneath*, peaked at #25 and sold a respectable 130,000 copies. The whole four-year adventure was captured in a film called *Strong Enough to Break*.

Other artists, like veteran folk-rocker Dean Friedman, do all their business on the Web. Friedman had one fair hit in the late 1970s, a song called "Ariel" that, because it was set amid landmarks familiar to New York suburbanites, became much bigger in the New York metropolitan area than anywhere else, but managed to go top 30 nationwide as well. His subsequent musical endeavors didn't go quite so well commercially, at least at home in the U.S. He remained something of a legend in England, but quickly discovered that you can't feed a family of four on legend. He moved on to interactive design, creating games for computers and working on the Nickelodeon TV show *Arcade*. When the Web came along, he put up deanfriedman.com and suddenly his fans had a nexus. Said Friedman:

> I knew they were out there, I just didn't have the means to reach them or they me. The Internet allows artists and audience to communicate directly and pass over the middlemen—the record companies, the distributors, etc. . . . I am selling CDs directly to these fans. I have sort of a cottage industry.

For his last CD, Friedman solicited advance sales from his coterie of fans worldwide on the World Wide Web. He used the funds to put together a studio and record the album. Fans that ordered it in advance got their names in the liner notes, a certificate of thanks, and a copy of the CD.

Certain movements in music, after a short time in the major label limelight as the next big thing, continue via artist-owned labels or independents. The poster children for these artists are the "jam bands" who tour incessantly, play to avid crowds in clubs and small auditoriums, and generally fly under the radar of the mainstream record business. Producer and label owner Vic Steffens said:

> I still contend that if you watch the developments in the jam scene, you can see that there is plenty of support for high-quality live music. If you think groups like Widespread Panic and Moe don't make money, you are mistaken. These groups are not going to tank because their last CD slipped below 500K. Not that I have ANY problem with 500K and up of CDs. . . . It's just not the only way.

Many of these DIY artists have discovered that the best way to get the word out is one contact at a time. To that end, some have even started to eschew clubs in favor of house concerts, where they perform for 40–80 people in a living room or family room. "I know artists who make a living doing just that!" said singer/songwriter Jenny Bruce; some of her compatriots might play 100 of these kinds of dates a year. "Yes, a living. From $30,000 to $150,000."

A circuit of some 300 of these "venues" has sprung up across North America, a genuine grassroots movement, linked via the Internet (check out houseconcerts.com). The door charge is $10 or $15 per person, most of which goes to the artist (the host serves snacks and drinks for money). That $400–$1,200 a night is a lot more than most artists could make in clubs. For the fans, this kind of concert offers something that music used to be the center of: community. Some of the homeowners who host these shows have repeat customers, and mostly these customers are people in their 30s to 50s, that lost audience, looking for an early night out close to home.

Those who can't host a concert can always host a listening party. These events take place in homes and dorms, as a means of getting people to preorder CDs. The host gets swag—T-shirts, CDs, concert tickets. The attendees get to hear some possibly cool music and hang out with friends in a party atmosphere. "The best promotion a band can ever get is for a fan to talk about them," said one band manager who uses these events to promote his bands' releases. "If a hard-core fan will spread the word to their community of friends, that's better than radio or MTV or anything."

Artists have begun finding nontraditional ways to sell their music to nontraditional niches. Tim and Ryan O'Neil, from New Prague, Minnesota, call themselves the Piano Brothers. They have found a niche audience of women 35 years of age and older. They've sold these women over a million CDs on their own Shamrock-N-Roll label. Having nothing to do with the traditional means of distribution, they sell their records through gift shops, grocery stores, craft shows, and wedding boutiques.

As indie labels proliferate, they have begun to take advantage of new media as well. In addition to selling their wares via the traditional means to the best of their ability—hiring independent distributors to get them into the chains that have room for them—they also sell them directly through their Web sites, often offering downloads as enticements or providing special deals directly to their known customers via e-mail.

Note also that some predict that the record industry might not merely become marginalized, but disappear altogether, Wolff's "quaintly anachronistic business, catering to an aging clientele, dying out as the clientele does." Music would still exist, of course, but would be ancillary to things like advertisements and movies. Recordings might still exist as stand-alone items, but in this scenario they would more likely be part of marketing campaigns, like the current one Toyota uses to promote its "youth brand," Scion. The company pays for the recording and production of young artists and distributes the records to clubs and college radio stations (where the DJ is still surviving, if not always thriving) and gives away compilations to potential customers. Companies will use music as branding and enticement.

Some artists will have larger ambitions, and we need artists like this. We need the Green Days of the world, the U2s, even the Hawthorne Heights, the groups that want to reach the most people with their music, and consequently sell truckloads of records without compromising what makes them special. I suspect, however, these artists will become fewer and further between. When they do build out of their niches and grow organically, to all but the most jaded music fans, they will be welcome.

Still, the odds are that most artists who put themselves out there won't make it. It may be because they don't market well, they can't reach their audience, or nobody appreciates the particular gift they think they might have. This, of course, is nothing new; it's as old as the music business itself. Even during the boom time for the record business, "The turnover rate of artists at large companies can approach 40 percent annually; that translates into a lot of broken dreams and box-loads of unsold records," Paul Bernstein observed in the *New York Times* in 1973.

The turnover rate has grown in the intervening quarter century, with the added twist that record company employees turn over far more frequently, leaving artists stranded at record companies without an advocate. Even major record companies face the turnover problem—a major part of Hanson's problems with UMG was that while the group was away, Mercury Records ceased to exist. Consider the fate of another UMG band, Edenstreet. They signed with A&M in 1997 and recorded a debut album, which was even sent out to press and radio. Three days before the album was set to ship, UMG shut down A&M Records entirely—very much the same way Mercury met its demise. No other UMG label picked up Edenstreet, sending the album to the limbo of unwanted recordings. "There are five guys sitting in Louisville," said one of the band members, "whose dreams have just been taken away on a whim. And it was so close—just three days."

The record business would seem to be entering a phase of what Dickens might call lesser expectations. As the greater part of the business struggles to deal with this, it trickles down to the artists as well. Even over 200 years ago, when the U.S. Constitution was written, its framers recognized the necessity of offering creative people an incentive to create, "[t]o promote the progress of science and useful arts, by securing for limited times to authors and inventors the exclusive right to their respective writings and discoveries." The question now becomes, how little incentive is the least for which an artist will create? At what point does an artist have to put aside creation for the business of making a living? Are "the useful arts" like music being "promoted" enough to ensure that they'll even exist on a professional level in 50 years?

The balance of art and commerce has always been a sticky problem for the creative person. Yet, to paraphrase Mark Twain, rumors of the record business's death have been greatly exaggerated. It is a time of radical change for the record business, and not many people are ready to step up and place their bets on the way things will shake out. But as Steffens put it:

At some point we are going to have to realize that the industry is never going to be the way it was. The old deals won't work, the old methods of delivery won't work. The old ways of supporting companies won't work, but music will find its way to the consumer, if the music is worthy and the people behind it have the desire.

"I really do believe," Majewski added, "that these are the most interesting times the industry has ever seen."

And as the old Chinese curse would have it, "May you live in interesting times."

Source Notes

Introduction

"Rock music had . . .": Neer, Richard, 2001.
Greek theater: Trumbull, Dr. Eric, 2001.
Roman theater: Boatwright, Mary T., 1990.
Minstrels: Frederickson, Jon, and James F. Rooney, 1990.
Church: Szendrei, Janka, 1986.
Guilds: Frederickson, Jon, and James F. Rooney, 1990.
"To promote the Progress . . .": U.S. Constitution.
Pianolas: Sanjek, Russell, and David Sanjek, 1996.

Part I: Playback and Payback: How the Record Business Drowned in Its Own Success

Chapter 1: Who's in Charge Here? You're Kidding!

1967 Record revenues: Sanjek, Russell, and David Sanjek, 1996.
"I started walking . . .": Smith, Joe, *Off the Record*.
Phil Spector: *World Musicians*, 1998.
Lester Sill: Lichtman, Irv, November 1994.
Liberty Records: Edwards, David, and Michael Callahan, 2001.
"I got stranded . . .": James, Etta, author's interview, 1988.
"Now, Leonard Chess . . .": James, Etta, author's interview, 1988.
"We got ripped . . .": Diddley, Bo, author's interview, 1996.
"It was a labor of love . . .": Hinte, Teri, October 16, 2005.
Prestige Records: Bowden, Marshall, 2003.

Chapter 2: Answering to the Stockholders, Not the Audience

"If you're not . . .": Cohen, Roger, 1992.
"It took several years . . .": Smith, Joe, 1988.

"Warner's Mo Ostin . . .": Yetnikoff, Walter, and David Ritz, 2004.

"Steve Ross realized . . .": Lowry, Tom, 2005.

Springsteen sales figures: Hagen, Mark, 1999.

"In 1967 or '68 . . .": Ertegun, Ahmet, author's interview, 1991.

"Deodato's *Prelude* . . .": Deutsch, Didier, author's interview, 1991.

"It's very nice . . .": Deutsch, Didier, author's interview, 1991.

PolyGram/Universal merger: Caslon Analytics, 2004.

"Everything that's wrong . . .": "Pointer," author's correspondence, 2006.

"Sony wanted their own software . . .": Yetnikoff, Walter, and David Ritz, 2004.

BMG buys RCA: *Communications Daily*, 1986.

"By pooling . . .": Sony Music, 2004.

UMG payroll cuts: Christman, Ed, 2004.

"Like the major . . .": Seybold, Patricia B., 2001.

Chapter 3: Who Does What to Whom: A Brief Tour of a Fictitious Record Company

"When I was doing . . .": Cohen, Stephanie, 2000.

CD release figures: "Optical Storage Media," 2003.

Chapter 4: Q: How Many A&R Guys Does It Take to Screw in a Lightbulb? A: We Can't Screw Anymore— They Cut Off Our Balls!

"Just so you're not . . .": Steffens, Vic, author's correspondence, 2005.

"I just knew . . .": Smith, Joe, 1988.

"In the days of . . .": Smith, Joe, 1988.

"Nobody really knew . . .": Smith, Joe, 1988.

"Maxwell Davis is . . ." Stoller, Mike, author's interview, 1995.

"They had this group . . .": Ertegun, Ahmet, author's interview, 1991.

"We figured we . . . : Stoller, Mike, author's interview, 1995.

"Budgets all over . . .": Anonymous former A&R person, author's correspondence, 2005.

Chapter 5: Charting the Course: How Changes in the Charts Changed the Biz

Billboard chart method: Mayfield, Geoff, 2002.

"For more than 30 . . .": Lander, Howard, 1991.

"We wanted to create . . .": Shallet, Michael, and Michael Fine, author's interview, 1992.

"Before you had . . .": Shallet, Michael, and Michael Fine, author's interview, 1992.

"Records slipped . . .": Shandler, Geoff, 2001.

Columbia University Study: Red Herring, 2006.

"The singles chart . . ." McAdams, Janine, 1992.

"We still get calls . . .": Shallet, Michael, and Michael Fine, author's interview, 1992.

"The SoundScan experience . . .": Shandler, Geoff, 2001.

Chapter 6: Control Issues: Did Home Taping Kill Music?

"It's a great scam . . .": Shamah, David, 2005.

"He showed it" Paul, Les, author's interview, 1992.

"When you tape something . . .": Weiss, George David, 1991.

Congress's reaction to DAT: Wikipedia, 2005.

"Gulf and Western Records . . .": Ripp, Artie, author's interview, May 8, 2004.

"We knew that CDs . . .": Rose, Don, author's interview, 1986.

"It was abysmal . . .": Rothchild, Paul, author's interview, 1992.

"The first few CDs . . .": Clark, Rick, 2002.

Sales figures: RIAA, 1999.

Chapter 7: Panic in the Suites: Napster, Grokster, and the Last Kazaa

"It will be Tower . . .": Rundgren, Todd, author's interview, 1997.

"Retailers have to be . . .": Gillen, Marilyn A., 1995.

"Until the appropriate balance . . .": Rosen Hilary, MCY Press release, July 1999.

"The Internet's threat . . .": Marsh, Dave, 1997.

"It was rooted . . .": Varanini, Giancarlo, 2000.

"I think the [record] . . .": Gal, Tsvi, op cite.

"Billy thought . . .": Crowly, Nina, 1999.

"There is no music . . .": Crowly, Nina, 1999.

Public perception of downloading: Rainie, Lee, Susannah Fox, and Amanda Lenhart, 2000.

CD sales figures: RIAA, 2004.

Annihilation Theory: Liebowitz, Stan, 2003.

"We're standing . . .": Ramone, Phil, author's interview, 1997.

"Traditional music distribution . . .": Bordowitz, Hank, 1999.

"The Internet is . . .": Cohen, Stephanie, 2000.

"Record companies stand . . .": Love, Courtney, 2000.

"Why does Metallica . . .": *Rock and Rap Confidential*, 2000.

"Artists standing up . . .": *Knowledge@Wharton*, 2002.

"Pioneer in the indexing . . .": MP3Board, 2000.

Figures on Internet and broadband penetration: Nielsen/Net Ratings survey, 2004.

Number of people subject to RIAA lawsuits: *Rock and Rap Confidential*, July 2005.

"The end result . . .": Greenblatt, Alan, 2003.

"The music industry . . .": Del Colliano, Jerry, PR Newswire, 2002.

"My understanding . . .": Zisk, Brian, author's correspondence, 2005.

Ratio of legal to P2P downloads: Hayes, Simon, 2005.

Ratio of CD sales to P2P downloads: Liebowitz, Stan, 2003.

"The main reasons . . .": Australian Associated Press, 2005.

Organisation for Economic Co-operation and Development Study: *The Economist*, 2005.

Harvard study: Oberholzer, Felix, and Koleman Strumpf, 2004.

"These same file sharers . . .": McBride, Terry, 2006.

"MP3 downloads . . .": Liebowitz, Stan, 2003.

"Abandon the 'Shock and Awe' . . .": Goldring, Fred, *Billboard*, 2005.

"Here's the social reason . . .": Doctorow, Cory, Address, 2004.

"Lawsuits against file sharers . . .": Dvorak, John, *PC Magazine*, 2004.

"We will no longer . . .": Laek, Andrew, Press Release, 2004.

"I get involved . . .": Cohen, Jonathan, 2005.

"It's nothing new . . .": Napoli, Lisa, 2003.

Chapter 8: 150 Records = 50 Percent of Revenue

Much of this chapter is based on Christman, Ed, 2001.

"We estimate . . .": Lindsey, Robert, 1975.

2005 figures: Christman, Ed, 2006.

Long tail: Anderson, Chris 2004.

"In the pop-prism . . .": Hinte, Terri, October 31, 2005.

Chapter 9: The Fable of the Elephant and the Rabbit: How the Indies Are Eating the Majors' Lunch

The math in this chapter is based on Albini, Steve, 1993.
"Record companies still . . .": Rundgren, Todd, author's interview, 1997.
"You don't need . . .": Bergman, Barry, author's interview, 2005.
"We're already into . . .": Cook, Stu, author's interview, 1997.
Victory Records figures on Thursday: Martens, Todd, 2006.
"These are great times . . .": Brancaccio, David, and Beatrice Black, 2002.

Part II: The Messy Suicide of Commercial Radio

Chapter 10: Airwaves of the People, for the People . . . Yeah, Sure

"After broadcast . . .": Corbett, Krystilyn, 1996.
Coolidge goes to Congress: Gruber, Frederick C., 1952.
The Radio Act "proclaimed that . . .": Gruber, Frederick C., 1952.
"It is the purpose . . .": Shelanski, Howard A., and Peter W. Huber, 1998.
Timeline of media ownership: Consumer's Union.
License renewal criteria: Shelanski, Howard A., and Peter W. Huber, 1998.

Chapter 11: Regulations? We Don't Need No Steenking Regulations

"Given the status . . .": Bates, Dr. Benjamin J., 1995.
Deregulation facts: Bates, Dr. Benjamin J., 1995.
Stations per market: DiCola, Peter, and Kristin Thompson, 2002.
Deregulation chart: DiCola, Peter, and Kristin Thompson, 2002.
"The recent passage . . .": SFX, 1996.
"Consider what could happen . . .": Lieberman, David, 2000.
"You cannot have . . .": Bohlert, Eric, 2002.
Radio stations are . . .": Seybold, Patricia B., 2001.
"In the next five . . .": Rundgren, Todd, author's interview, 1992.

Chapter 12: The Death of the DJ: The Curse of Selector

"Computers were just . . .": Neer, Richard, 2001.

Chapter 13: *The Process: How Songs Really Get on the Radio*

"As much as people . . .": Ahrens, Frank, 2004.

"Call-out has become . . .": Palmese, Richard.

"Theoretically, those trips . . .": Bohlert, Eric, 2001.

"The real problem . . .": Greenman, Ben, 2004.

"One always had to be wary . . .": Neer, Richard, 2001.

Chapter 14: *Payola Isn't Dead. It Always Smelled Like That*

"The TOBA was . . .": Price, Sammy, author's interview, October 1989.

Strawbs story: Neer, Richard, 2001.

"The music business . . .": Yetnikoff, Walter, and David Ritz, 2004.

"Questionnaire . . .": *New York Times*, 1924.

"I was a song plugger . . .": Gayles, Juggy, author's interview, 1988.

"The cry that . . .": Ackerman, Paul, 1955.

"I had to get . . .": Smith, Joe, 1988.

"A guy who will go unnamed . . .": Smith, Joe, author's interview, 1988.

"Guys at the radio . . .": Smith, Joe, author's interview, 1988.

"Black artists . . .": Greenman, Ben, 2004.

"I was out . . .": Gayles, Juggy, author's interview, 1988.

"George Furness and me . . .": Gayles, Juggy, author's interview, 1994.

Promoting "the public interest . . .": Communications Act Ammendment
    of 1960.

"The radio formats . . .": Smith, Joe, author's interview, 1988.

"They all took . . .": Gayles, Juggy, author's interview, 1988.

"The practice of payola . . .": Associated Press, 1967.

"We have become . . .": Lindsey, Robert, 1975.

"It may not be exactly . . .": Halberstam, David, 1961.

David Wynshaw: Lichtenstein, Grace, January 20, 1973.

"I took all the artists . . .": Dannen, Fredric, 1991.

"It's a nice way . . .": Lichtenstein, Grace, July 22, 1973.

"If Joni Mitchell . . .": Lichtenstein, Grace, July 22, 1973.

Payola penalties: Communications Act Ammendment of 1960.

Payola "corrosive to the integrity . . .": Morris, Chris, and Alexander
    Woodson, 2005.

"Please be advised . . .": *Rock and Rap Confidential*, October 2005.

"Make sure Donnie . . .": Gross, Daniel, 2005.

Misrepresenting "their identities . . .": Sony/BMG, 2005.

"The difference between . . .": Greenman, Ben, 2004.

"I ran a test . . .": Lotz, I. C.

"A well-worn truism . . .": Greenman, Ben, 2004.

Chapter 15: We Don't Do Payola. We Let the Independent Promotion Companies Handle It

"I worked for Epic . . .": Gayles, Juggy, author's interview, 1988.

"I know what . . .": Yetnikoff, Walter, and David Ritz, 2004.

Claims against Isgro: Rohter, Larry, 1990.

"The artists were furious . . .": Yetnikoff, Walter, and David Ritz, 2004.

"When I saw . . .": Yetnikoff, Walter, and David Ritz, 2004.

Koppleman hiring Isgro: Lichtman, Irv, 1993.

"In 1983 or '84 . . .": Waller, Don, 2001.

"There is a greater reliance . . .": Zuckerman, Steven, 2004.

Isgro sent to jail: Morris, Chris, 2000.

"Record companies that want . . .": Brancaccio, David, and Beatrice Black, 2002.

McClusky as businesslike: Bohlert, Eric, 2001.

"We now recognize . . .": Clear Channel, 2003.

"Strong relationships . . .": Clear Channel, 2003.

An effort to "dodge. . .": Leeds, Jeff, 2005.

Upper echelon management involvement: Morris, Chris, and Alexander Woodson, 2005.

McClusky's other interests: Leeds, Jeff, 2005.

"Some things we think about now . . .": Zuckerman, Steven, 2004.

"A song without significant . . .": Pareles, Jon, 1990.

Chapter 16: Arbitron Rated #1 in Symphonic-Punk-Country-Disco—Fragging the Format

"When you agree . . .": Bonko, Larry, 2005.

Chinese listener figures: Arbitron, 2005.

Clear Channel's New York City stations: Arbitron ratings via *Radio and Records* Online, 2005.

"What has happened . . .": Smith, Joe, author's interview, 1988.

"The Commission is . . .": Federal Communications Commission, 1934.

Number of stations by format: Farrish, Bryan, 2000.

"Now there are people who . . .": Smith, Joe, author's interview, 1988.
"It's a tool . . .": Bonko, Larry, 2005.

Chapter 17: Are you Sirius? Can Satellite Radio, Webcasting, and Podcasting Save Broadcasting (or Even Themselves)?

WorldSpace's satellites: Sarma, Ripunjoy Kumar, 2005.
XM's satellites: Margolis, Lynne, 2005.
WorldSpace mission: Sarma, Ripunjoy Kumar, 2005.
XM and Sirius's terrestrial signals: Sarma, Ripunjoy Kumar, 2005.
Satellite subscriber perks: Margolis, Lynne, 2005.
Satellite penetration figures: Heine, Paul, July 22, 2005.
Stern's Sirius contract: Westfeldt, Amy, 2005.
Stern subscribers: Heine, Paul, July 22, 2005, and Wilkowe, Ellen S., 2005.
Growing number of Web radio stations: Okoli, Christina.
"The growth potential . . .": Zeidler, Sue, 2005.
"To win . . .": Heine, Paul, November 11, 2005.
Paul Allen: Johnson, Gene, 2005.
"It's all about creating context . . .": Johnson, Gene, 2005.
More rules for webcasters: *Digital Millennium Copyright Act*.
Operating at a loss: Zeidler, Sue, 2005.
KEXP podcasts: Johnson, Gene, 2005.
"It's apparent . . .": *FMQB*, 2005.
Podcast and profit: Shields, Mike, 2005.
KEXP cell signal: Johnson, Gene, 2005.
"Once Internet radio's . . .": UPI, 2005.
Ford car radio: Microsoft and Ford, 2005.

Part III: Retailing Records

Chapter 18: Rock and the Hard Place: Records Become a Commodity and Face Real Estate Prices and Profit Margins

Description of late '40s record stores: Mabry, Donald J., 1990.
Record sales in the '20s and '30s: Shelton, Robert, 1958.
"I thought [records] . . .": Barron, James, 1991.

"I said to myself . . .": Barron, James, 1991.

Turntable giveaway: Barron, James, 1991.

Number of customers in Goody's store: Sanjek, Russell, and David Sanjek, 1996.

Goody's sales by 1955: Barron, James, 1991.

Record clubs: *The Billboard*, 1955.

"No royalty . . .": "Independent Record Company Contract.

Advertising: Horowitz, Is, November 1955.

"A minute of music . . .": Shelton, Robert, 1958.

"The happy tunes . . .": Shelton, Robert, 1958.

Goody in Chapter 11: Barmash, Isadore, 1969.

"A low margin . . .": Rood, George, 1965.

Industry growth: Rood, George, 1965.

"The end of the upward . . .": Rood, George, 1965.

Goody out of bankruptcy: Barmash, Isadore, 1969.

"They loved each other . . .": Barmash, Isadore, 1988.

"I agreed . . .": Barmash, Isadore, 1977.

Jack Eugster: Palmieri, Christopher, 1993.

Russ Solomon: Serwer, Andy, 2004.

Tower's growth: Serwer, Andy, 2004.

"Our company policy . . .": Solomon, Russ, author's interview, 1993.

Eugster's sales: Palmieri, Christopher, 1993.

Record-store sales percentages: RIAA, 1999, and RIAA, 2005 (profile).

NYC retail rental costs: Fashion Center, 2003.

Vegas retail rental costs: Kirk, Patricia L., 2004.

Mall retail rental costs: Hazlett, Curt, January 1, 2003.

CD margins: Christman, Ed, 2003–2005, and Podmolic, Mary Ellen, 2003.

"On Fiona Apple . . .": Christman, Ed, 2005.

"Hemorrhaging money . . .": Serwer, Andy, 2004.

Sales figures pre-9/11: National Association of Record Merchandisers "Device Ownership," October, 2001.

Sales figures post 9/11: RIAA, 2005 (profile).

Best Buy buys Musicland: Serwer, Andy, 2004.

Sales figures lower than 10 years earlier: RIAA, 1999, and RIAA, 2005 (profile).

"This industry . . .": Podmolic, Mary Ellen, 2003.

"Wherehouse and Sam Goody . . .": Green, Frank, 2005.

"The industry views. . .": Breen, Bill, 2003.

"CBGB's was not. . .": Archives of Contemporary Music, 2005.

"In our case . . .": Williams, Paul, 2004.

"You will never . . .": Rundgren, Todd, author's interview, 1992.

"The Web eliminates . . .": Napoli, Lisa, 2003.

Chapter 19: Censorship: Wal-Mart Tippers the Scales

Wal-Mart record sales figures: Strauss, Neil, 1996.

"For the sake . . .": Smith, Brian K., 2005.

"Our customers . . .": Strauss, Neil, 1996.

The Alleys, Prince, and the PTA: Marsh, Dave, 1985.

Twisted Sister video "was simply meant . . .": Harrigan, Richard, 1985.

"It's not going to affect . . .": Harrigan, Richard, 1985.

"The PMRC proposal . . .": Zappa, Frank, 1985.

Ritual de lo Habitual cover: Strauss, Neil, 1996.

"If you're an artist . . .": Browne, David, 1990.

"You may need to show . . .": Marsh, Dave, 1985.

Chapter 20: A Voyage Down the Amazon.com

"Breadth of selection . . .": Williams, Mark London, 1998.

Computer penetration: U.S. Census Bureau, 2004.

Number of Web servers and people on the net: Lewis, Peter H., 1994.

Online in 1994: Lewis, Peter H., 1994.

"CDNow was founded . . .": CDNow, 1997.

Geffen linking to CDNow: Lichtman, Irv, December 1994.

CDNow revenues: *Advertising Age*, 1995.

Newbury and Rosen online: *Billboard*, 1995.

Music as the most popular thing to buy on the Web: Pelline, Jeff, 1995.

"A three-minute song . . .": Burnett, Scott, author's interview, 1997.

"If you don't know . . .": Evenson, Laura, 1998.

Webnoize study: Seybold, Patricia B., 2001.

"Five years out . . .": Burnett, Scott, author's interview, 1997.

Part IV: Technology

Chapter 21: We Recorded This in Only Three Months! From One Mic to 128 Tracks

"Some people think . . .": Rundgren, Todd, author's interview, 1985.

"A lot of guys . . .": Paul, Les, author's interview, 1992.

"The whole point . . .": Smith, Joe, 1988.

New independent record companies: Parmenter, Ross, 1952.

"I paid for production . . .": Smith, Joe, 1988.

"Gouging a record . . .": Paul, Les, author's interview, 1992.

"The Octopus . . .": Paul, Les, author's interview, 1992.

"Who needs . . .": Credited to Phil Ramone.

Beatles recording and three track: Morin, Cari, 1988.

"I cannot see . . .": *Record World Magazine*, 1971.

"I started . . .": Bongiovi, Tony, author's interview, 1985.

"We invested millions . . .": Verna, Paul, 1998.

"You never win . . .": Verna, Paul, 1998.

"During the heyday . . .": Fast, Larry, author's correspondence, 2005.

"The folks that . . .": Steffens, Vic, author's correspondence, 2005.

Customer retention: Costello, Daniel, 2000.

"One studio owner . . .": Verna, Paul, 1998.

"In some cases . . .": Steffens, Vic, author's correspondence, 2005.

"Right now, the market . . .": Droney, Maureen, 2002.

"When computer and hard-disk . . .": Walsh, Christopher, 2005.

"You can buy . . .": Walsh, Christopher, 2000.

"Many producers and artists . . .": Walsh, Christoper, 2004.

Unique Studios: Walsh, Christopher, 2004.

"In a rising market . . .": Petersen, George, 2005.

"It is the musicians and singers . . .": Bongiovi, Tony, author's interview, 1985.

Chapter 22: The Internet: Friend, Foe, or Just a Tool?

"The Internet is definitely . . .": Cohen, Stephanie, 2000.

Arctic Monkeys: Pfanner, Eric, 2006.

"The Web is a fabulous . . .": Robertson, Thomas Dolby, 2000.

"In artist development . . .": Nelson, Chris, *New York Times*, 2003.

"There will be a lot of hidden . . .": Rundgren, Todd, author's interview, 1992.

"I'd rather have . . .": Rundgren, Todd, author's interview, 1985.

"I can write music . . .": Rundgren, Todd, author's interview, 1997.

"I'm leaving . . .": Love, Courtney, 2000.

"People are under the collective . . . : Top 40 Charts.com, 2005.

"The exciting part . . .": Bowie, David, and Emma Brockes, 1999.

"Clap Your Hands . . .": McBride, Terry, 2006.

"With the creation . . .": Morin, Armand, PR Newswire, 2005.

"When we were trying . . .": Matens, Todd, *Billboard*, 2006.

"The lack of control . . .": Bowie, David, and Emma Brockes, 1999.

"What bothers me . . .": Cohen, Stephanie, 2000.

"In 1985 . . .": Cohen, Stephanie, 2000.

"We should thank the heavens . . .": Sutton, Dan, author's correspondence, 1997.

"Now there is a generation . . .": D'Agostino, Debra, 2005.

"The only successful . . .": Wells, Matt, 2001.

The shopping pleasure principle: Manning, Robert D., Derek V. Price, and Henry J. Rich, 1997.

"It's like saying home shopping . . .": Ramone, Phil, author's interview, 1997.

"Human nature requires . . .": Gillen, Marilyn A., 1995.

P2P ratios: Orlowski, Andrew, 2005.

Canadian P2P figures: Canadian Recording Industry Association, 2005.

Downloaders buy: Miller, Karen Lowry, 2005.

Rise in sales: BBC News, 2005.

"In mid 2004 . . .": Winkler, Peter, and Laura Schooler, 2005.

"However valid . . .": Goldring, Fred, 2005.

Grokster ruling "important psychologically . . .": Goldring, Fred, 2005.

MySpace: Ahrens, Frank, 2004.

"Fifteen years ago . . .": Pepper, Tara, 2005.

"Sales of 20,000 . . .": Pepper, Tara, 2005.

"A record company can underwrite . . .": Rundgren, Todd, author's interview, 1997.

"An artist is not required . . .": Keefe, Bob, 2005.

"Physical product has . . .": Noguchi, Yuki, 2005.

"The future has never been . . .": Duhigg, Charles, 2004.

Chapter 23: Hardware and Software: On Demand and on Your Hip

"Right now, you can't . . .": Ice-T, 2000.

"I had my record out . . .": Ice-T, 2000.

"Disruptive technology should . . .": Christensen, Clayton M., 2000.

"You'll always have a certain . . .": Solomon, Russ, author's interview, 1993.

"Rather than rush . . .": Griesman, Dwight, author's interview, 2000.

"Personal TV . . .": *InfoGuia Juegos*, 2000.

Idrema's closing: Hall, Michael, 2001.

SongBank: Wild, 2005.

"The reality of the marketplace . . .": Griesman, Dwight, author's interview, 2000.

Ted Cohen's car stereo: Cohen, Ted, author's interview, 2002.

Four generations of iPod: Self, Jonathan, and Jason Snell, 2004.

IPod sales: Top 40 Charts.com, 2005.

Two weeks of music based on a 20-gig iPod.

MP3 player penetration: Schadler, Ted, and Sally M. Cohen, 2005.

Purchased downloads: Schadler, Ted, Josh Bernoff, Sally Cohen, and Jennifer Joseph, 2005.

Mobile phone penetration in U.S.: Wikipedia entry on Mobile Phones.

Mobile phone penetration in Europe: Telecomworldwire, 2005.

Developing ringtones for sale: Simon, Ralph, 2005.

"Once considered . . .": Ringtones.It, 2005.

"That's something the artists . . .": Bruno, Anthony, 2005.

"Artists are playing . . .": Bruno, Anthony, 2005.

CSI: New York promotion: Turner, Cynthia, November 2005.

Stones album on card: Duhigg, Charles, 2004.

Barenaked on a Stick: *Seattle Post-Intelligencer*, 2005.

Part V: We, the Audience

Chapter 24: A Touch of Grey: Boomers Grow Up and Grow Old

"When the Who . . .": Mabe, Chauncey, 2005.

"A baby boomer and. . .": Goldberg, Danny, 2005.

"Rock 'n' roll became . . .": Mabry, Donald J., 2004.

Herb London: Cockrell, Dale, 1986.

"The baby boom generation . . ." Manchester, Joyce, 1988.

"Baby boomers literally . . .": Adler, Jerry, 2005.

"People like us, who grew up . . .": Bauder, David, 1992.

"Now in middle age . . .": Frey, William H., 2001.

Dylan and McCartney: Paoletta, Michael, November 19, 2005.

CD sales to boomers: RIAA, 2005 (profile).

"The older demographic . . .": Goddard, Peter, 1996.

Chapter 25: The Lost Audience: How the Music Business Broke Faith with Its Main Supporters

Norah Jones Grammys: GRAMMY.com.

Norah Jones sales: RIAA.com.

Putumayo and Barry Manilow sales figures: SoundScan.

Sales to adults in 2003: Consumer profile RIAA.com.

Chapter 26: An Embarrassment of Riches: Entertainment Options Today—"Hey, Kid, Wanna Buy a Record or a Video Game?"

"If kids aren't . . .": Amdur, Meredith, 2004.

Video games to overtake music business: *Industry Analyst Reporter*, 2005.

Record sales figures: RIAA, 2005 (statistics).

Video game sales figures: Entertainment Software Association, 2005.

College survey: National Association of Record Merchandisers, "College Market," October 2001.

Homes with TVs: Roberts, Donald F., Ulla G. Foehr, and Victoria Rideout, 2005.

Boys and video games: Billings, Gwen, November 22, 2005.

Kids and PCs: Roberts, Donald F., Ulla G. Foehr, and Victoria Rideout, 2005.

Americans online: Stone, Brad, 2005.

IMs: Roberts, Donald F., Ulla G. Foehr, and Victoria Rideout, 2005, and Billings, Gwen, December 7, 2005.

Mobile phones: Schadler, Ted, and Sally M. Cohen, 2005.

Time online: Lopez, Maribel D., Ted Schadler, Jennifer Joseph, and Sally Cohen, 2005.

Media consumption: Roberts, Donald F., Ulla G. Foehr, and Victoria Rideout, 2005.

Two media: Billings, Gwen, December 7, 2005.

Kids with mobile phones: Billings, Gwen, November 22, 2005.

Cell accessories: Billings, Gwen, November 22, 2005.

"We'll see a time . . .": Alterio, Julie Moran, 2005.

Video game value: Allan, Keri, and David Cole, 2004.

"It's pretty obvious . . .": Ritholtz, Barry, 2004.

DVD consumer figures: Rothman, Wilson, 2004.

"Our central strategy . . .": High, Mamau, 2005.

"The impact . . .": High, Mamau, 2005.

"Maybe I'm slow . . .": Christman, Ed, 2005.

Part VI: Money

Chapter 27: Music Education: Buddy, Can You Spare a Dime?

Government funding: Associated Press, 2006.

"Music is a specialized . . .": Yoh, William H., Jr., 1996.

First-grade study: Gardiner, Martin, Alan Fox, Faith Knowles, and Donna Jeffery, 1996.

"Students with coursework . . .": Nelson, T. J., 2005.

Bronx parochial school: Dickinson, Dee, 1993.

Texas commission and Gallup: Nelson, T. J., 2005.

"The other choices . . .": Lindelof, Bill, 2004.

"School districts statewide . . .": Carr, Lynette, 2005.

VH-1 pianos: Nelson, T. J., 2005.

"The reason for that . . .": Lindelof, Bill, 2004.

"Children in the vulnerable . . .": Zappa, Frank, 1985.

Chapter 28: The Orlando Phenomenon: Boy Bands and Bad Girls Made to Order

"The band made its . . .": Turner, Cynthia, September 2005.

"I decided I needed . . .": Smith, Joe, 1988.

"The strategy was . . .": Smith, Joe, 1988.

The Archies: Jahn, Mike, 1969.

The Archies in 1969: Bronson, Fred, 1985.

"The incredible thing is . . .": Smith, Joe, 1988.

"Artie told me . . .": Passy, Charles, 2001.

"The *Mickey Mouse Club* was. . .": Abbot, Jim, 2002.

"Until God stops . . ." Rayner, Ben, 2001.

"*American Idol* amounts. . .": Dumenco, Simon, 2003.

"The industry is only . . .": Llewellyn Smith, Caspar, 2005.

Chapter 29: Breaking the Star = Breaking the Bank

Bruce's first record: Bordowitz, Hank, 2004.

Cost of breaking a hit: G, Scott, 2005.

Carly Hennessy: Ordoñez, Jennifer, 2002.

"We've never been . . .": Newman, Melinda, 2005.

"Labels used to thrive . . .": Ponti, Jack, author's correspondence, 2005.

"I'd say managers . . .": Bergman, Barry, author's interview, 2005.

"The group I am managing . . .": Majewski, Ed, Author's correspondence, 2005.

"Fans cannot download . . .": Majewski, Ed, author's correspondence, 2005.

"Major labels can't . . .": Ponti, Jack, author's correspondence, 2005.

"People want something . . .": Rawls, Lou, author's interview, 1989.

Chapter 30: The Video Revolution: Looks Aren't Everything; They're the Only Thing

"He said, 'I don't mind . . .' ": Nispel, Marcus, author's interview, 1991.

"Things which used to count . . .": Banks, Jack, 1997.

Video statistics: Banks, Jack, 1997.

"There's a band . . .": Lekberg, Jason, author's correspondence, 2005.

"I have two bands . . .": Banks, Jack, 1997.

"I'm very uncomfortable . . .": Clark, Rhodri, 2005.

"We want to break . . .": Paoletta, Michael, November 12, 2005.

Temple of the Dog video: Woletz, Robert G., 1992.

Cost of indie video: Banks, Jack, 1997.

Cost of a major video: Banks, Jack, 1997, and Schwartz, Lara, 2007.

"You do music videos . . .": Nispel, Marcus, author's interview, 1991.

"Certain artists . . .": Schwartz, Lara, author's correspondence, 2006.

Video "all done on desktop . . .": Rundgren, Todd, author's interview,
1992.
"From now on . . .": Cohen, Stephanie, 2000.
"Cactusflower" video: Rickwood, Lee, 2005.
"Videos are nothing but . . .": Nispel, Marcus, author's interview, 1991.
"You're making . . .": Banks, Jack, 1997.
MTV/Microsoft joint venture: Tymkiw, Catherine, 2005.

Chapter 31: Contacts and Contracts: Why an Artist Can Go Gold One Day and Be Flipping Burgers the Next.

"Today I want . . .": Love, Courtney, 2000.
"I got tired . . .": Shocklee, Hank, author's interview, 2002.
"One has to be . . .": Jacobson, Jeffrey, author's correspondence, March
2006.
"Signing isn't trivial . . .": "...Get Signed" Cumberland, Rob, 2005.
"Your lawyer doesn't . . .": "...Get Signed" Cumberland, Rob, 2005.
"It's the story . . .": "Sponge" Cumberland, Rob, 2005.
Monkey points: Adler, Tim, 2004.
Hootie and the Blowfish: Fisher, Anne B., 1996.
Korn/EMI deal: Garrity, Brian, 2005.
"Korn not only loses . . .": Marsh, Dave, 2005.
Fake Science: Delvecchio, Rick, 2005.

Conclusion: The Bilious Stew of the Music Business at the Turn of the Millennium—and Hope for Deliverance

"The Record industry . . .": Taubman, Howard, 1942.
"They made lots . . .": Wolff, Michael, 2002.
"Soon you'll be grateful . . .": Wolff, Michael, 2002.
"Marketing and promotion costs . . .": RIAA.com, 2003.
Marketing vs promotion costs: *Washington Post*, 1995.
"The recording industry . . .": O'Connor, Timothy, 2005.
"Part of the reason . . .": Majewski, Ed, author's correspondence, 2004.
"Henceforth . . .": Rundgren, Todd, author's interview, 1997.
Hanson: Levine, Robert, 2005.
"I knew they were out there . . .": Friedman, Dean, 2003.
"I still contend . . .": Steffens, Vic, author's correspondence, 2005.

"I know artists . . .": Bruce, Jenny, author's correspondence, 2005.

House concerts: Strauss, Neil, 1999.

"The best promotion . . .": Soukup, Elise, 2005.

Piano Brothers: Nelson, Lizz, 2004.

Scion record: Halliday, Jean, 2005.

"The turnover rate . . .": Bernstein, Paul, 1973.

"There are five guys . . .": Bauder, David, 1999.

"At some point . . .": Steffens, Vic, author's correspondence, 2005.

"I really do believe . . .": Majewski, Ed, author's correspondence, 2005.

Bibliography

Abbot, Jim. "Orlando: Best Known as a Breeding Ground for Boy Bands, the City Has Plenty More Talent to Offer." *Billboard*, December 21, 2002.

Ackerman, Paul. "300,000 Spins a Day Throw Music Industry into Whirl." *The Billboard*, November 12, 1955.

Adler, Jerry. "Turning 60." *Newsweek*, November 14, 2005.

Adler, Tim. "Net Profits Make a Monkey Out of Producers." *Screen Finance*, August 25, 2004.

Advertising Age. "Selling CDs Successfully." November 20, 1995.

Ahrens, Frank. "Technology Repaves Road to Stardom." *Washington Post*, May 2, 2004.

Albini, Steve. "The Problem with Music." *Maximum Rock and Roll* 166 (1993).

Allan, Keri, and David Cole. "Up, Up, and Away! Game Industry Forecasts Stay Bright." *Electronic Gaming Business*, March 10, 2004.

Amdur, Meredith. "Teens Spent 15% Less on CDs." *Daily Variety*, February 11, 2004.

Arbitron. "Arbitron Releases Results of Chinese Language Radio Listening in New York and Los Angeles." Press release, June 1, 2005.

Archives of Contemporary Music. Press release, October 6, 2005.

Associated Press. "New Budget Plan Squeezes Education, Medicare." February 6, 2006.

Associated Press. "Tax Court Rules Payola Is Not Deductible Expense." January 24, 1967.

Australian Associated Press. "People Prefer to Buy CDs—Survey." August 9, 2005.

Anderson, Chris, "The Long Tail" *Wired*, October 2004

Banks, Jack. "Video in the Machine: The Incorporation of Music Video into the Recording Industry." *Popular Music*, October 1997.

Barmash, Isadore. "American Can Plans to Buy Sam Goody." *New York Times*, December 14, 1977.

Barmash, Isadore. "At 85, Sam Goody Longs for a New Business." *New York Times*, June 13, 1988.

Barmash, Isadore. "Music Merchant Bullish on Youth and Technology." *New York Times*, July 9, 1969.

Barron, James. "Sam Goody, Who Started Chain of Record Stores, Is Dead at 87." New York Times, August 9, 1991.

Bates, Dr. Benjamin J. "The Economic Basis for Radio Deregulation." Paper presented at Popular Culture Association, Philadelphia, April 1995.

Bauder, David. "Adapting to a Graying Marketplace." Associated Press, February 14, 1992.

Bauder, David. "The Hard Realities of a New World in the Music Business." Associated Press, April 22, 1999.

BBC News. "US Sees Growth in CD Sales Market." January 6, 2005.

Bernstein, Paul. "What Happens to Rockers Who Don't Make It?" *New York Times*, November 4, 1973.

Billboard. "Interactive Briefs: Boston Retailer Goes Online." October 14, 1995.

The Billboard. "Results of Clubs Jell Slowly. 61 Percent Still Opposed to Project." December 3, 1955.

Billings, Gwen. "Benchmark Mobile Entertainment Study." *Cynopsis: Kids*, November 22, 2005.

Billings, Gwen. "The First Amendment Reigned Supreme." *Cynopsis: Kids*, December 5, 2005.

Billings, Gwen. *Cynopsis: Kids*, December 7, 2005.

Boatwright, Mary T. "Theaters in the Roman Empire." *Biblical Archaeologist*, December 1990.

Bohlert, Eric. "Fighting Pay-for-Play." *Salon*, April 3, 2001.

Bohlert, Eric. "Is Clear Channel Selling Hit Singles?" *Salon*, June 25, 2002.

Bonko, Larry. "A Radio Listener Is Heard by Arbitron." *Virginian*, August 13, 2005.

Bordowitz, Hank. *The Bruce Springsteen Scrapbook*. New York: Kensington/Citadel Books, 2004.

Bordowitz, Hank. "The Future Is Here: Goodbye CDs?" *Gallery*, 1999.

Bowden, Marshall. "Visions of Miles (review of *The Miles Davis Story on DVD*)" PopMatters.com, November 26, 2003.

Bowie, David, and Emma Brockes. "David Bowie in His Own Words: Not Afraid of the Internet." *Guardian*, January 20, 1999.

Brancaccio, David, and Beatrice Black. *Marketplace,* American Public Media (Radio), June 27, 2002.

Breen, Bill. "What's Selling in America." *Fast Company*, January 2003.

Bronson, Fred. *The Billboard Book of Number One Hits.* New York: Billboard Books, 1985.

Browne, David. "The Music Business Watches Its Own Step." *New York Times*, September 23, 1990.

Bruno, Anthony. "Ringtones Still Have Plenty of Room to Grow." *Billboard*, September 24, 2005.

Canadian Recording Industry Association. "Recording Industry Launches Campaign to Protect and Promote Products of the Mind, Citing Results of Two National Polls." September 29, 2005.

Carr, Lynette. "Keep the Arts in School." *Pittsburgh Post-Gazette*, June 22, 2005.

Caslon Analytics. "Ketupa.net Media Profile: PolyGram, Decca and DG." www.ketupa.net/polygram2.htm, June 2004.

CDNow. "CDNow Announces Free Music for Life." Press release, October 21, 1997.

Christensen, Clayton M. *The Innovator's Dilemma.* New York: HarperBusiness Books, 2000.

Christman, Ed. "2005 Sales Data: Long Tail Is Wagging." *Billboard*, March 18, 2006.

Christman, Ed. "FTC Removes Final Hurdle to Merger of Sony and BMG." *Billboard*, August 7, 2004.

Christman, Ed. "Not Much Yule Cheer for Music Business." *Billboard*, January 11, 2003.

Christman, Ed. "Retail Pays for UMG's Price Cut." *Billboard*, September 12, 2003.

Christman, Ed. "Retail Track, Margins Shrink as CDs Vie with Other Media." *Billboard*, November 19, 2005.

Christman, Ed. "Retail Track: SoundScan Numbers show .35 percent of Albums Account for More Than Half of All Units Sold." *Billboard*, April 28, 2001.

Clark, Rhodri. "Talent or Looks." *Western Mail,* June 18, 2005.

Clark, Rick. "Gus Dudgeon, 1942–2002." *Mix,* October 2002.

Clear Channel. "Clear Channel Cuts Ties with Independent Promoters." Press release, April 9, 2003.

Cockrell, Dale. "Review: Closing the Circle: A Cultural History of the Rock Revolution." *American Music,* Winter 1986.

Cohen, Jonathan. "Lennon Catalog to Make Digital Debut." *Billboard.biz,* November 8, 2005.

Cohen, Roger. "A $78 Million Year: Steve Ross Defends His Paycheck." *New York Times Magazine,* March 22, 1992.

Cohen, Stephanie. "Peter Townshend Interview." Edited by Hank Bordowitz. MCY.com, 2000.

Communications Act Ammendment of 1960 86 P.L. 752. 74 Stat. 889.

Communications Daily. "Bertelsmann AG Buys Rest of RCA Records from GE." September 10, 1986.

Costello, Daniel. "New Measures of CRM Performance" *CRM Magazine,* October 2000.

Consumer's Union, "History." hearusnow.org.

"Contract Between King David Distributors and Galaxy Records." June 5, 1969.

Corbett, Krystilyn. "The Rise of Private Property Rights in the Broadcast Spectrum." *Duke Law Review,* December 1996.

Crowly, Nina. "*Mass Mic* Responds to RIAA E-mail Re: mp3." *Mass Mic,* January 5, 1999.

Cumberland, Rob. "How Do I Get Signed? What You Should Know About Contracts." Bemuso.com, 2005.

Cumberland, Rob. "The Money Sponge: Why Can't the Major Labels Sell Enough Records?" Bemuso.com, 2005.

D'Agostino, Debra. "The Sound of Change." *CIO Insight,* January 5, 2005.

Dannen, Fredric. *Hit Men,* New York: Vintage Press, 1991.

Delvecchio, Rick. "Fake Science Searches for New Stars." *San Francisco Chronicle,* November 11, 2005.

Dickinson, Dee. "Music and the Mind." *New Horizons for Learning,* 1993.

DiCola, Peter, and Kristin Thompson. *Radio Deregulation: Has It Served Citizens and Musicians?* Washington, DC: Future of Music Coalition, 2002.

Digital Millennium Copyright Act. Public Law 105-304, *U.S. Statutes at Large* 112 (1998): 2860.

Doctorow, Cory. "Cory Responds to *Wired* Editor on DRM" boing boing.com, December 29, 2004.

Droney, Maureen. "Survival of the Fittest." *Mix*, October 2002.

Duhigg, Charles. "Music Is Listening to Him." *Los Angeles Times*, November 23, 2004.

Du Lac, J. Freedom. " 'Hey Jude'? Duude." *Washington Post*, November 14, 2005.

Dumenco, Simon: "The Un-Star System." *The New Yorker*, September 8, 2003.

Dvorak, John C. "Ode to Napster, Music's Last Hope." *PC Magazine*, March 16, 2004.

The Economist. "A Market for Ideas." October 20, 2005.

Edwards, David, and Michael Callahan. "The Liberty Records Story." Liberty.com, January 20, 2001.

Entertainment Software Association. Year End Figures (Report). 2005.

Evangelista, Benny. "Hell Freezes Over as Jobs Crosses PC Line." *San Francisco Chronicle*, October 17, 2003.

Evenson, Laura. "Amazon.com Makes Major Music Push." *San Francisco Chronicle*, June 11, 1998.

Farrish, Bryan. "Radio Airplay 101." Music Biz Academy.com, October 2000.

Fashion Center. "Economic Profile 2003."

Federal Communications Commission. "Radio Entertainment Format Changes." Mass Media Bureau, publication 40.

Fidelity Investments. "Music Icon and Investment Leader Team Up to Help Keep Music Education Alive in Schools." Press release, October 18, 2005.

Fisher, Anne B. "Record Clubs Face the Music." *Fortune*, April 29, 1996.

FMQB. "Bridge Ratings Study: Podcasting Elevates Litening." November 14, 2005.

Frederickson, Jon, and James F. Rooney. "How the Music Occupation Failed to Become a Profession." *International Review of Aesthetics and Sociology of Music*, December 1990.

Frey, William H. "Boomer Havens and Young Adult Magnets." *American Demographics*, September 2001.

Friedman, Dean. "Fan Funded DIY Records." Panel at the Global Entertainment and Media Summit, May 2003.

G., Scott. "Indie Artists Meet Clear Channel Execs." Ezine @rticles (ezinearticles.com), October 25, 2005.

Gardiner, Martin, Alan Fox, Faith Knowles, and Donna Jeffery. "Learning Improved by Art Training." *Nature*, May 23, 1996.

Garrity, Brian. "Korn's 'Twisted' Deal." *Billboard*, November 12, 2005.

Gillen, Marilyn A. "Sony CEO Stresses Retail Role in Digital Future." *Billboard*, January 7, 1995.

Goddard, Peter. "Boom Gloom Makes Music Business Nervous." *Toronto Star*, February 21, 1996.

Goldberg, Danny. "Excerpt of New Introduction from Forthcoming Paperback Edition of My Book." DannyGoldberg.com, January 10, 2005.

Goldring, Fred. "Editorial: After Grokster, Can Music Business Save Itself?" *Billboard*, July 16, 2005.

GRAMMY.com. Grammy Award Winners. Graser, Marc. "Did Somebody Sing McDonald's? Adversongs Urge Fast Food into Hip-hop Lyrics." *Crain's Chicago Business*, April 4, 2005.

Green, Frank. "Q&A Eustaquio Kirby, Owner of Gary's Record Paradise." *Escondido (CA) Union-Tribune*, October 23, 2005.

Greenblatt, Alan. "Will the Major Music Labels Survive the Digital Age?" *CQResearcher*, November 21, 2003.

Greenman, Ben. "Q&A: The Price of Payola." *The New Yorker Online Only*, July 5, 2004.

Gross, Daniel. "What's Wrong with Payola?" *Slate*, July 27, 2005.

Gruber, Frederick C. "Radio and Television Ethical Standards." *Annals of the American Academy of Political and Social Science*, March 1952.

Hagen, Mark. "Interview." *Mojo*, January 1999.

Halberstam, David. "Some in FTC Say Payola Is Ended." *New York Times*, February 5, 1961.

Hall, Michael. "Indrema CEO Discusses the Close of His Company." *Linux Today*, April 12, 2001.

Halliday, Jean. "Scion Brand Enters the Music Business." *Crain's Automotive News*, April 4, 2005.

Harrigan, Richard. "The Capitol Hill Rock War. Emotions Run High as Musicians Confront Parents' Group at Hearing." *Washington Post*, September 20, 1985.

Hayes, Simon. "Music for a Song, Quick Sharp or Web Piracy Continues." *The Australian*, September 10, 2005.

Hazlett, Curt. "More Bad News for Retailers: Rising Rent." *Retail Traffic*, January 1, 2003.

Heine, Paul. "Satellite Stampede: The Competition Zone." *Billboard Radio Monitor*, July 22, 2005.

Heine, Paul. "Winning on the Web." *Billboard Radio Monitor*, November 11, 2005.

High, Mamau. "In Search of All the Young Men with Big Bulging Wallets." *Financial Times*, May 24, 2005.

Hinte, Teri. *Berkeley Item* 265 (October 16, 2005).

Hinte, Teri. *Berkeley Item* 266 (October 31, 2005).

Horowitz, Is. "Going to Be a Record Fight. Independents Smack Big Labels." *The Billboard*, November 19, 1955.

Horowitz, Is. "Long-Play Records to Chalk Up Peak Volume This Year." *The Billboard*, December 3, 1955.

Ice-T. "Speech to MP3 Summit." June 20, 2000.

Industry Analyst Reporter. "Interactive Entertainment Industry to Rival Size of Global Music Business, Says DFC." November 9, 2005.

InfoGuia Juegos. "Interview with Yana Kushner About the Indrema L600 Entertainment System." March 26, 2000.

Jahn, Mike. "The Archies Are Fictional, but Their Success Is Not." *New York Times*, November 5, 1969.

Johnson, Gene. "Internet Helps Indie Radio Spread Out." *Associated Press*, October 27, 2005.

Keefe, Bob. "Napster Verdict: Music Business Changed Forever." *Atlanta Journal-Constitution*, October 2, 2000.

Keefe, Bob. "Warner to Start Digital 'E-label.'" *Atlanta Journal-Constitution*, August 23, 2005.

Kiley, David. "Is Mickey D Getting a Bad Rap?" Edited by Ira Sager. *Business Week*, April 18, 2005.

Kirk, Patricia L. "A Tale of Two Markets." *Retail Traffic*, May 1, 2004.

Knowledge@Wharton. "Peer-to-Peer Music Trading: Good Publicity or Bad Precedent?" October 2002.

Lander, Howard. "A Letter from the Publisher. *Billboard* Debuts Piece Counts on Two Music Sales Charts" *Billboard*, May 25, 1991.

Leeds, Jeff. "Music Promoter to Abandon a Radio Policy He Developed." *New York Times*, November 3, 2005.

Levine, Robert. "Rage Against the Record Label: The Hanson Brothers Make a Film." *New York Times*, October 21, 2005.

Lewis, Peter H. "Companies Rush to Set Up Shop in Cyberspace." *New York Times*, November 2, 1994.

Lichtenstein, Grace. "Payola Jury Asks Testimony on Tips." *New York Times*, January 20, 1973.

Lichtenstein, Grace. "Record Industry on Coast Shaken by Payola Scandal." *New York Times*, July 22, 1973.

Lichtman, Irv. "Lester Sill, Rock Era Publishing Great, Dies at 76." *Billboard*, November 12, 1994.

Lichtman, Irv. The *Billboard* Bulletin. *Billboard*, December 3, 1994.

Lichtman, Irv. The *Billboard* Bulletin. *Billboard*, March 13, 1993.

Lieberman, David. "Entertainment Clout Builds: Clear Channel's Purchase of SFX Entertainment Creates a Radio, Billboard and Live Performance Titan." *USA Today*, March 1, 2000.

Liebowitz, Stan. "Will MP3 Downloads Annihilate the Record Industry? The Evidence So Far." Paper, School of Management, University of Texas at Dallas, June 2003.

Lindelof, Bill. "Budget Knell for the Arts." *Sacramento Bee*, March 20, 2004.

Lindsey, Robert. "Payola Threatens Recording Profits." *New York Times*, July 23, 1975.

Llewellyn Smith, Caspar. "Feelin' Free." *Observer Music Monthly*, September 18, 2005.

Lopez, Maribel D., Ted Schadler, Jennifer Joseph, and Sally Cohen. "Entertainment Grabs Youths' Online Time." Young Consumers and Technology, Forrester Research, July 29, 2005.

Lotz, I. C. "Dick Clark over a Chinese Luncheon." *Fusion Magazine*.

Love, Courtney. "Speech to Digital Hollywood Online Entertainment Conference." May 16, 2000.

Lowry, Tom. "Jamming with Jac, Seymour, and Ahmet." *Business Week Online*, August 8, 2005.

Mabe, Chauncey. "Why Can't Baby Boomers Learn How to Age Gracefully?" *Sun-Sentinel*, November 20, 2005.

Mabry, Donald J. "Rise and Fall of Ace Records: A Case Study in the Independent Record Business." *Business History Review*, Autumn 1990.

Mabry, Donald J. "Rock 'n' Roll: The Beginnings." Historical Text Archive (www.historicaltextarchive.com), April 30, 2004.

Manchester, Joyce. "The Baby Boom, Housing, and Financial Flows." *American Economic Review*, May 1988.

Manning, Robert D., Derek V. Price, and Henry J. Rich. "Concierge or Information Desk: Teaching Social Stratification Through the Malling of America." *Teaching Sociology*, January 1997.

Margolis, Lynne. "Why Satellite Radio Is Beaming." Cox News Service, August 10, 2005.

Marsh, Dave. "The Cradle Will Rock." *Rock and Roll Confidential*, February 1985.

Marsh, Dave. "Deal Memo: Korn." Holler If Ya Hear Me hollerif.blogspot.com/ September 27, 2005.

Marsh, Dave. *Rock and Rap Confidential*, August 1997.

Martins, Todd. "Lonely No More" *Billboard*, February 25, 2006.

Mayfield, Geoff. "How the Music Charts Are Compiled." *Billboard*, December 28, 2002.

McAdams, Janine. "BDS, SoundScan Now Form Basis for R&B Charts." *Billboard*, December 5, 1992.

McBride, Terry. "Editorial: The New Frontier." *Billboard*, April 15, 2006.

Microsoft and Ford. Joint press release, November 1, 2005.

Miller, Karen Lowry. "EMI: Inside a Makeover." *Newsweek*, September 26, 2005.

Morin, Cari. "The Evolution of Beatles' Recording Technology." Paper, Northwestern University, Evanston, IL, 1988.

Morris, Chris. "Labels' Future in Doubt After Isgro's Sentencing." *Billboard*, September 23, 2000.

Morris, Chris, and Woodson, Alexander. "News. Music." *Hollywood Reporter.com*, July 27, 2005.

MP3Board. "MP3Board Files Counter Claim Against RIAA. Creates New Digital Rights Technology." Press release, July 7, 2000.

Napoli, Lisa. "Think the Debate on Music Property Rights Began with Napster? Hardly." *New York Times*, September 22, 2003.

National Association of Record Merchandisers. "The College Market: Content Spending and Device Ownership." *NARM Research Briefs*, October 2001.

National Association of Record Merchandisers. "Retail Sales: Terrorism Alters the Outlook." *NARM Research Briefs*, October 2001.

Neer, Richard. *FM: The Rise and Fall of Rock Radio*. New York: Villard Books, 2001.

Nelson, Chris. "Upstart Labels See File Sharing as Ally, Not Foe." *New York Times*, September 22, 2003.

Nelson, Lizz. "Building Up into a Crescendo of Successful Sales: How Two Brothers from a Small Town Sold Over 1 Million CDs—Without a Major Label." PR Newswire, December 13, 2004.

Nelson, T. J. "Dumbing Down, the Dwindling Funding of the Arts." World Music Central (www.worldmusiccentral.org), March 9, 2005.

Newman, Melinda. "The Beat—Savoy Plucks Vollenweider." *Billboard*, March 25, 2005.

New York Times. "The Indelible Pietro." June 19, 2005.

New York Times. "Questionnaire Reveals Radio Beneficial to Music Industry." March 23, 1924.

Nielsen/Net Ratings survey, 2004.

Noguchi, Yuki. "Warner Music Turns to Web." *Washington Post*, November 11, 2005.

Oberholzer, Felix, and Koleman Strumpf. *The Effect of File Sharing on Record Sales: An Empirical Analysis*. Cambridge, MA: Harvard Business School, 2004.

O'Connor, Timothy. "File Share Plaintiff Plans Own Defense." *Journal News*, December 11, 2005.

Okoli, Christina. "What Is Web Radio?" Answer Bank UK. www.the answerbank.co.uk.

"Optical Storage Media." In *How Much Information? 2003*. Regents of the University of California, October 27, 2003.

Ordonez, Jennifer. "Pop Singer Fails to Strike a Chord Despite the Millions Spent by MCA." *Wall Street Journal*, February 26, 2002.

Orlowski, Andrew. "For Every DRM Download, 16 P2P Swaps." *The Register*, June 23, 2005.

Palmieri, Christopher. "Media Merchant to the Baby Boomers." *Forbes*, March 15, 1993.

Paoletta, Michael. "Making the Brand: Financial Firms See Payoff in Aging Stars." *Billboard*, November 19, 2005.

Paoletta, Michael. "MTV Taps Consultant as President/COO." *Billboard*, November 12, 2005.

Paoletta, Michael. "Q&A: Christina Norman." *Billboard*, August 27, 2005.

Pareles, Jon. "Money Talks, Top 40 Listens." *New York Times*, September 2, 1990.

Parmenter, Ross. "Economics of Records." *New York Times*, March 9, 1952.

Passy, Charles. "Waiting for Lou Pearlman." *Palm Beach Post*, July 29, 2001.

Pelline, Jeff. "Marketers Flocking to Sell Music on the Internet." *San Francisco Chronicle*, November 28, 1995.

Pepper, Tara. "Making Their Own Breaks." *Newsweek*, September 26, 2005.

Petersen, George. "What's Going On?" *Mix*, April 2005.

Pfanner, Eric. "A British Invasion for the Digital Age." *International Herald Tribune*, March 12, 2006.

Podmolic, Mary Ellen. "Music Retailers Hear Sour Notes." *Crain's Chicago Business*, May 26, 2003.

PR Newswire. "Instead of Suing over Downloadable Music—the Music Business Should Take the High Road." August 27, 2002.

Radio and Records Online (www.randr.com). Ratings for New York. Accessed November 14, 2005.

Rainie, Lee, Susannah Fox, and Amanda Lenhart. "13 Million Americans 'Freeload' Music on the Internet. One Billion Free Music Files Now Sit on Napster Users' Computers." Internet Tracking Report, Pew Internet and American Life Project, June 8, 2000.

Rayner, Ben. "Manufacturing Music for Teenage Fanatics." *Toronto Star*, April 1, 2001.

Record World Magazine. "George Martin Speaks Out." January 30, 1971.

Red Herrin. "Herd Shapes Music Tastes." February 9, 2006.

RIAA. Press Release on DiMA, 2000.

RIAA. "1998 Consumer Profile." Recording Industry Association of America, 1999.

RIAA. "2003 Consumer Profile." Recording Industry Association of America, 2004.

RIAA. "2003 Year End Statistics." Recording Industry Association of America, 2004.

RIAA. "2004 Consumer Profile." Recording Industry Association of America, 2005.

RIAA. "2004 Year End Statistics." Recording Industry Association of America, 2005.

RIAA.com. "Cost of a CD." 2003.

RIAA.com. Gold and platinum searchable database.

Rickwood, Lee. "John Gold's 'Cactusflower' Video." *Video Systems,* November 2005.

Ritholtz, Barry. "DVD Sales Cannibalizing CD Sales." The Big Picture (bigpicture.typepad.com), March 1, 2004.

Roberts, Donald F., Ulla G. Foehr, and Victoria Rideout. *Generation M: Media in the Lives of 8–18 Year-Olds.* Henry J. Kaiser Family Foundation, 2005.

Robertson, Thomas Dolby. "The Upside of Music on the Web." RIAA.com, 2000.

Rock and Rap Confidential. "R.U.A. Criminal?" July 2005.

Rock and Rap Confidential. October 2005.

Rock and Rap Confidential. 2000.

Rohter, Larry. "Payola Case Dismissed by Judge." *New York Times,* September 5, 1990.

Rood, George. "Holiday Expands Recording Sales." *New York Times,* December 19, 1965.

Rothman, Wilson. "I Don't Rent. I Own." *New York Times,* February 26, 2004.

Sanjek, Russell, and David Sanjek. *Pennies from Heaven.* New York: Da Capo Press, 1996.

Sarma, Ripunjoy Kumar. "Why Should I Tune in to Satellite Radio?" *Economic Times*, July 26, 2005.

Schadler, Ted, Josh Bernoff, Sally Cohen, and Jennifer Joseph. "Musical Youth: Still Stealing, but Also Buying." Young Consumers and Technology, Forrester Research, September 15, 2005.

Schadler, Ted, and Sally M. Cohen. "Young Consumers Love Their Devices." Young Consumers and Technology, Forrester Research, July 28, 2005.

Schwartz, Lara. *The Billboard Guide to Music Video*. New York: Watson Guptil Books, 2007 (from the manuscript).

Seattle Post-Intelligencer. "Barenaked Ladies Distributing New Release via USB Flash Drive." November 22, 2005.

Self, Jonathan, and Jason Snell. "Rock and Scroll." *Macworld*, October 2004.

Serwer, Andy. "Music Retailers Are Really Starting to Sing the Blues." *Fortune*, March 8, 2004.

Seybold, Patricia B. *The Customer Revolution*. New York: Crown Business Books, 2001.

SFX. "SFX Broadcasting and Multi-Market Radio Announce Final Acquisitions to Complete the $223 Million Liberty Broadcasting Transaction." Press release, February 9, 1996.

Shamah, David. "Exposed! The Dark Side of 8-Tracks and CDs." *Jerusalem Post*, July 12, 2005.

Shandler, Geoff. "Book Scandal." *The Industry Standard*, July 2, 2001.

Shelanski, Howard A., and Peter W. Huber. "Administrative Creation of Property Rights to the Radio Spectrum." *Law and Economics*, October 1998.

Shelton, Robert. "Happy Tunes on Cash Registers." *New York Times*, March 16, 1958.

Shields, Mike. "Tracking Down the Podcast People." *Mediaweek*, November 15, 2005.

Silverman, Tom. "Addressing B'nai B'rith Panel Discussion on Independent Record Companies." 1996.

Simon, Ralph. "Commentary: Sounding Off on Ringtones." *Billboard*, October 1, 2005.

Smith, Brian K. "An Assault on Retailers." *Billboard*, November 26, 2005.

Smith, Joe. *Off the Record*. New York: Warner Books: 1988.

Sony/BMG. Memo to all employees, October 24, 2005.

Sony Music. "Sony Music Entertainment and BMG Unite to Create Sony BMG Music Entertainment." Press release, August 5, 2004.

Soukup, Elise. "Bands: An Idea as Fresh as Mom's Tupperware." *Newsweek*, June 20, 2005.

Soundscan Album Sales Report. April 29, 2005.

Stone, Brad. "Hi-Tech's New Day." *Newsweek*, April 11, 2005.

Strauss, Neil. "Acoustic Music, Live from the Living Room." *New York Times*, November 8, 1999.

Strauss, Neil. "Wal-Mart's CD Standards Are Changing Pop Music." *New York Times*, November 12, 1996.

Szendrei, Janka. "The Introduction of Staff Notation into Middle Europe." *Studia Musicologica Academiae Scientiarum Hungaricae*, 1986.

Taubman, Howard. "Black Discs by Millions." *New York Times*, January 18, 1942.

Telecomworldwire. "Global Cellular Connections Reach Two Billion." September 19, 2005.

Top 40 Charts.com. "MP3 and More." October 25, 2005.

Trumbull, Dr. Eric W. "Ancient Greek Theater." Introduction to Theatre Online Course (novaonline.nv.cc.va.us/eli/spd130et/ancientgreek.htm), Northern Virginia Community College, 2001.

Turner, Cynthia. *Cynopsis*, November 30, 2005.

Turner, Cynthia. *Cynopsis*, September 9, 2005.

Tymkiw, Catherine. "MTV, Microsoft Plan Service to Rival iTunes." *Crain's New York Business* (online), December 12, 2005.

UPI. "Motorola Adding Internet Radio to Phones." July 25, 2005.

U.S. Census Bureau. *Statistical Abstract of the United States: 2004–2005*. Washington, DC, 2004.

U.S. Constitution art. I, sec. 8, cl. 8.

Van Zandt, "Little" Steven. *Little Steven's Underground Garage* 44, WQXD February 2, 2003.

Varanini, Giancarlo. "Q&A: Napster Creator Shawn Fanning." *ZDnet Music*, March 2, 2000.

Verna, Paul, "Studio Monitor: Room with a View's Closing Illustrates Harsh Realities." *Billboard*, October 24, 1998.

Waller, Don. "The JMA Q&A." *Billboard*, August 18, 2001.

Walsh, Christopher. "Studio Monitor: 2005 Turns Rough on Pro Audio Field." *Billboard*, March 12, 2005.

Walsh, Christopher. "Studio Monitor: Behind the Severe Drop in Studio Bookings." *Billboard*, December 30, 2000.

Walsh, Christoper. "Studio Monitor: DAW Advances Challenge Business Model." *Billboard*, December 25, 2004.

Washington Post. "Why It Costs . . . for a Hit CD." February 15, 1995.

Weiss, George David. "Address to the B'nai B'rith Music Entertainment and Media Unit." 1991.

Wells, Matt. "Red Herring Research Study Doubts Napster Success." Red Herring Research, May 31, 2001.

Westfeldt, Amy. "Stern Taken Off the Air after Promoting Move to Sirius." *Associated Press*, November 7, 2005.

Wikipedia. "Digital Audio Tape." Accessed October 26, 2005.

Wikipedia. "Mobile Phones." Accessed February 9, 2006.

Wild. "MediaGear SongBank Review." GeekExtreme.com, May 24, 2005.

Wilkowe, Ellen S. "Many Morris Fans Plan to Follow Howard Stern in Move to Satellite." *Daily Record*, November 20, 2005.

Williams, Mark London. "Online Shipping Enters Comfort Zone." *Daily Variety*, May 19, 1998.

Williams, Paul. "HMV to Close Final US Store." *Music Week*, November 6, 2004.

Winkler, Peter, and Lara Schooler, eds. "Global Entertainment and Media Outlook: 2004–2008" PricewaterhouseCooper, 2005.

Woletz, Robert G. "A New Formula: Into the 'Bin.' Out Comes a Hit." *New York Times*, August 2, 1992.

Wolff, Michael. "Facing the Music." *New York*, June 10, 2002.

World Musicians: Current Biography. H. W. Wilson Company: Bronx, NY, 1998.

Yetnikoff, Walter, and David Ritz. *Howling at the Moon*. New York: Broadway Books, 2004.

Yoh, William H., Jr. "Music Education: The Cornerstone to Developing a Well-Rounded Individual." *Massachusetts Music News*, Winter 1996.

Zappa, Frank. "Statement to Congress." Testimony in "Record Label-ing," hearing before the Senate Committee on Commerce, Science, and Transportation, 99th Cong., 1st sess., September 19, 1985.

Zeidler, Sue. "Casting the Net." *Reuters*, June 26, 2005.

Zimmerman, Kevin. "Who Fears Peer-to-Peer?" *Cablevision*, February 12, 2001.

Zuckerman, Steven. "Interview with Jerry Lembo." Totalaccesslive.com, 2004.

Original Sources

"Anonymous former A&R person." Author's correspondence, October 18, 2005.

Bergman, Barry. Author's interview, December 12, 2005.

Bongiovi, Tony. Author's interview, 1985.

Bruce, Jenny. Author's correspondence, December 14, 2005.

Burnett, Scott. Author's interview, July 17, 1997.

Cohen, Ted. Author's interview, March 2002.

Cook, Stu. Author's interview, 1997.

Deutsch, Didier. Author's interview, 1991.

Ertegun, Ahmet. Author's interview, June 13, 1991.

Fast, Larry. Author's correspondence, June 17 and 18, 2005.

Gayles, Juggy. Author's interview, November 5, 1988.

Griesman, Dwight. Author's interview, August 2000.

James, Etta. Author's interview; October 1988.

Lekberg, Jason. Author's correspondence, 2005.

Majewski, Ed. Author's correspondence, April 7, 2004, and October 24, 2005.

McDaniel, Elias (a.k.a. Bo Diddley). Authors interview, 1996.

Nispel, Marcus. Author's interview, August 16, 1991.

Paul, Les. Author's interviews, 1992.

"Pointer" (anonymous West Coast media executive). Author's correspondence, 2006.

Ponti, Jack. Author's correspondence, December 9 and 10, 2005.

Ramone, Phil. Author's interview, July 17, 1997.

Rawls, Lou. Author's interview, August 1989.

Rose, Don; Author's interview, 1986.

Rundgren, Todd. Author's interviews, 1985, June 20, 1992, and July 1997.

Schwartz, Lara. Author's correspondence, 2006.

Shallet, Michael, and Michael Fine. Author's interview, June 1992.

Shocklee, Hank. Author's interview, 2002.

Smith, Joe. Author's interview, November 1988.

Solomon, Russ. Author's interview, September 1993.

Steffens, Vic. Author's correspondence, September 11, October 15, and November 26, 2005.

Sutton, Dan. Author's correspondence, 1997.

Zisk, Brian, Author's correspondence, 2005.

Index

A&M Records, 13, 163
A&R (Artist & Repertoire)
    changing role of, 30
    role of, 21–22, 32, 33
    success and failure in, 29
A2P Internet subscription service (artist to public),
        278. *See also* Internet; online business model
Abdul, Paula, 253
Abramson, Herb (Atlantic Records), 6
actors, popularity of singing actors, 239–240
ADA (Alternative Distribution Alliance), 79
Adams Media Research report, 227
adult demographic, targeting, 219–222
"adult pop" format, explanation of, 91
advances
    decrease in, 183
    example of, 73
    payment of, 22
    recouping, 23
African American artists
    exposure of, 110
    success of, 114
AfriStar satellites, use of, 135
"After the Ball" (Stephen Foster), 105
Aguilera, Christina, 239, 241
A-ha, 123
"Ain't She Sweet" (the Beatles), 6
airwaves, ownership of, 83–85
Aladdin (Maxwell Davis), 31
Albini, Steve (producer), 73–74
albums
    breaking even on major labels, 68
    low sales of, 44
    recovery of production costs from sales of, 67
Alexander, Gavin (technologist), 243
Alive, (Armand Morin), 188–189
Allen, Paul (Experience Music Project), 138
Alleys, relationship to "1999" (Prince), 159–160
allofmp3.com, potential violations related to, 62–63
Alpert, Herb and Jerry Moss (A&M Records), 13
"Also Sprach Zarathustra" (Deodato), 14
Alternative Distribution Alliance (ADA), 79
AM stations, ownership of, 88
Amazon (David Risher), 167–168
American Bandstand, significance of, 30, 33
American Can Company, purchase of Sam Goody by,
        149
American Idol, debut of, 243
Amoeba Records, success of, 154–155
Ampex, relationship to Les Paul, 176–177
Anderson, Chris (*Wired* magazine), 69
Anderson, Ray, 122–123
Animals, 175, 181–182
"announcers," DJs as, 91–92
Anthony, Polly, 29, 33
Apple, Fiona, 152
Apple Computer (Steve Jobs), 191–192, 205
Apple Corps versus Apple Computer trademark, 207
Arbitron
    report on radio listeners on Web, 138
    tracking radio listeners with, 129–133
Arcade Fire, 188
Archie comic books, 240
Archies, ("Sugar, Sugar"), 240
ARChive of Contemporary Music (Bob George), 155
Arctic Monkeys, success on Internet, 186
"Ariel" (Dean Friedman), 279–280
Armone, Joseph, 121
Armstrong, Louis ("What a Wonderful World"), 43
Artist Formerly Known as Prince
    "1999," 159
    availability of music online, 57–58

Crystal Ball, 188
    NPG Music Club, 188
artists
    cost of getting on charts, 246
    deals for, 78
    development of, 20, 247–250
    exposure of black artists, 110
    failure of, 282
    net payments to, 74–75
    ownership of labels by, 279
    relationships with record companies, 268–269
    role of, 18
    success and failure in, 29
ASCAP, position on rock and roll, 109–110
AsiaStar satellites, use of, 135
Asylum Records (David Geffen), 114
Atco Records (Ahmet Ertegun), 6
Atkinson, Paul, 32
Atlantic Records, 6, 13, 30
audiences, reaching, 246
Audio Home Recording Act of 1992, 43–44
Audio Layer 3 compression protocol, adoption of, 47
AudioRevolution (Jerry Del Colliano), 60–61
Austin, Michael Lee, 188
Avallone, Francis, 238
Avalon, Frankie, 30, 238

baby boomers, impact on music business, 211–215
Bach, Johann Sebastian, xix
back office and front office flowchart, 24
Backstreet Boys, 70, 242
Bagdasarian, Ross, 5
Baker, Chet, 13
bands, budgeting, 74–75
Barenaked Ladies (*Barenaked on a Stick*), 206
Barenaked on a Stick (Barenaked Ladies), 206
Barone, Richard (the Bongos), 190
BDS (Broadcast Data Systems)
    monitoring of songs by, 38–39
    relevance to radio, 100
Beastie Boys, 54
Beatles, 31
    "Ain't She Sweet," 6
    first studio recordings of, 177
Beatles catalog, availability of, 65
benchmarks in radio, examples of, 125
Benedetti, Nicola (violinist), 254
Benson, George, 13
Bergmann, Barry (Music Managers Forum-US), 77,
        247
Bernstein, Paul (*New York Times*) on turnover rate of
        artists, 282
Bertelsmann Music Group
    acquisition of Music Boulevard by, 168
    acquisition of RCA Records by, 16
Best Buy, purchase of Musicland by, 154
Betamax (Sony), failure of, 16
Big Champagne digital music tracking company, 65
Big Daddy, 79
"big six," reduction to "big four," 17
Billboard
    Christman, Ed on music sales analysis, 66–69
    Lander, Howard, 36
    Newman, Melinda, 246
    Rossi, Terri, 39
    celebration of Jeff McClusky's 20th anniversary, 125
    location of, 35
    music videos on, 252
    Paul Verna on recording studios, 181
    relationship to SoundScan, 26
Billboard releases, conference calls held after,
        102–103